BUILDING STRONGER SCHOOL COUNSELING PROGRAMS:
Bringing Futuristic Approaches into the Present

Editors & Contributors
C.D. Johnson
Sharon K. Johnson

Foreword by Donald G. Hays

This publication was funded in part by the U.S. Department of Education, Office of Educational Research and Improvement, Contract No. ED-99-CO-0014. Opinions expressed in this publication do not necessarily reflect the positions of the U.S. Department of Education, OERI, or ERIC/CASS.

Contents

Section 1: Embracing the Community

Section 2: Counseling for Employability

Section 3: Considering Multicultural Issues

Section 4: Staying the Course

Section 5: Preparing Student Support Professionals

Section 6: Riding Political and Technological Currents

Preface I

Over the years ERIC/CASS has striven to produce books that offer compelling ideas and practices which have not become commonplace within the counseling literature. We see our role as an ERIC clearinghouse as being a purveyor of information which by its freshness and cogency can bring about significant positive changes in the programs and practices of those who use them.

This book, edited by two very visionary authors, Drs. C.D. Johnson and Sharon K. Johnson, brings together an array of authors whose chapters will provide the reader with a bountiful cache of new perspectives and exciting approaches. There is much to be excited about in this book and a great number of ideas and practices which warrant the reader's immediate adoption and use. I believe that readers will come away from reading/using this publication with a new vision of what counseling and guidance in schools can and should be. Few of us will be the same for having read it. And that is a good test of the worth of a book.

An especially satisfying aspect of producing this publication has been the participation of the American School Counselor Association (ASCA) as a co-publisher. ERIC/CASS and ASCA have a long and successful history of collaboration on a wide variety of initiatives, e.g., publications, conferences, participation in one another's committees, etc.

Kwok-Sze Richard Wong has shown himself to be most adept in facilitating win/win ASCA and ERIC/CASS initiatives. This book is further testimony to how our collaboration is highly contributive to producing viable resources for school counselors.

If this publication proves to be the stimulus to thought and action that we anticipate, you very likely will be seeking the means to follow through on the interest generated by your reading. On the back cover is a visual of the ERIC/CASS award-winning Gateway Websites, which offer online full-text resources on a wide array of counseling relevant topics.

Garry R. Walz, Ph.D.
ERIC/CASS Co-Director

Preface II

School counseling is a dynamic, ever-changing profession. Almost since its inception, school counseling has continually evolved to meet the needs of students in a society that is constantly in flux.

The last half of the 20th Century saw a revolution in the school counseling profession. It moved from strictly college and career placement to development of the total student. And the nature of school counseling programs changed. School counselors were no longer isolated individuals providing services in schools. They were no longer mental health specialists who only responded to the needs of the students. School counselors became integral parts of comprehensive counseling programs that were woven into the very fabric of education. School counselors infused personal and social development into the daily curriculum, knowing that personal and social development leads to higher academic achievement, which helps prepare students for fulfilling careers.

C.D. Johnson and Sharon Johnson have been two of the most prominent leaders in the school counseling movement. In this book they have brought together some of the most influential thinkers in school counseling to anticipate future trends that must be addressed now. Concepts such as school counselors in the community, counseling to prepare students for employability and technology will be as crucial in the future as academic achievement, multicultural diversity and school counselor preparation are today and will continue to be in the future.

The American School Counselor Association is proud to collaborate with ERIC/CASS to produce this important book. Just as ASCA and ERIC have helped shape the school counseling profession during the past five decades, the principles explored in this book will drive the profession for years to come.

Kwok-Sze Wong
Executive Director
American School Counselor Association

Foreword:

The Future of Counseling

The future is about change. And change is more important to the human species now than in previous generations due to its rapidity. To describe counseling in the future is a challenge, and for our authors to do so will reflect their mindsets of how change takes place.

To begin with, the future does not exist! There is no future except in the mind of each human being. What we believe about the future depends upon our own experiences of the past and what is happening to us now. To speculate about the future as our authors have is to take a degree of risk. They come from a variety of fields, and thus you will find a diversity of thought. As you read through the chapters, you will note that some authors believe there will be few changes from what we are experiencing today. Changes will be *incremental*; that is, we will make small accretionary changes of a short-term nature as we resolve problems that arise. It is important to take care of today before we can deal with the issues of tomorrow.

Others see what might be called *transitional* changes. The future will be different, but during the period from now to then, the changes will be orderly and linear, progressing one step at a time. Transitional changes rely upon Newtonian thinking, using a linear, left-brain, and rational approach. In essence, we know where we are going and are making plans to get there. In fact, we have a strategic plan to accomplish our mission and our vision.

Still others envision *transformational* change. The future will be as different from today as AD 2000 is from 2000 BCE! Transformational change is based on recently identified quantum physics and chaos theory, wherein one uses whole-brain thinking, is intuitive, and looks for patterns of relationships within a larger environmental context. Whose belief system will prevail will be determined as we move forward in time.

As you begin the journey of futures thinking, consider how each author believes the future will unfold. What occurs in this foreword is a preview of what will occur in the chapters. The intent is to pique your interest and to provide a flavor of the approaches used to describe what counseling might resemble in the future. The book is divided into six sections: Embracing the Community, Counseling for Employability, Considering Multicultural Issues, Staying the Course, Preparing Student Support Professionals, and Riding Political and Technological Currents. Johnson and Johnson summarize by posing the thought that future student support programs may be faced with either distinction or extinction.

In section 1, Embracing the Community, Wickwire begins by considering how one studies the future. She looks at what probable, possible, and preferred futures mean. She speaks to emerging and continuing trends: expansion of electronics, growth of distance learning, emphasis on competencies and skills, movement toward standards, inculcation of lifelong learning, and reconstruction of work and career. Addressing the counseling profession in the future, Wickwire states that "the counseling profession will respond and initiate, exercising combinations of authentic, visionary, cultural, quality, and service leadership (based on modeling, ideas, interpersonal factors, excellence, and systems support, respectively)." She goes on to predict that "the student of tomorrow will need to be aware of, understand, and apply behavior and learning (in career, work, family, education, and leisure areas) with the goal of mastering the following qualities, skills, and areas of knowledge . . . ," and she lists an array of descriptors. "The counselor of tomorrow will have the same needs for awareness, understanding, and application in behavior and learning as the student of tomorrow, plus the capacity to assist the student to meet those needs. The counselor will be a continuous learner and an accomplished change agent." Some of the areas of concern to the proposed counselor of tomorrow are leadership, systems, domains, treatments, delivery systems, and evaluation. "Counselors are ultimately responsible for futures in the counseling profession, although factors in the external environment may play major roles. Counseling futures could range from obliteration to modification to renaissance, depending, in part, on the posture and action of those in the profession." Wickwire concludes with the prediction that "counselors will make the final choices regarding survival, maintenance, or enhancement of the counseling profession."

DuFour, Guidice, Magee, Martin, and Zivkovic speak to the problem of prognostication, especially in the school sector. The group believes that basic transformation is needed and cites research to that effect. They mention three emerging national trends, including (a) the learning organization, (b) greater personalization and individualization of services, and (c) the pervasiveness and power of technology. After describing the "factory model" that no longer can meet the challenges of the present and the future, the authors turn to some principles of the learning organization and posit that student services departments of the future will function as learning organizations. Four questions need to be answered to lay the foundation of a learning organization: "Why do we exist?" "What does the department hope to become?" "What are our values and how do we make a commitment to a shared vision?" and "Which steps will we take, when will we take them, and how will we measure their impact?" Collaborative teams will be engaged in collective inquiry as to the success and well-being of individual students, the effectiveness of programs in meeting the needs of each student, and the effectiveness of the team itself.

Bemak proposes community learning centers (CLCs) within the school. These CLCs, with "students studying interdisciplinary subject areas in small groups," would be led by teachers and staff who would facilitate learning. There would be more integration with families and the community. He expects that "principals, teachers, parents, and community personnel of the future will be clear about what a counselor does and how those activities contribute to the educational mission of the school." Bemak suggests the school counselor of the future will assume a leadership role in his or her assigned CLCs and "will be responsible for educating teachers, administrators, and parents about issues such as child development, mental health as it relates to academic achievement, cultural learning styles, career development and opportunities, college placement, course tracking, group process and relationships, community relations, and family dynamics as they relate to school performance." To serve as a guide for students, teachers, principals, parents, administrators, and community members, the counselor would need "more extensive consultation training with an emphasis on the collaborative process, and a newly developed skill area that provides the tools for school counselors to be guides and facilitators of process rather than content experts."

Allen talks about counseling and its future as seen by those who live in the present. From there she tells of the storyteller who "takes tales from the past and retells them, making them relevant to the future." Referring to Joseph Campbell's power of myths in our daily lives, she tells of three myths—one for each of the past three decades. There is the *hero myth* of the 1970s, the *victim myth* of the 1980s, and the *stepchild myth* of the 1990s. She asks the question, "Are these myths a proper legacy for the twenty-first century?" She answers that question with a new myth for the twenty-first century: *counseling in community*, which requires a new paradigm for counseling. Allen suggests the best strategy for "a counseling paradigm is paradigm pliancy— divergent thinking, brainstorm planning, and creative envisioning." This new paradigm must take into account the global economics of the century; human rights issues; the diversity of various cultures, races, and nationalities; the interconnection of systems; and technology as a means of communication. "The paradigm must be amenable to change, use the best techniques and methodologies to facilitate that change, be flexible enough to take the energy of the age and flow with that energy, and employ the very best leaders to light the way." Within the counseling in community myth and paradigm, Allen speaks to five key components: global community, spiritual foundations, counseling methodology, organizational structure, and leadership. "Counseling will be alive in the twenty-first century, but its metamorphosis may challenge the comfort level and stretch the imagination of the twentieth-century counselor." Allen then closes with a quote from Franklin Delano Roosevelt: "The only limit to our realization of tomorrow will be our doubts of today. Let us move forward with strong and active faith."

Anderson proposes a community involvement model for developmental guidance. His thesis is based on the work of the Search Institute's "40 research-based, key internal and external factors that support healthy development." The factors are called *assets*, many of which are correlated with risk-taking and thriving behaviors in students. In addition, "the 40 assets show a strong resemblance to a guidance-program set of goals and objectives." Anderson cites the book *All Kids Are Our Kids*, written by Peter Benson, the president of Search Institute. In his book, Benson details a plan for communities to rebuild the developmental infrastructure for children. This enables intergenerational relationships, which are at the heart of asset building. Thus, according to Anderson, counselors need to move out into the community with a community-based guidance program. He does caution us that "although the potential benefits of a community-based guidance program grounded in an assets approach are relatively clear, the challenges are significant. To get out of the traditional office and into the community is the biggest paradigm shift."

Section 2, Counseling for Employability, contains two articles. Ammon begins with an introduction to the Arizona Comprehensive Competency-Based Guidance (CCBG) program model. She then turns to her experience with the National Occupational Information Coordinating Committee (NOICC) Adult Career Portfolio in a business and industry setting. Her conclusion, as it relates to the future, is that "the human need for counselor interaction related to career development will persist into 2021." She turns to her Career Decidedness Study and relates its salient points and implications for career guidance in 2021:

- Career counseling is interactive and, optimally, client need determines the counseling intervention.
- Career guidance interventions that help employees raise their level of career decidedness would facilitate their completion of a career plan.
- The composite of evaluations from both the Portfolio Group Session and eight-hour Career Development Class interventions evidenced a high degree of customer satisfaction; employees continued to request those interventions.

She believes that the CCBG will continue to be viable in the future "if (schools and school counselors) work with business and industry advisory council members to understand project work and new job titles, and to build into their models the concept of career resilience as related to the career and educational domains."

Another issue concerning the future is the workplace and the preparation of those who will be required to meet the challenges therein. Toepfer stresses that it is essential to identify the skills and information today's youth will need to qualify for evolving work and career opportunities. Those skills and information then have to be articulated into effective pre-K through grade 12 programs of learning experiences. He then addresses systemic educational concerns. Much of his comments focus on the middle-level educational efforts. He asserts that "the singular focus on academic standards risks creating (a) a surplus of overqualified people for employment opportunities requiring academic preparation, and (b) a substantial population of others unable to achieve those standards who have not developed other employability skills. More than preparing rocket scientists, our society needs to provide all students with basic technological literacy." Toepfer speaks to the need for a "zero-defect" model that assists students according to their own needs and interests, at their own pace.

Diversity is a major issue today, as it will be in the future. Section 3, Considering Multicultural Issues, addresses the issue of diversity—an issue of great concern as we continue to move into a global society. Lindsey, Robins, and Lindsey offer a "cultural proficiency model" in which "educators and students will know they are valued, and they will involve community members in the school to facilitate their own cultural understanding." On a continuum that consists of six points, ranging from cultural destructiveness to cultural proficiency, "cultural proficiency is the endpoint . . . , the point at which educators and the school environment will optimally facilitate effective cross-cultural interaction." The authors describe culturally proficient behavior in detail as a model for future student support providers.

Tarver Behring "dreams of a systemic multicultural approach by the field of school counseling in the twenty-first century." According to her, "culture is defined in terms of membership in subgroups based on gender, ethnicity, socioeconomic status, religion, sexual orientation, and handicapping conditions; each group has values, beliefs, norms, traditions, language, and other features that are distinct and that define the group." She asks what multiculturally inclusive school counseling services might look like in the twenty-first century and creates a number of examples. She looks "forward to the time when a multicultural worldview is infused into all aspects of the educational system, so that we no longer need to use the word *multicultural* to describe specific services."

As I state in the beginning of this foreword, approaches to the future differ. There are those who believe that what we have now will be viable in the future. Section 4, Staying the Course, addresses this possibility. Gysbers describes a model for comprehensive guidance programs as an "example of a current and widely used student-centered program in the schools that is specifically designed to facilitate students' personal, career, and academic development with strong support from and in collaboration with parents, teachers, administrators, and community members, including personnel in the business and labor communities." For Gysbers, "the same organizational structure for guidance that works today will work in 2021," although he does acknowledge that some guidance activities will change as society and individuals change. Furthermore, "staying the course with the basic organizational structure . . . will provide the consistency, continuity, and common language to allow us finally to show the student results we have anticipated for so long."

Gazda says that student support programs will be related to the kind of schools in existence at the time. In looking ahead, he describes the Georgia Partnership for Excellence in Education's *Next Generation School Project,* in which he participated as a member of the "Re-invent Secondary Education" ad hoc team. He lists "seven vital change criteria that a school system could use to organize itself differently in order to be more effective." These criteria include (a) self-paced learning, (b) mastery-based progress, (c) nontracking placement, (d) continuous progress, (e) total reorganization commitment, (f) external influence, and (g) cooperative learning. He notes that these seven criteria are incorporated in the Corsini 4-R School model and addresses that model in detail. It appears to Gazda that change will occur very slowly over the next 20 years. He does not see any radical changes but believes the "next 20 years could be a transitional period during which many different options are tried until the more effective models emerge."

A current role of the school counselor is that of promoting academic achievement. Hanson contends that in this role, counselors "will more fully define academic support in terms of building and providing programs and interventions that will directly engage the learning needs of children." One aspect of this endeavor is to help the school become a learning community and periodically assess the learning climate of the school. Hanson emphasizes a number of specific skills that are building blocks to successful learning and indicates how the counselor will help children and parents address these skills. The skills noted include goal setting, time management, task analysis, memory and listening skills, note taking, test taking, strategies for reading comprehension and writing, and others.

What kind of counselor shall we have in the future? Section 5, Preparing Student Support Professionals, considers the implications of future-oriented counselors. House, Martin, and Ward suggest that counselor educators must prepare school counselors to be leaders and advocates. "It is critical that school counselors move beyond their current roles as helper-responders in order to become proactive leaders and advocates for the success of all students in schools." Essentially, counselor educators are to help produce "action-oriented critical thinkers." House, Martin, and Ward go on to establish a rationale for the changes based on addressing an achievement gap "between poor and minority students and their more advantaged peers." The current school counselor preparation programs are discussed, leading to recognition that counselor educators need to "move to a proactive approach that addresses systems change." But first, counselor educators must examine their personal beliefs and their beliefs about the need for change and how systems change. House, Martin, and Ward offer a number of questions to be addressed by counselor educators as well as goals for school counselor preparation, followed by a proposal for a mission-driven model to revise the preparation curriculum. Among the essential elements the authors describe as important to changing the counselor education curriculum are the following: "(a) criteria for selection and recruitment of candidates for counselor preparation programs; (b) curricular content, structure, and sequence of courses; (c) method of instruction, field experiences, and practice; (d) induction process into the profession; (e) working relationships with community partners; (f) professional development for counselor educators; (g) university–school district partnerships; and (h) university–state department of education partnerships."

Dear also addresses the preparation of counselors and reminds us that every school has an obligation to accept every student living within a certain district. With such diversity, schools must be at the forefront of helping all children develop the basic skills and qualities necessary in society: "The student of the year 2021 should leave the K–12 system as an academically, socially, and psychologically balanced, civic-minded person ready to enter society and become a responsible, productive individual with basic skills in reading, writing, and thinking critically, as well as competence in the use of computers and other emerging technologies." The future pupil service provider is to be the catalyst to "a better relationship, agreement, and level of commitment among the *learners, teachers,* and the *end users* of the person being taught." Dear identifies what each of these categories must "bring to the table" in order to accomplish what needs to be done. The basic concept of learners, teachers, and end users applies to institutions of higher education, in which the learners are credentialed-counselor candidates, the teachers are counselor educators, and the end users are the public schools that will employ the learners. Counselors must be experts "in the two extremes of the human behavioral continuum. On the one end are such behaviors as motivation, self-esteem, personal growth, nurturing, positive reinforcement, and support; on the other end are crisis prevention and intervention, conflict management and mediation, problem solving and decision making, and the development of refusal skills." He encourages student counselors to foster student leadership throughout the K–12 system: "Ultimately, counselors and other support staff of 2021 should not only work hard to acquire certain skills and competencies, but they should also work toward assisting students to acquire those same competencies."

As to individuals with disabilities, Orange and Brodwin draw upon recent federal legislation (Americans with Disabilities Act and Individuals with Disabilities Education Act) to build their vision of the future. The authors' vision is based on four premises: "(a) that every public school will have support services for students with disabilities; (b) that rehabilitation counselors will be available for these students in every school; (c) that architectural barriers that impede access for people with disabilities to move freely about their environment will no longer exist; and (d) that U.S. society will adopt a philosophy of total inclusion of people with disabilities in all aspects of life and living, including public education." They state that the goals of the legislation will be realized by the year 2021. They speak to the issues of inclusion and integration. To ensure that these issues are addressed in the public school sector, accommodations must be made. "Disability has broad sociocultural implications that go beyond the physical, mental, and emotional limitations." In the future, "Public school personnel . . . realize that sociocultural considerations include discrimination in education and employment." The authors talk about "assistive technology" that "has helped provide persons with disabilities greater independence in the areas of social, educational, vocational, and leisure-time pursuits." Empowerment philosophy will have been adopted by the public school system in 2021; this philosophy is based on four tenets: (a) "Each individual is of great worth and dignity"; (b) "all people have equal opportunities to maximize their potential and are deserving of help from society, whenever necessary, to achieve this potential"; (c) "people strive to grow and change in positive ways"; and (d) "individuals are free to make their own decisions about managing their lives and futures."

Hallberg sees five major trends in the future that provide a context for college counseling: (a) "computer dominance"; (b) "the university without a place"; (c) "the university as a source of societal power and, therefore, money"; (d) "the narcissism of individuality"; and (e) "the faculty as entrepreneurs." While there is positivism in computer dominance, there is also a downside. The university, as a place, will cease to exist. Research money will increase the power of universities and research faculty, but faculty will spend more time in company labs than on campus. The student as a consumer will have more power as an individual to determine when, where, what, and how he or she will learn. Faculty will emerge as entrepreneurs, and tenure will cease. Librarian faculty will emerge as key professionals in the acquisition of information. The lecture method will be passé. "Moreover, good teaching and research will be inextricably tied to individual student progress." Hallberg goes on to look at four major trends in higher education counseling. The new organization of 2021 "will be much like the new organization suggested in the trends stated above: entrepreneurial and computer driven." According to Hallberg, "the new century will demand new skills in three areas. First, we [school counselors] will need new skills related to changing behavior, not merely presenting information. Second, we will need to move from therapy to direct teaching of content; and third, we will need to move from being artists to being scientists."

Finally, we come to an arena that is relatively new for counselors. Section 6, Riding Political and Technological Currents, takes the reader on a trip that will challenge the typical counselor's belief system. One might question school counseling within a political arena, but Rowell makes a case that "the future of school counseling is bound to political processes interwoven with the contemporary education reform movement and with the social and economic conditions of the emerging global economy." He offers an analysis of the future of school counseling via two paths: institutional theory and progressive social commentary. In response to general criticism of school counselors who do not want to engage in the political arena, Rowell asks that they consider an alternative view that politics are unavoidable and "it is essential for us to learn to do our politics wisely—with care, skill, and humility—on behalf of, first and foremost, children and youth." In conducting a political analysis, Rowell delves into contemporary school reform agenda, the professionalization of school counseling, and the relationship between counseling and the critical social and economic issues of the twenty-first century.

Mitchell and Hardy begin by looking to the past 20 years and the strides we have made in technology. With that in mind, they indicate that it might be difficult to project what the next 20 years will look like. They note that "computer capacity has doubled (and halved in price) roughly every 18 months for the past 50 years." With increasing capacity, new forms of computers will evolve, and with these, new ways of dealing with life will develop. Telecommunications will evolve to a point that we will have "Homo cyberneticus": people who are online—always! "In short, easy and inexpensive access to the Internet should have the same revolutionary effect on everyday life that the access to electricity did half a century ago. . . . It will simply permeate every aspect of human functioning." Biotechnology and artificial life is the third area (computer science and telecommunications being the first and second) that Mitchell and Hardy consider influential on the future of guidance programs. They point out that "among the predictions floating around is that ultimately we will carry around our entire genetic makeup on a handy CD. A trip to the doctor's will entail an examination of the information on the CD, rather than a physical. . . . Once we start cloning ourselves and selecting the genetic characteristics of our children, it is anyone's guess as to what is likely to happen to humans."

Unfortunately, when Mitchell and Hardy turn to the impact of these trends on guidance programs of the future, they return to reality quickly with the knowledge that schools (where guidance programs now exist) will not have changed much. Although they see great potential for change, they qualify all "statements with words such as *could* and *might* because schools (and their associated guidance programs) are notoriously slow to change." How services will be offered depends on how schools will change and on how the services might be provided within or without the school structure.

Anticipating and forecasting what student support services and counseling will be like in the future is difficult. One can sense future scenarios within most of the chapters. No one controls the future, and no one knows what will happen tomorrow—let alone 20 years from now. There are three kinds of futures according to the futurists: probable, possible, and preferable. If one believes in projecting trends, then the *probable* future will occur. According to most of the authors, it is *possible* for the scenarios they offer to occur. But it is the *preferable* future that we should be seeking, which includes many of the ideas and concepts offered in this book.

Donald G. Hays, Ph.D.
Professor of Education (Retired)
University of La Verne, California

Introduction:

Student Support Programs for the Future— The Call for New Paradigms

C. D. Johnson & Sharon K. Johnson

Most student support professionals maintain an established "role and function" approach to their work. They address change by adding on to their list of responsibilities, then they are slowly consumed by stress and overload. To better understand the current dilemma of counselors, one need only trace the history of school-based student support services. Initially counselors were advisers, charged with assisting students to identify a vocation that matched their personal characteristics. Later, students' mental health was added to school concerns in response to public concern over dysfunctional children, and counselor-training programs expanded to include therapeutic skills to help counselors work with students and their families. In the 1990s, all school personnel were encouraged to refocus their efforts on academic achievement, and counselors began to actively teach students how to study, take tests, plan their educational career, and learn to focus on academic success. These additional responsibilities changed the traditional role of the school counselor without removing any of the former demands. By following "The Calf Path" (Johnson & Johnson, 1983)—that is, blindly continuing tasks that formerly were part of the counseling profession—counselors find their visions become limited in scope and flexibility as they struggle to fulfill all of the expectations with few resources and little help. Populations they serve get the same treatment regardless of differences in values, culture, family structures, or economy. As a result of maintaining the status quo, systemic changes necessary to fully utilize current technology and other resources are perceived as a threat. It seems that each professional group has its own "path," thereby creating territoriality and hindering collaboration toward achieving the delineated mission of the organization. Yet collaboration is paramount in forming a learning community in which each member is committed to the single purpose of the organization (Senge, 1990).

The Calf Path

one day through the primeval wood
a calf walked home as good calves should

but made a trail all bent askew,
a crooked trail as calves all do.
since then three hundred years have fled,
and I infer the calf is dead.

but still he left behind his trail,
and thereby hangs my moral tale.

the trail was taken up next day
by a lone dog that passed that way;

and then a wise bellwether sheep
pursued the trail o'er vales and steep
and drew the flock behind him, too
as good bellwethers always do.

and from that day, o'er hill and glade.
through these old woods a path was made.

and many men wound in and out,
and dodged and turned and bent about.

and uttered words of righteous wrath
because 'twas such a crooked path;

but still they followed . . . do not laugh.
the first migrations of that calf.
this forest path became a lane.
that bent and turned and turned again.
this crooked lane became a road,
where many a poor horse with his load
toiled on beneath the burning sun
and traveled some three miles in one.

and thus a century and a half
they trod the footsteps of that calf.

the years passed on in swiftness fleet;
the road became a village street;   and this, before men were aware.
       a city's crowded thoroughfare.

       and soon the central street was this
       of a renowned metropolis.

the men two centuries and a half
trod in the footsteps of that calf.
a hundred thousand men were led
by one calf near three centuries dead.

for men are prone to go it blind
along the calf-paths of the mind
       and work away from sun to sun
       to do what other men have done

       they follow in the beaten track,
       and out and in, and forth and back.

       and still their devious course pursue,
       to keep the path that others do

       they keep the path a sacred groove
       along which all their lives they move,

       but how the wise old wood gods laugh
       who saw the first primeval calf!

Sam Walter Foss, 1896

With the identified situation as it exists today, traditional methods of changing the role or function of professional groups within an organization are doomed to failure. To develop a new paradigm, we must address the importance of creating effective metaphors with which to build our collective future as professionals. The metaphor we suggest is *coherent ecology*, a term selected to provide a framework or blueprint for building learning communities that ensure each individual is significant and has a sense of belonging. To ensure that our students achieve this goal, the collective body of student support personnel and individual professionals must achieve new perspectives.

Building a coherent ecology is dependent upon an environment where everyone is significant and everyone belongs. To belong one must contribute and be appreciated.

> We have only begun the process of discovering and inventing the new organizational forms that will inhabit the twenty-first century. We need the courage to let go of the old world, to relinquish most of what we have cherished, to abandon our interpretations about what does and doesn't work. As Einstein is often quoted as saying: "No problem can be solved from the same consciousness that created it. We must learn to see the world anew." (Wheatley, 1994, p. 3)

Some of the identified current changes that affect our social institutions—including education, community, police, health, armed services, and all other government agencies—provide a glimpse of the world as it is developing. These changes can lead the way to the new coherent ecology or, if seen as threats to the status quo, can result in extinction for current institutions. The intent of this publication is to provide information that will facilitate breaking away from the traditional calf path of exclusion to creating a new vision of inclusion. The authors were given the following query: "How do you envision student support programs in the year 2021?" Each author's response to this question adds his or her unique perspective to the task ahead, the task of redesigning student support programs for the future to ensure all students will be prepared for productive citizenship.

References

Foss, S. W. (1896). The calf path. *Whiffs from wild meadows*. Boston: Lee and Shepard.

Johnson, C., & Johnson, S. (1983). Competency-based training of career development specialists, or let's get off the calf path. *Vocational Guidance Quarterly, 30* (4).

Senge, P. (1990). *The fifth discipline: The art and practice of the learning organization*. New York: Currency Doubleday.

Wheatley, M. (1994). *Leadership and the new science: Learning about organization from an orderly universe*. San Francisco: Berrett-Koehler Publishers.

About the Authors

C. D. "Curly" Johnson, Ph.D., has been a consultant for more than 30 years in the areas of education, counseling, mental health, and business. Currently president of Professional Update, an educational and business consulting firm, Dr. Johnson has consulted in 30 states and 16 countries on a variety of programs, including results-based school counseling, marriage and family counseling, student development, group counseling, and school-home partnerships. He has authored and co-authored books and articles in the areas of at-risk students and potential dropouts, family practices, parent-school partnerships, group leadership, therapeutic techniques, career development, program evaluation, and management for results. He resides and runs an active consultant practice from his residence in San Juan Capistrano, California. Dr. Johnson is the recipient of several achievement awards from national and state professional associations including PTA, NCDA, CACD, and CASC.

Sharon K. Johnson, Ed.D., is retired from her position as professor and coordinator of the Counseling and Educational Leadership Program within the Division of Administration and Counseling at California State University, Los Angeles. She has consulted nationally and internationally with educational and business organizations, as well as co-authoring articles and books in the areas of parent-school partnerships; group counseling;

program development and evaluation; management training; marriage, family, and child counseling; career development; and multicultural issues. Dr. Johnson is a former teacher and school counselor, and was director of pupil services for the Howard County Public Schools in Maryland for 10 years. She has been active in many national and state professional associations, including PDK, AAUW, ASCD, AERA, and multiple divisions of ACA, representing group work specialists, counselor educators and supervisors, career development professionals, and school counselors. She is past president of the California Association of Counselor Educators and Supervisors, the Los Angeles chapter of Phi Delta Kappa, and the California Association for Counseling and Development.

BUILDING STRONGER SCHOOL COUNSELING PROGRAMS:

Bringing Futuristic Approaches into the Present

Section 1:

Embracing the Community

Chapter One

Current Trends and Their Implications for Futures in the Counseling Profession

Pat Nellor Wickwire

Contributors to this volume were invited to consider the nature of student support offerings in the year 2021. Using today's paradigm for school systems, children born in 2001 will have completed high school by that time. They will be employed, completing community college or specialized training, enrolled in a university or college, or engaged in a combination of educational and employment ventures. The task of projecting 20 years into the future is both sobering and thought provoking.

This chapter includes basic information about the study of futures, a brief examination of some of the trends likely to affect student support offerings, and some ideas and predictions regarding the counseling profession. Finally, a concluding statement includes a caveat for the counseling profession about approaching futures.

The Study of Futures

In developing predictions, futurists study, interpret, and select probabilities, possibilities, and preferences (Bishop, 1998). This forecasting is based on assumptions and current known information that appear relevant to a given area. In making predictions, futurists consider trends, critical events, and choices (Bishop, 1998). In noting trends, futurists assume evolution. In projecting critical events, they assume unpredictability. In acknowledging choices, they assume influence.

Each potential future situation can be identified as probable, possible, or preferred. *Probable futures* assume likelihoods given the lack of surprising and cataclysmic events and given reasonable and consistent choices. *Possible futures* assume various

3

combinations of trends, events, and choices in outlining multiple alternative plausible futures. *Preferred futures* assume that certain trends, events, and choices will or will not occur. Given these assumptions, futurists create scenarios with plot lines, themes, and descriptors of anticipated interim and end conditions. In doing so, they interpret elements of relevant physical, scientific, social, emotional, moral, economic, political, educational, work, and other environments. Futurists' beliefs range on a continuum from a deterministic, accommodating, "let it happen" attitude to a generative, focused, "make it happen" outlook.

Predictions can be made with greater ease, accuracy, and definitiveness in some areas than in others. Confidence in prediction is directly related to the probabilities of gradual evolution, unpredictable happenings, and control. Furthermore, confidence in prediction is likely to be greater in information-based areas than in areas that are inference based or opinion based. Time and timing are influential factors, and short-term forecasting is generally simpler and more accurate than long-term forecasting.

Emerging and Continuing Trends

Certain social and educational trends are likely to affect the future of education, and with it, counseling. These trends relate to electronics and computers; distance learning; the emphasis on competencies, skills, and standards; lifelong learning; and work and career changes, among others.

Expansion of Electronics

Electronics are heavily used for information, communication, commerce, and entertainment (Kraut et al., 1998). The computer and the Internet are following the telephone and the television in changing the social and economic fabric of home, community, and work. Well established as a harbinger of the information-knowledge-service era, the computer is a contributor to globalization and to many other changes throughout the United States and the world. Currently, 66% of U.S. employees work in all areas of services; by the year 2000, 44% are projected to be in data services alone (Pritchett, 1998).

The impact of the Internet on the lives of individuals is not yet fully known, and varying opinions exist about the "high-touch" (human contact) correlates of high technology. For example, in a review of literature regarding human factors and electronics use, Kraut et al. (1998) found both negative and positive effects of technology on socialization. In a field trial with 169 participants in 93 households in their first years of Internet use, researchers found decreases in family participation and size of social circle, and increases in depression and loneliness. This has been framed as increasing isolation (Sleek, 1998a), and warnings about the effects of virtual versus real worlds have been issued (Sleek, 1998b).

In a similar vein, Polka (1997) reminded readers of the need for balance between high tech and high touch, and identified five attitudinal correlates of the human side of technological change: challenge, commitment, control, creativity, and caring. He recommended that these five characteristics be present in innovation and reform in education. Others have recommended the inclusion of educators, including counselors, in the implementation of technology in educational settings (Hartman, 1998).

As a result of the digital revolution, intelligent tutoring systems, personalized learning modules, and voice recognition are beginning to be used in learning (Bassi, Cheney, & Lewis, 1998). The "plug-in" school—with modules blending responsibilities, functions, activities, and tasks of home, work, and school—may be technologically possible (Pesanelli, 1993). Interactive simulations may be sponsored by and replicative of whole communities and their component parts (Page, 1998).

Growth of Distance Learning

One consequence of the increasing use of electronic technology is the advancement of distance learning. The coincidence of time, place, and personnel is no longer essential to the content, process, and structure of education. Virtual universities are multiplying and, in some cases, supplanting in-residence and on-site institutions as locations of study. Major industries are now offering virtual training and education. New jobs and job titles are appearing, such as distant-site facilitator, management sponsor, and technology supporter (Abernathy, 1998). Web-based training is underway, using web-specific technology, training methods, and standards compliance (Black, 1998).

Emphasis on Competencies and Skills

On the human side, one major trend in employment is the emphasis on competencies and skills, with employment being

5

earned by way of accomplishment and productivity, with a corresponding de-emphasis on personality traits, and the loss of entitlement therein. The federal government and business and industry are developing organization-specific competency and sequential skill packages for work and training applications (Wickwire, 1995). In the high-performance workplace, employees are expected to have competencies related to resources, interpersonal relationships, information, systems, and technology, as well as foundations of basic work skills, thinking skills, and desirable personal qualities. Schools are implementing instructional and assessment programs designed to teach active learners foundation, employability, transferable, and transition-management skills and competencies (Secretary's Commission on Achieving Necessary Skills, 1991). Organizations such as the Business Coalition for Education Reform (1997), which is supporting the use of transcripts in hiring for employment, are involved in the effort to implement these programs in schools.

Emphasis in employment is shifting away from the normal curve and individualized approaches of differential psychology and toward the approaches of the management sciences and the psychology of education and behavior (McLagan, 1997; Mirabile, 1997). Important now are competencies and skills for high-quality, productive performance. Important now are knowledge of content; skills in processes, including specific tools, tasks, and activities; skills in facilitative, contributory attitudes and behaviors, such as teamwork; and skills leading to desired results and output (McLagan, 1997). Employers identify core competencies and superior performance indicators; organizational vision, mission, goals, and objectives are prominent, along with flexibility in employment.

Competency modeling is becoming a science with its own vocabulary and methods, and job analysis is being conducted through direct observation, critical incident analysis, job function analysis, focus group research, work methods analysis, interviews, job inventories and checklists, and position-analysis questionnaires (Mirabile, 1997). Competency models are constructed in different ways with different degrees of detail depending upon their purpose, function, and practicality. For example, construction of a competency model may begin with identifying success factors, followed by developing behavioral descriptors, rank ordering of factors by criticality, and establishing proficiency levels for factors.

<u>Emphasis on Standards</u>

Closely allied to the movement toward skills and competencies is the movement toward standards, with accountability and assessment becoming bywords in public, legislative, professional, and consumer domains. The federal government has spearheaded a drive toward the development and adoption of national education standards; most states have responded by developing and adopting state education standards. Associations and agencies have also developed and adopted standards (Campbell & Dahir, 1997; Wickwire, 1996). In addition, some two dozen industries are developing standards under agreements with the National Skill Standards Board ("ASTD Works," 1998; Wickwire, 1995).

The establishment of standards is generally initiated with content standards followed by performance standards and, thus, carries assessment and evaluation components. Standards are designed to identify the subject matter to be learned, the level to which it is to be learned, and the applications for which it is to be learned. Standards are also designed to measure the degree and the nature of the learning, to recycle and modify educational approaches until learning occurs, to evaluate the entire approach systematically and to make needed changes, and, ultimately, to institute reforms in education for more focused acquisition of learning and more defined accountability for what one learns and how one uses this learning.

The move toward standards has led to wider experimentation and innovation in assessment and evaluation by an increasing number of professionals. For example, *value-added alternative assessment* may take the forms of the portfolio, demonstration, exhibit, criterion-referenced testing, or performance assessment scored with rubrics. Moreover, different methods of evaluation are being developed for the different purposes of evaluating these five levels; reaction, learning, behavior, results, and output. The effort to develop evaluation methods has been accompanied by examination of and experimentation with systems, policies, and practices such as social promotion, transitions from school to career, private operation of public schools, teacher preparation and placement, school choice, world competition, community service, and preschool offerings ("Making the Grade," 1998).

Standards-based education reform is touted as a means (a) to increase equity for all; (b) to add clarity for all stakeholders regarding expectations for learning; (c) to offer an internally integrated and consistent system of planning, delivery, and evaluation; and (d) to provide for individual and organizational consequences of reaching or not reaching standards (Panasonic Foundation & American Association of School Administrators, 1998). Under standards-based reform, educational institutions could become learning organizations, learning communities, and continuing laboratories within which to study and apply the bases of learning.

Inculcation of Lifelong Learning

Lifelong learning is a significant trend that is focused on the development of human capital and social capital. Individuals, organizations, and communities are expected to invest in formal and informal education and training, to the ends of individual and group satisfaction, success, and productivity. Continuous lifelong learning is now essential for individual, organizational, community, state, and national economic growth ("Multifaceted Returns," 1998).

The learning organization (e.g., institution, agency, corporation) is part of the concept of lifelong learning. In the learning organization, a unique synergy drives a systematic search for collective learning in order to achieve constructive results and output. Ideally, employers and employees learn and share openly; they review their beliefs and values, behaviors, solutions, and the connections among them; and they work together to improve productivity (Calvert, Mobley, & Marshall, 1994). Continuous improvement is a goal.

In the lifelong-learning paradigm, the learning organization adopts a knowledge-based culture with databases to support members of the organization in decision making about policy, programs, and operations. Adding value, developing intellectual capital, and achieving results and outcomes are important; structures, systems, and processes are internally consistent (Tecker, Eide, & Frankel, 1997).

Reconstruction of Work and Career

Paradigms for career and work are changing (Wickwire, 1993); serial, mobile employment is becoming more frequent and job changes more rapid; contingent work and cybernetic work spaces are increasing; passion, action, and entrepreneurism are becoming necessary; expectations for flexibility, responsiveness, and quality are rising; specific high-performance skills, such as problem solving, are increasingly being targeted; and lifetime job entitlement is no longer either certain or expected (Pritchett, 1998). In 1970, the usefulness of a worker's skills diminished by half over 15 years; today, that figure is 2 to 3 years ("Talking Trends," 1998).

Matching of individual assets, attitudes, and aspirations to employer needs for personal qualities, skills, and outcomes in work and career continues. Ongoing self-knowledge, self-assessment, self-development, and self-management based on knowledge of one's inner world and the outer environment are required for self-sufficient career and work in the information-knowledge-service era (Borchard, 1995). Increasingly, individuals need to add value for employment by advancing and enhancing their portable skills. To meet change in work and career, they need to release dependence on traditional systems and to create their own fluid options (Kaye & Farren, 1996).

Other Trends
Change. Change is a significant overriding trend. The current speed, frequency, complexity, and scope of change require commitment, vigilance, capacity to learn, adaptability, and renewal. Managing organizational change requires leadership strategies centered on customers and driven by mission, value, and behavior (Trahant, Burke, & Koonce, 1997).
Information. The creation of information is accelerating and its availability increasing. More information has been produced in the last 30 years than in the last 5,000 years; one weekday edition of the New York Times includes more information than the average person in seventeenth-century England would encounter in a lifetime (Pritchett, 1998). Knowledge is becoming a commodity; industries are managing knowledge by building knowledge repositories, using knowledge for discussion and learning, offering knowledge-transfer services, and encouraging knowledge appreciation through sharing. Some organizations are initiating positions such as chief knowledge officer, director of intellectual capital, and chief learning officer (Bassi et al., 1998). More rapid access to extensive information results in both positive and negative effects, including increased or decreased effectiveness and accuracy, sensory overload, and anxiety caused by information overload.
Additional trends. Additional trends are numerous, among them are changes in global relationships, age and cultural demographics, family structure, socioeconomics, patterns of socialization, and leisure opportunities and choices. Partly in

reaction to the information-knowledge-service era, the existential-experiential-spiritual era is beginning.

The Counseling Profession in the Year 2021

Counseling as a formal discipline is a late nineteenth- and early twentieth-century invention, created in part because of the shift from the agricultural age to the industrial age. Industrialization brought increasing urbanization, immigration, migration, and differences in work and family. Needs for information about occupational options arose, and interest in social, economic, and educational issues grew. Vocational guidance and the measurement of individual differences began, as responses to trends of the time (Herr, 1997).

Today's trends, as discussed above, include the expansion of electronics and rise of distance learning; the movement toward competencies, skills, standards, and lifelong learning; and the reconstruction of work and career. Trends also include changes in the nature of change, information, globalism, demographics, socioeconomics, family, socialization, and leisure. The information-knowledge-service age is burgeoning and evolving toward the existential-experiential-spiritual age.

These trends need response, as did those of a century ago. The counseling profession will respond and initiate, exercising combinations of authentic, visionary, cultural, quality, and service leadership (based on modeling, ideas, interpersonal factors, excellence, and systems support, respectively) (Schwahn & Spady, 1998). Various counseling futures are possible. The needs of the student are paramount in studying and selecting futures to pursue.

The Student of Tomorrow

The student of tomorrow will need to be aware of, understand, and apply behavior and learning (in career, work, family, education, and leisure areas) with the goal of mastering the following qualities, skills, and areas of knowledge:

1. Purpose, vision, mission, goals, expected outcomes, and outputs
2. Partnership, teamwork, conflict resolution, problem solving
3. Flexibility, adaptability, resiliency, self-management
4. Initiation, involvement, sense of ownership, responsibility

10

5. Change management, inquiry, innovation, continuous improvement, renewal
6. Leadership, decision making, options discovery and selection
7. Technology, organization facilitation, systems implementation
8. Openness, responsiveness, communication, consistency
9. Alertness, high performance, quality, productivity, accountability
10. Recognition of complexity, multiple-skill mastery, skill transferability, transition management
11. Content, process, structure, results

As the knowledge-information-service age matures and dovetails into the existential-experiential-spiritual age, the student will seek to add high-touch efforts to balance high-tech, to increase rewarding social and personal involvement and contributions in the home and in the community, to become part of the service community with integrity, to clarify the relevance of morality to behavior and learning, to explore matters of personal and societal ethics, to test systems and structures of living and working, to identify and experience the effects of these systems and structures on the affective domain, and, in general, to seek a variety of new experiences that will enhance breadth and in-depth capacities to think, know, feel, be, and do.

The Counselor of Tomorrow

The counselor of tomorrow will have the same needs for awareness, understanding, and application in behavior and learning as the student of tomorrow, plus the capacity to assist the student to meet those needs. The counselor will be a continuous learner and an accomplished change agent.

The counselor is likely to continue the following professional models, with pragmatic, updated twenty-first-century adaptations.

1. Leadership: authentic, visionary, cultural, quality, service-based (Schwahn & Spady, 1998)
2. Systems: programs, services, content, processes, structures, policies, procedures, operations
3. Domains: affective, cognitive, academic-educational, career-vocational-work, personal-social
4. Treatment: prevention, development, remediation, crisis intervention

5. Service delivery: assessment, diagnosis, planning and preparation, implementation-monitoring, evaluation-recycling
6. Evaluation: formative, summative, reaction, learning, behavior, results, outcomes-outputs

In working with individuals, groups, agencies, organizations, and communities, the twenty-first-century counselor will maintain the vision of the optimal development of human potential, and the mission of developing and delivering theory, practice, ethics, guidelines, standards, laws, and regulations that are consonant with the vision. The counselor will seek content, process, and structure that support mass customization of counseling services with customer-oriented quality. The counselor will respond to ever-increasing expectations for accountability in programs and services, and to increasing competition within the human development field.

The counselor will strive to embrace change and an increasing number of options as opportunities and challenges. Like others, the counselor will work under conditions with high expectations for on-demand communications, decisions, problem solving, and other actions. The counselor will recognize the complex trend toward multiples: causes, options, success factors, intelligences, models for practice, and others. The counselor will use technology productively, for example, to forecast and evaluate alternative client futures, to obtain immediate feedback on emotionality of clients, or to monitor client choices. The counselor will be called upon to create means to balance high tech with high touch, and to lead in establishing a culture of caring, commitment, and responsibility. The counselor will apply both the science and the art of counseling.

The counselor will be expert in the development and enhancement of the person, the environment, and person-environment interaction. Major roles of the counselor will revolve around the creation, location, and dissemination of information and other resources; the creation, location, delivery, and brokering of strategies for the modification of client behavior and learning patterns; and the creation, location, delivery, and brokering of strategies for intervention into valences in the environment.

The counselor will continue to fulfill various functions and may work under different job titles as, perhaps, alliance creator, career and work competencies educator, consultant for self-actualization, excellence agent, experience designer, human development artist, information broker, insight developer, interventionist, leadership development specialist, learning facilitator, life planner, option designer and locator, predictor of behavior, problem-solving skills builder, scanner-mover of environment, situation clarifier, social intelligence planner, student advocate, systems designer, trainer in decision making, or whole life monitor.

Within education systems, the counselor will have equivalent status and influence with other educators. Management support services, curriculum and instruction support services, and student support services will have equivalent responsibility and authority; each of these three structural components will, in turn, have its own management, curriculum and instruction, and student services. Schools will be more open and fluid institutions, and responsibility for seamless informal and formal education will be shared by learner, home, business and industry, community, and school.

Counseling Futures

Counseling is about being or becoming a whole person. Counseling is about self-sufficiency and connectedness; about knowing when, how, and where to find information, assistance, and support; and about being responsible for self. Counseling is about value-added programs and services, and about results and outcomes. Counseling is about selecting and offering the best possible theory and practice to create the best possible desired changes for clients.

In a preferred future for the year 2021, the counseling profession will operate from planned systems, programs, and policies, as opposed to operating on a situational basis. Counseling will first determine desired results, outcomes, or outputs, and then determine content, process, and structure. Specialized counseling strategies keyed to results will be used; these strategies will have been tested against characteristics of the organism and the environment. Probabilities of the effects of given strategies in given situations with given clients will be known. An advanced, sophisticated grid may be available for the selection and application of strategies for the specific anticipation of keyed outcomes.

Counselors will conceptualize futures scenarios and test alternative futures that support utilization of information and other resources, modification of learning and behavior, and modification of environment. For example, in one possible counseling future, counseling could be conceived according to a model with a results-based taxonomy; this could add clarity and common understanding for client and counselor about the goals and objectives of the counseling experience. Both client and counselor could agree upon specific, measurable, achievable, realistic, and time-specific objectives. Such a taxonomy could include the following types:

1. Relationship-based
2. Achievement-based
3. Knowledge-based
4. Inquiry-based
5. Creativity-based
6. Leadership-based
7. Motivation-based
8. Accommodation-based
9. Values-based
10. Support-based
11. Action-based
12. Skills-based
13. Anchor-based
14. Mission-based
15. Service-based
16. Vision-based

After client and counselor reach consensus on the themes for the results of counseling, they could develop content, process, and structure, and select and follow through on key strategies. Evaluation of effectiveness, then, could be clearly constructed and conducted by both client and counselor according to client change related to the chosen theme.

This approach could firmly place the focus on results; presumably, process and structure known empirically to have high probabilities for success could be implemented. The framework could apply to the individual, group, agency, or institutional client, and to both direct and indirect interventions. Counselor leadership could ultimately participate actively in policy making, and function in earned and deserved positions of increased span of influence.

Concluding Statement

Counselors are ultimately responsible for futures in the counseling profession, although factors in the external environment may play major roles. Counseling futures could range from obliteration to modification to renaissance, depending, in part, on the posture and action of those in the profession.

Focused convergent and divergent study and action regarding possible, probable, and preferred futures are recommended. This attention is best directed through a proactive approach to defining and creating demonstrable, marketable results that meet client needs. Counselors will make the final choices regarding survival, maintenance, or enhancement of the counseling profession.

References

Abernathy, D. J. (1998, September). The www of distance learning: Who does what and where? *Training and Development, 52*(9), 29–31.

ASTD works to develop national kill standards. (1998, November/December). *ASTD Advance,* 2.

Bassi, L., Cheney, S., & Lewis, E. (1998). Trends in workplace learning: Supply and demand in interesting times. *Training and Development, 52*(11), 51–75.

Bishop, P. (1998, June/July). Thinking like a futurist. *The Futurist, 32*(5), 39–42.

Black, D. (1998, June/July). Live and online: A wbt primer. *Training and Development, 52*(9), 36, 38.

Borchard, D. (1995, January/February). Planning for career and life: Job surfing on the tidal waves of change. *The Futurist, 29*(1), 8–12.

Business Coalition for Education Reform. (1997). *Making academics count* [Brochure]. Washington, DC: National Alliance of Business.

Calvert, G., Mobley, S., & Marshall, L. (1994, June). Grasping the learning organization. *Training and Development, 48*(6), 37–43.

Campbell, C. A., & Dahir, C. A. (1997). *National standards for school counseling programs.* Alexandria, VA: American School Counselor Association.

Hartman, K. E. (1998, October 28). Technology and the school counselor: Have we left someone out of the revolution? *Education Week, 18*(9), 40, 43.

Herr, E. L. (1997). Perspectives on career guidance and counseling in the twenty-first century. *International Association of Educational and Vocational Guidance Bulletin, 60,* 1–15.

Kaye, B., & Farren, C. (1996, February). Up is not the only way. *Training and Development, 50*(2), 49–53.

Kraut, R., Patterson, M., Lundmark, V., Kiesler, S., Mukopadhyay, T., & Scherlis, W. (1998). Internet paradox: A social technology that reduces social involvement and psychological well-being? *American Psychologist, 53*(9), 1017–1031.

Making the grade. (1998, August 6). *Global Network Trend Letter, 17*(16), 1–4.

McLagan, P. (1997, May). Competencies: The next generation. *Training and Development, 51*(5), 40–45.

Mirabile, R. J. (1997, August). Everything you wanted to know about competency modeling. *Training and Development, 51*(8), 73–77.

The multifaceted returns to education. (1998, June). *National Alliance of Business Workforce Economics Trends: The Business Voice on Workforce Development,* 1–6.

Page, D. (1998, September/October). John Gage: Tapping the unstoppable capability of people. *Converge: Education and Technology Fast Forward, 1*(1), 38–39.

Panasonic Foundation & American Association of School Administrators. (1998). When standards drive change. *Strategies for School System Leaders on District-Level Change, 5*(2), 1–16.

Pesanelli, D. (1993, September/October). The plug-in school: A learning environment for the twenty-first century. *The Futurist, 27*(5), 29–32.

Polka, W. S. (1997, Winter). High-tech + high-touch = twenty-first century educational success. *Educational Horizons, 76*(2), 64–65.

Pritchett, P. (1998). *New work habits for a radically changing world: 13 ground rules for job success in the information age.* Dallas, TX: Pritchett and Associates.

Schwahn, C. J., & Spady, W. G. (1998). *Total leaders: Applying the best future-focused change strategies to education.* Arlington, VA: American Association of School Administrators.

Secretary's Commission on Achieving Necessary Skills. (1991). *What work requires of schools: A SCANS report for America 2000.* Washington, DC: U.S. Department of Labor.

Sleek, S. (1998a, September). Isolation increases with Internet use. *American Psychological Association Monitor, 29*(3), 1, 30, 31.

Sleek, S. (1998b, September). New cybertoast: Here's MUD in your psyche. *American Psychological Association Monitor, 29*(3), 30.

Talking trends: Emphasizing the human in human resources. (1998, November). *American Management Association International Human Resources: Organization Development, 1*(7), 4–5.

Tecker, G., Eide, K., & Frankel, J. (1997, August). In pursuit of a knowledge-based association. *Association Management, 49*(8), 122–130.

Trahant, B., Burke, W. W., & Koonce, R. (1997, September). 12 principles of organizational transformation. *Management Review,* 17–21.

Wickwire, P. N. (1993). America at school and work in the 1990s: Career education: An opportunity. *Youth Policy, 15*(6–7), 16–23.

Wickwire, P. N. (1995). Consortia develop voluntary skill standards with DoL and DoE. *AACE Bonus Brief.* Hermosa Beach, CA: American Association for Career Education.

Wickwire, P. N. (1996). Voluntary content, performance, and skill standards: A resource directory. *AACE Bonus Brief.* Hermosa Beach, CA: American Association for Career Education.

Wickwire, P. N. (Ed.). (1997). Careers, education, and work today. *AACE Forum: Trend Watch.* Hermosa Beach, CA: American Association for Career Education.

About the Author

Pat Nellor Wickwire is president of the American Association for Career Education, president of the California Association for Measurement and Evaluation in Counseling and Development, and editor of the *CACD Journal.* She is past president of the California Association for Counseling and Development, CACD Education Foundation, California Women's Caucus, and Los Angeles County Personnel and Guidance Association. She is past Research and Knowledge chairperson of the American Counseling Association, and member of the World Future Society. She has served as school counselor, school psychologist, coordinator of guidance and psychological services, director of student services and special education, and administrator of a multidistrict special education consortium. Pat is a frequent presenter, consultant, and author on topics related to career, education, work, counseling, management, leadership, gender, writing, futures, and ethics. She has advanced degrees from The University of Texas at Austin and The University of Iowa. Listed in *Who's Who in America,* she has been honored with awards from the California Association for Counseling and Development, National Career Development Association, and Association for Multicultural Counseling.

Chapter Two

The Student Support Team as a
Professional Learning Community

Richard DuFour, Aida Guidice, Deborah Magee
Patricia Martin, & Barbara Zivkovic

Predicting the future is always risky business. Consider the following predictions:

> "When the Paris Exhibition closes, electric light will close with it and no more will be heard of it."
> —Erasmus Wilson, Oxford University, 1878

> "Heavier than air flying machines are impossible."
> —William Thomson (Lord Kelvin), President of the Royal Society, 1895

> "There is not the slightest indication that nuclear energy will ever be obtainable."
> —Albert Einstein, 1932

> "I think there is a world market for about five computers."
> —Thomas Watson, founder of IBM, 1943

> "You ain't going nowhere, son—you ought to go back to driving a truck."
> —Jim Denver, manager of the Grand Ole Opry, to Elvis Presley, 1954

If prognostication is fraught with difficulty in general, anticipating the future of public schools and their programs in tumultuous times is particularly challenging. The ability of public schools to engage in significant, fundamental change is

19

increasingly being called into question. In his review of the research on school innovation, David Perkins (1992, p. 205) arrived at the "profoundly discouraging" conclusion that "almost all educational innovations fail in the long term." Thus, research would seem to support the argument that the schools of the future are likely to look very much like schools of the present.

Another perspective, offered both by friends and foes of public schools alike, predicts the imminent demise of public education. Phil Schlechty (1997, p. ix) is among the school reformers who warn educators that unless they move quickly to transform their schools in dramatic ways, "public schools will not be a vital component of America's system of education in the twenty-first century." The president of the Kettering Foundation echoed that sentiment when he wrote: "The research forces me to say something that I never thought I would say—or even think. The public school system as we know it may not survive into the next century" (Matthews, 1997, p. 741).

There is a third possibility—the possibility that public schools will neither remain as they are nor become extinct, but will undergo fundamental changes. While we acknowledge that this transformation is not inevitable, we do believe that it is possible. Furthermore, student services programs can be affected by and contribute to this transformation.

Three emerging national trends could serve as a catalyst for fundamental change in student services programs. First, throughout most of the twentieth century, the industrial model has dominated American thinking about organizational development. There is now growing recognition, however, that the concept of the learning organization offers a superior model for enhancing the effectiveness of institutions and the people within them. Second, there is a movement away from standardization and uniformity toward greater personalization and individualization of services in both the private and public sectors. Third, the pervasiveness and power of technology are changing standing operating procedures in all areas of life. If student services programs learn to function as a critical component of a learning organization, if they focus on providing more personalized services, and if they capitalize on the potential of technology, they will undergo significant changes between now and 2021.

The School as a Learning Organization

American schools were organized according to the concepts and principles of the prevalent organizational model of the late nineteenth and early twentieth century—the factory model. This model was based on the premise that one best system could be identified to complete any task or solve any organizational problem. It was management's job to identify the one best way, to train workers accordingly, and then to provide the supervision and monitoring to ensure that workers would follow the prescribed methods. Thus, a small group of people could do the thinking for the entire organization. The model demanded centralization, standardization, hierarchical management, a rigid sense of time, and accountability based on adherence to the system.

Schools were designed to mirror the same characteristics, and the factory model in traditional public schools is still much in evidence today. Schools continue to focus on procedures rather than results, following the assumption that if they adhere to the rules—teaching the prescribed curriculum, maintaining the correct class sizes, using the appropriate textbooks, helping students accumulate the right number of course credits, and following district procedures—students will learn what is intended. Little attention is paid to determining whether the learning has actually taken place. Schools remain preoccupied with time and design, organizing the class period, school day, and school year according to rigid schedules that must be followed. Teachers and their opinions are still considered insignificant in many schools. It is left to the *thinkers* of the organization to specify what is to be taught and then to provide the supervision to ensure that teachers do as they are told. Student services personnel typically have even less autonomy and are expected simply to apply uniform policies and procedures rather than use their professional judgment.

The factory model may have served schools well when they were not intended to educate large numbers of students to a high level. The fact that large numbers of students dropped out of school prior to graduation or failed to develop essential skills was not viewed as a cause for great alarm as long as these students had ready access to unskilled jobs in industry regardless of their educational level. But the decline of unskilled jobs in industry and the arrival of the information age have left schools with a model that is ill-equipped to bring students to the high levels of learning necessary to function as productive citizens in the twenty-first century.

The incongruity of the factory model assumptions with the demands on contemporary public education has led to a growing movement to bring the principles of a learning organization to schools. Consider the following:

> Organizations that build in continuous learning in jobs will dominate the twenty-first century. (Drucker, 1992, p. 108)

> The most successful corporation of the future will be a learning organization. (Senge, 1990, p. 4)

> The new problem of change . . . is what would it take to make the educational system a learning organization—expert at dealing with change as a normal part of its work, not just in relation to the latest policy, but as a way of life. (Fullan, 1993, p. 4)

> The Commission recommends that schools be restructured to become genuine learning organizations for both students and teachers; organizations that respect learning, honor teaching, and teach for understanding. (National Commission on Teaching and America's Future, 1996, p. 198)

> We have come to realize over the years that the development of a learning community of educators is itself a major cultural change that will spawn many others. (Joyce & Showers, 1995, p. 3)

> If schools want to enhance their organizational capacity to boost student learning, they should work on building a professional community. (Newmann & Wehlage, 1995, p. 37)

> We argue, however, that when schools attempt significant reform, efforts to form a schoolwide professional community are critical. (Louis, Kruse, & Raywid, 1996, p. 13)

Rarely has research given school practitioners such a consistent message and clear sense of direction. Now those practitioners face the challenge of bringing the characteristics of a learning organization to life in their schools. Those characteristics include:

1. clarity of purpose, shared vision, collective commitments and values, and common goals;
2. collaborative teams engaged in collective inquiry;
3. a focus on results; and
4. a structure and culture that fosters continuous improvement.

Let's examine each of these areas to identify how the student support team of the future can help transform traditional schools into learning communities.

Laying the Foundation of a Learning Organization

Because student services departments of the future will function as learning organizations, they will attend to the four questions that serve as the foundation or building blocks of such organizations. The first of these questions, "Why do we exist?" will challenge members of the department to reflect upon and articulate the fundamental purpose or mission of the department. Addressing this question is the first step in clarifying priorities, giving direction to members of the department, and establishing a results orientation. Clarity of purpose and a willingness to work together in the pursuit of that purpose are essential to a learning organization.

The second issue that student services departments will address is the question of what the department hopes to become, or its vision of its future. Department members will work collaboratively in an effort to describe in detail how they will "look" in the future. They will visualize themselves in action and develop a compelling, attractive future for the department toward which they are committed to working. This clearly articulated, shared vision will identify ideals and establish benchmarks that enable members of the department to be proactive in their work with students, parents, and teachers. Furthermore, this vision for the department will complement and reinforce both the vision that has been developed for the school and the effort to articulate the knowledge, dispositions, and characteristics the school hopes to develop in each student. In short, the student services department of the future will be more effective in achieving results because it will have taken the time to identify the results it is striving to obtain in a credible, compelling shared vision.

The third building block, collective commitments or values, challenges members of the student services department to consider the attitudes, behaviors, and commitments they must demonstrate in order to achieve their shared vision. *Vision* describes aspirations of a desired future state, and *values* describe commitments that people are prepared to make today. The focus of these value statements will be internal rather than external. Instead of citing the deficiencies in students, parents, teachers, society, and so forth, or engaging in the "if only" approach to school improvement ("if only our load were cut in half, then we could do the job"), each member of the student services team will concentrate on what he or she can do to advance the department as it works to better serve students.

The fourth building block that will be in evidence when a department is functioning as a learning organization is developing clear and specific goals. The goals building block raises the questions, "which steps will we take, when will we take them, and how will we measure their impact?" Although this may appear to be the most pragmatic component of the building blocks, goals can contribute to the creation of a learning organization only if they are built upon the three precursors. Furthermore, the identification of clear, measurable, ambitious performance goals represents a critical link to another characteristic of a learning organization—effective collaborative teams (Katzenbach & Smith, 1993).

When the members of a student services department have seriously discussed these questions and arrived at consensus on answers to each question, they will have established the foundation of a learning organization. Although much work will remain if the department is to be transformed, that work will have the benefit of a solid foundation.

Collaborative Teams Engaged in Collective Inquiry

Collaborative teams have been described as "the basic building block of the intelligent organization" (Pinchot & Pinchot, 1993, 66), the "essence of a learning organization" (Dilworth, 1993, 252), and "the critical component for every enterprise— the predominant unit for decision making and getting things done" (Senge, Ross, Smith, Roberts, & Kleiner, 1994, 354). The student services department of the future will recognize that no one staff member can or should hope to meet all the complex needs of students through isolated, individual efforts. Therefore the department will be organized into collaborative work teams that might include counselors, social workers, and deans. These teams will engage in ongoing collective inquiry in at least three areas: the success and well-being of individual students, the effectiveness of programs in meeting the needs of each student, and the effectiveness of the team itself.

Focusing on the Individual Student

The success and well-being of each student will be the primary focus of the student support department of the future. Each member of the team will have instant access to every student on the team's caseload, including each student's grades, progress reports, participation in activities, attendance, discipline referrals and consequences, anecdotal records, goals, four-year plans, parent information, and so forth. The teams will conduct weekly meetings and engage in informal daily contact regarding their students because regular, ongoing communication is the lifeblood of effective teams. The team will develop procedures and systems to monitor each student, will respond promptly to any student who requires additional support, and will work collaboratively to develop an individualized plan for students who are struggling in the standard program. Some of the questions that will drive the collective inquiry of the team might include the following:
- Has the student identified his or her goals?
- Is the student achieving his or her goals and reaching his or her potential through the existing program?
- Is there evidence that this student is having difficulty or needs additional support?
- Would the student benefit from a different program?
- What can we do to meet the needs of this student better?

Assessing the Effectiveness of Programs

A learning community is characterized by a perpetual disquiet, a constant search for a better way. Thus, student services teams will engage in an ongoing assessment of the programs that are in place to meet the needs of students. The goal of this assessment is to develop multiple programs and interventions that respond to the diverse needs of students. Rather than focusing on molding students to fit existing programs, the team will focus on developing programs to meet the individual needs of students. Questions that will drive the collective inquiry of

the team might include the following:
- Do existing programs meet the needs of all students?
- What evidence are we monitoring to ensure that students' needs are being met?
- Are the monitoring systems sufficiently comprehensive?
- How can we use input from students, faculty, and parents to develop more effective programs?
- How can we improve upon the results we are currently getting?

Assessing the Effectiveness of the Team

The student services team will demonstrate the following characteristics of effective teams: Members will be guided by shared purpose, will clarify each member's role and responsibilities, will articulate operational norms or protocols for working together, will establish meeting formats and agendas, will identify specific performance goals, and will agree upon the criteria they will use in assessing the achievement of those goals. Furthermore, they will engage in ongoing discussions and assessments of the functioning of the team itself. Questions that will drive the collective inquiry of the team might include the following:
- Are we truly functioning as a team?
- Are we maintaining an appropriate balance between advocacy for our individual positions and inquiry regarding the thinking of others on the team?
- Have we clarified and are we fulfilling our individual and collective responsibilities?
- Do we need to meet more frequently?
- Do we need to expand our membership or work with other teams?
- Are we achieving our goals?
- How can we be more effective as a team?

A student support team at work is illustrated in the following scenario.

A high school counselor visits the support team of a junior high school in late spring to review the status of students who will be assigned to that counselor's team as they enter the high school in the fall. One of the entering freshman boys has been identified by the junior high school team as a student who may have difficulty with the transition to high school. He has a history of poor academic achievement and has demonstrated some social-emotional issues.

Upon returning to the high school, the counselor reviews the student's records and the anecdotal observations of the junior high school staff with the other members of his student support team, a social worker, and the dean. The team decides to recommend a specialized summer school program on study skills for the student. Team members also conclude that assigning the student to a small, monitored study hall with an instructor who teaches study strategies would benefit the student during the school year. The counselor contacts the student and his parents and invites them to come to the school to discuss the upcoming transition to high school. The student works with the counselor and parents to articulate his goals for high school. The parents agree that the summer school class may be beneficial and enroll their son in the program. They also endorse the small study hall for their son.

The student has a successful summer school session and begins the regular school year. The student support team discusses him at their first meeting of the year. Team members delegate monitoring responsibilities to assess his transition to high school as well as his success in his classes. Teachers are asked to provide weekly updates on the school's computerized system for monitoring grades and behavior. At a subsequent meeting, the student support team discusses the student's progress and determines that he needs more support. The counselor contacts the parents and advises them of the team's recommendations. With the parents' approval, the counselor and social worker invite the student to attend a support group for freshman, and he is moved to a more intensive study skills program where a teacher not only monitors each student's homework, but also provides ongoing communication with parents, teachers, and the student support team. The counselor arranges for tutoring for the student before school to help him complete missing assignments. The counselor also convinces the student to join the stage crew for the upcoming fall play. The student begins to show improvement that is noted at the next meeting of the support team. The team decides he would benefit from some positive reinforcement. They convene a meeting with his teachers and parents and congratulate him on his improvement. The team invites ideas as to what might be done to help the student maintain his success. As time goes on, the student and his progress are continually assessed, new strategies are developed and implemented as needed, and the cycle continues.

It has been said that schools foster a culture of isolation, but the student services department of the future will be characterized by a culture of collaboration. Teams will work with teachers, students, and parents in an ongoing effort to monitor the success of each student, the effectiveness of the school's programs, and the effectiveness of the team itself. They will be relentless in their efforts to promote conditions that support the success of each student.

A Focus on Results
The primary reason for becoming a learning community is to achieve dramatically better results for each student. Student services personnel must be relentless in their efforts to assess the needs of each student; to identify the barriers and obstacles that interfere with student success; and to work with students, parents, the student support team, and faculty to develop strategies for overcoming those barriers. Most important, they must assess their efforts on the basis of results rather than intentions. In many schools, the contemporary counselor is not called upon to present evidence of effectiveness. In others, counselors cite the number of programs they have initiated or the amount of student and parent contact they have had as evidence of their success. But the student services program of the future will insist that the effectiveness of the department be assessed on the basis of student success. Efforts and initiatives will be subjected to ongoing assessment on the basis of tangible results.

The American School Counselor Association (1997) has articulated the results student services programs should seek in the National Standards for School Counseling Programs. These standards include the areas of academic, career, and personal and social development:

Academic Development
Standard A: Students will acquire the attitudes, knowledge, and skills that contribute to effective learning in school and across their life span.

Standard B: Students will complete school with the academic preparation essential to choose from a wide range of substantial post-secondary options, including college.

Standard C: Students will understand the relationship of academics to the world of work and to life at home and in the community.

Career Development
Standard A: Students will acquire the skills to investigate the world of work in relation to knowledge of self, and to make informed career decisions.

Standard B: Students will employ strategies to achieve future career success and satisfaction.

Standard C: Students will understand the relationships among personal qualities, education and training, and the world of work.

Personal-Social Development
Standard A: Students will acquire the attitudes, knowledge, and interpersonal skills to help them understand and respect others.

Standard B: Students will make decisions, set goals, and take the necessary actions to achieve goals.

Standard C: Students will understand safety and survival skills.

A Commitment to Continuous Improvement

Articulating results is a critical step in developing the results orientation of a learning community, but the ongoing monitoring of the desired results is equally important. In most organizations, what gets monitored gets done. As Phil Schlechty (1997, p. 111) observes, "People know what is expected by what is inspected and respected . . . evaluation and assessment, properly conceived, are key elements in building . . . a result-oriented, self-regulating environment." The student services department that is serious about improving its programs' effectiveness will move beyond articulating desired results. Its members will identify indicators that offer evidence of improvement, will develop systems to monitor those indicators on a continual basis, and will revise programs and procedures based on their ongoing analysis of the information they are gathering. This monitoring will go beyond the traditional tracking of credits toward graduation to include examining trends in grades; analyzing student performance on state and national tests; helping the student to develop and implement academic and career goals, and complete career exploration programs; administering personality, attitude, and learning style inventories; ensuring student participation in cocurricular activities and service projects; administering student satisfaction surveys, parent satisfaction surveys, and faculty satisfaction surveys; reviewing discipline and attendance records; and encouraging students to write reflections on their school experience as they approach graduation. Because many of the goals of a student services department extend beyond graduation, it is imperative that the monitoring process include follow-up studies of graduates. These studies might include annual focus groups of randomly selected alumni to discuss their level of satisfaction with the preparation their school has given them and their identification of areas needing improvement. It might also include a phone survey of randomly selected students one year and five years after their graduation to assess their school experience.

This constant monitoring will be driven by the department's commitment to continuous improvement. While members will take time to celebrate evidence of improvement, they will be characterized by a persistent disquiet with the status quo and a constant search for more effective ways to achieve the desired results. They will recognize that becoming a professional learning community represents not a project to complete, but a way of conducting their day-to-day business, forever.

Technology

As our world moves through the twenty-first century, it will continue to become increasingly technologically advanced. Internet connections will be as ubiquitous as telephone lines. All educators, even those in the most remote parts of our country, will be connected to others using voice mail, electronic mail, and the Internet. Students in the year 2021 will be able to interact with multimedia devices, computer simulations, and virtual reality and obtain information from experts in any field in any nation. Interactive programs will offer virtual experiences of historical events (Cornish, 1996). Technology will bring cooperative learning to a global scale. Schools will be linked so that students in rural Iowa will be able to "attend" a lecture given by a history professor in Great Britain using Internet-based videoconferencing. If teenagers in the most remote part of Siberia are curious about life in an American city, they will be able to e-mail students in Chicago, obtain virtual tours of the neighborhoods, and learn about the city's past through digital video and imaging. Conversations with other teenagers will be instantaneously translated into their own language.

There are those that contend that the availability of technology will make the educator and the student services department obsolete, that children from a very early age will be able to learn from a computer at home and will never again set foot in a school building. We disagree with that prediction. Although technology will be an integral part of the professional learning organization, adolescents will continue to have a developmental need to experience success, build relationships, gain social experiences, and increase in emotional maturity. Students in the future will continue to require one-on-one guidance, supervision, and personal discussion, and student services personnel will be positioned to fill this need.

Counselors in the professional learning environment of 2021 will use technology to track instantaneous information about their students and their students' learning progress throughout their academic career. Students will have individualized education plans that begin when they are very young, and the information about how they learn most effectively will travel with them throughout their academic development. Strengths will be capitalized on as weaknesses are addressed. Annual goals will be set for each person, and all members of the school community will assist students in achieving their potential. Students will enter each phase of schooling with a plan that will be continually reviewed and modified as the student matures.

The student services department of the future will use technology to its greatest potential as well. Time and distance will no longer limit the work that people do. Imagine the following scenario that illustrates the student services department of the future at work:

> Sandy is a student who has been a hard worker and has done very well in school for the past 11 years. She has been a model student, earning the praise of her

parents and teachers. She has always seemed to motivate herself, asking for help when she needs it and taking advantage of the educational opportunities around her. Sandy is now at the end of her junior year. Last week, Sandy's wireless Personal Digital Assistant alerted her that she had received three grades in math and two grades in English below her 94% average. The system displayed the trend and suggested helpwork (teacher-planned additional curriculum) to assist her in improving her performance. Even with the additional assistance, however, Sandy's lower performance continues and the system notifies her counselor, Mr. Reed.

Mr. Reed reviews Sandy's performance report and discusses Sandy's performance with her English and math teachers. They note that there had been a gradual decline in her grades and a change in her attitude toward her coursework. Although she hasn't ignored her assignments, she has not been working up to her usual standards. She seems somewhat depressed and anxious about something, but she has not responded to any of the questions that concerned faculty asked her.

Mr. Reed confers with the other members of Sandy's student support team to see if any other problems have surfaced and to collaborate on possible solutions. The team decides to have Mr. Reed meet with Sandy to investigate her recent downward trend and her change in attitude. Sandy talks openly with Mr. Reed, and he discovers that she is apprehensive about college and what she will do there. The career and vocational assessment system had analyzed her educational history, grade level portfolios, personality, and learning style and suggested several career fields in which she might be successful, but she is still anxious about what college and the future hold for her. While Mr. Reed is talking to Sandy, Ms. White, Sandy's social worker, videoconferences with Sandy's parents to see if they have noticed any difference in their daughter and to see if anything is going on in the family that might explain the sudden change. Sandy's parents express a concern that they have seen the same change in their daughter and are not sure what may be the cause. Every time they ask, she says she is nervous about college, but she never elaborates. The team is able to confer once again and decides to hold a meeting with Sandy, her parents, and her teachers.

Mr. Reed instructs his Personal Digital Assistant to coordinate a meeting with all the interested parties. The system compares the schedules of the invited persons and finds a time slot when they are free to meet. The Personal Digital Assistant then schedules the room and alerts the invited parties of the meeting place and time. At the meeting, Sandy's teachers express their concerns about her schoolwork, and the team explores Sandy's anxiety about the future. Instead of waiting for Sandy's parents to come to school, the team and teachers are able to meet that afternoon with Sandy's mother and father through a videoconference that Sandy attends.

Sandy apologizes to the group but admits that she is extremely anxious about college. She has never visited a school and is worried that she will not be able to succeed in the colleges to which she has decided to apply. Her parents express their frustration that they do not have the time or the money to visit every college that interests Sandy. If she were able to narrow down her choices to one or two colleges, personal visits to the colleges would be more realistic. The team brainstorms with the family to find ways to get Sandy back on track and to help alleviate Sandy's anxiety about college. Sandy agrees to visit the paraprofessional tutor for help with English and math for the next few days after school. Her teachers feel this will give her a chance to succeed again in these classes. They agree to send e-mails to the student support team to update them on Sandy's progress.

Mr. Reed also makes an appointment for Sandy to come into the office during her lunch period to take an in-depth virtual tour of the two universities in which she is most interested. He shows her how to investigate the major options, the admission requirements, and the different buildings on campus. He also demonstrates how to access a video chat room in order to speak with students and faculty. Sandy videoconferences with an admissions officer to ask questions about the admission process. Sandy finds that this combination of virtual tours, chat rooms, and videoconferences is very informative, and she decides to use it to explore other universities. Gradually her concerns begin to diminish.

As this example illustrates, the student services department of the future will respond to problems immediately. They will quickly spot and address a downward trend. Time and distance will be less of a hindrance in problem solving, and all concerned parties will be able to participate in the education of a child. Technology will not eliminate the need for student services personnel but instead will be a powerful tool in helping them to be more effective in helping all students achieve their goals.

Conclusion

There will be those who contend that this description of the student services department of the future lacks imagination and does not represent a radical departure from current best practice. There is some validity to that criticism, but we feel that our image presents a good news–bad news message to practitioners. The good news is that the best programs have already begun to move in this direction and are demonstrating many of the characteristics we describe in this chapter. The bad news is that although best practice is acknowledged, very few schools actually implement that practice. It is a mistake to wait for the passage of time or for some act of divine intervention to transform student services programs. Those who want a decidedly more effective program in the year 2021 will begin the hard work of implementing best practice today. Time won't change our departments; we will have to do it ourselves, and there is no reason to wait.

References

American School Counselor Association. (1997). *The national standards for school counseling programs.* Alexandria, VA: Author.

Burris, D. (1993). *Technotrends: How to use technology to go beyond your competition.* New York: HarperCollins.

Cornish, E. (1996). The cyberfuture: 92 ways our lives will change by the year 2025. *The Futurist, 30*(1), 27–44.

Dilworth, R. (1995). The DNA of the learning organization. In C. Sarita & J. Renesch (Eds.). *Learning organizations: Developing cultures for tomorrow's workplace*. Portland, OR: Productivity Press.

DuFour, R., & Eaker, R. (1998). *Professional learning communities at work: Best practices for enhancing student achievement*. Bloomington, IN: National Educational Service.

Drucker, P. (1992). *Managing for the future: The 1990s and beyond*. New York: Truman Talley Books.

Fullan, M. (1993). *Change forces: Probing the depths of educational reform*. London: Falmer Press.

Joyce, B, & Showers, B. (1995, May). *The Developer*. Oxford, OH: National Staff Development Council.

Katzenbach, J., & Smith, D. (1993). *The wisdom of teams: Creating the high performance organization*. New York: Harper Business.

Louis, K. S., Kruse, S., & Raywid, M. A. (1996). Putting teachers a the center of reform. *NASSP Bulletin, 80,* 580.

Matthews, D. (1997). The lack of a public for schools. *Phi Delta Kappan, 78,* 10.

National Commission on Teaching and America's Future. (1996). *What matters most: Teaching for America's future*. New York: Author.

Newmann, F. & Wehlage, G. (1995). *Successful school restructuring: A report to the public and educators by the Center for Restructuring Schools*. Madison: University of Wisconsin.

Perkins, D. (1992). *Smart schools: From training memories to educating minds*. New York: The Free Press.

Pinchot, G., & Pinchot, E. (1993). *The end of bureaucracy and the rise of the intelligent organization*. San Francisco: Berrett-Koehler Publishers.

Schlechty, P. (1997). *Schools for the twenty-first century: Leadership imperatives for educational reform.* San Francisco: Jossey-Bass.

Senge, P. (1990). *The fifth discipline: The art and practice of the learning organization.* New York: Doubleday Currency.

Senge, P., Ross, R., Smith, B., Roberts, C., & Kleiner, A. (1994). *The fifth discipline fieldbook: Strategies and tools for building a learning organization.* New York: Doubleday.

About the Authors

Dr. Richard DuFour is superintendent of Adlai Stevenson High School District 125 in Lincolnshire, Illinois, and the author of *Professional Learning Communities at Work: Best Practices for Enhancing Student Achievement.*

Patricia Martin, Debbie Magee, Aida Guidice, and Barbara Zivkovic were members of the Student Services Department of Stevenson High School who helped to build the pyramid of interventions that has become a model for providing students experiencing difficulties with additional time and support. **Patricia Martin** and **Debbie Magee** continue to serve in leadership roles in Stevenson's Student Services Department. **Aida Guidice** is now director of pupil personnel service for Bartlett High School in Bartlett, Illinois. **Barbara Zivkovic** is a counselor at Lake Forest High School in Lake County, Illinois. To learn more about the nationally-recognized program of Stevenson High School contact Debra Magee at dmagee@district125.k12.il.us or visit the Stevenson website at www.district125.k12.il.us

Chapter Three

Paradigms for Future School Counseling Programs

Fred Bemak

To establish a context for envisioning the school counselor of 2021, it is first necessary to envision the public school of the future. Many of today's schools in the United States have fallen behind the pace of technological, ecological, social, and economic advances. We maintain large institutions, which for many of our youth have been ineffective, despite the fact that in the mid-1990s, the United States spent $275 billion on public K–12 education. This is particularly striking considering that expenditures on public education have been declining since 1950, which may contribute to problems such as an increasing group of students who are at risk of school failure (Carlson, 1996; Dryfoos, 1990); increased violence and crime in the schools (U.S. Department of Education, 1998); high rates of teenage pregnancy (Dryfoos, 1990); drug-infested environments (Kirst, 1991); and school climates that students and faculty experience as unsafe and dangerous (U.S. Department of Education, 1998). A report by The Education Trust (1998) clearly documents the discrepancy in academic achievement between minority students and White students and between students from lower socioeconomic classes and those from middle and upper classes. However, the problems of schools are not specific only to poor districts and areas with high concentrations of minority students. Other factors affecting all schools, in addition to problems based on economic conditions, include pedagogy; politics of communities and school boards; training for educational professionals; and the lack of clarity regarding educational missions, which neglect values and cultures of learning that reflect the whole person.

Demographics and societal changes also have great influence on schools. It is anticipated as we move forward through the next two decades that a number of societal, technological, educational, and philosophical changes will significantly affect schools. I would suggest that nuclear families as we know them today will dramatically change; children in special education classes will be mainstreamed and exceed the current figure of 19%; technological advances will prevail in school cultures and play a major role in education; and communities will more effectively define their role in partnerships with schools and assist in local management.

Currently, children spend only 19% of their time connected with schools. I suggest that this figure will significantly increase. In addition, there will likely be an exploration of shifting time schedules for schools, with openings and closings at different times throughout the day and night that are more reflective of research regarding children's biological rhythms, more responsive to activities outside the current limited scope of school days, and more convenient to parents' schedules. Within the school itself, I see a trend that moves away from the large institutional educational structures as we see them today, with an emphasis on redesigning them into small learning centers within the larger establishment. These smaller learning centers will operate more like the universities of today, with small departments having specializations and themes in different areas. Within this configuration, teachers will have different roles to facilitate learning, rather than teach learning. They will assume more of the roles of facilitator, helper, and mentor, while relying heavily on technology as a teaching vehicle. Similarly, the principal's role will become one of a consensus manager, bringing together leadership teams of respective staff in the schools to provide collaborative guidance, leadership, and vision. Technological advances will allow teachers more time and communication with parents, because the computer linkages of the future will follow the development of phones and televisions, whereby almost all homes are wired to technology, including those of families from low-income backgrounds. Subsequently, school counselors will play a different role than they do today. I suggest that within the context of these changes, future public education systems must address changing educational, social, and psychological problems, and I contend that it is the school counselor who must lead the way to tackle these issues.

Following in the Footsteps
of Public Psychiatric Hospitals

An analogy of the transformation of schools may be the evolution of the large public psychiatric institutions.

Contemporary schools could be viewed as similar to large public psychiatric hospitals of the past, which were developed to accommodate large numbers of patients, with the aim of serving the most people at the least expense. They adopted all the worst qualities of institutionalization, with dehumanizing practices that were more concerned with the maintenance of the institutional rules and regulations than the care or treatment of the patients. The realization that the goals of psychiatric treatment were not being met, and people were not being released or growing and developing as a result of these large institutions, led to deinstitutionalization and humanization of these facilities. Smaller facilities in public and private hospitals, group homes, independent apartment living, and other forms of deinstitutionalized care were developed in an attempt to shift from the larger, less effective institutions to more effective treatment models.

This may parallel the modern day reality of large numbers of schools, many of which are experiencing problems similar to those of the former large public psychiatric institutions: These problems include emphasis on social control and cost, deterioration of standards, not attaining goals, and dehumanization. Some schools may be viewed as large, oftentimes unmanageable, institutions, sometimes without success in meeting their goals to educate students, and sometimes with more of an emphasis on social control than on education (Gonzalez & Darling-Hammond, 1997). In some regions, the environment both inside and outside of schools has become unsafe, leading to a greater emphasis on control. There is an increasingly concerted effort to focus on records and documentation of goal attainment in the schools, with neglect of the human values, influences, interpersonal relationships, and qualities that comprise the culture of any school environment. These issues oftentimes result in schools falling short of meeting the goals for academic achievement, as well as frustration and disillusionment of teachers and staff; more rigid and unreasonable rules and procedures as a reaction to the difficulties in meeting educational goals; and even, in some instances, neglect of educational goals in attempts to control the environment better. Furthermore, escalating crises, rather than education, may dominate time and energy in many schools.

Community Learning Centers

To address these issues, I propose that schools restructure to form Community Learning Centers (CLCs). The CLCs would consist of students studying interdisciplinary subject areas in small groups. Teachers and staff would guide and facilitate learning, and each CLC would be part of a larger school. The culture of each CLC would be important in teaching about values, community, and learning, in concert with traditional academic subjects, and each CLC would contribute to the larger school environment, which would house multiple CLCs. CLCs and schools would be far more integrated with the community and families of students, through technology and classes that are not bound by the institutional walls. Time spent on school-related activities would be up from today's 19% to about 45%, and schools would be far more accessible and flexible with schedules, including offering long evenings and weekends as optional times to learn.

Questions for Reflection

If CLCs are to be the design of the future, a number of questions are raised regarding the future school counselor. Within this framework, is there school counseling? If so, what do counselors do and what kind of programs do they design? What is their mission? What are their goals, and are these goals compatible with the objectives of the educational facilities where counselors work? How is the counselor's job defined and structured? What kind of hours do counselors keep, and is their job focused on working with students, teachers, parents, administrators, businesses, community personnel, or others?

What to Be Called: Identity Issues

A first and immediate concern that has significant implications for job and identity is what to call guidance counselors. Currently, they are called both school counselors and guidance counselors. I would suggest that the term *guidance counselor* will be replaced by *school counselor*. This relates to past associations with the word *guidance* and the implication that it is more vocationally focused in accordance with the vocational and school guidance movements of the past (Bemak, 2000), which originated with Frank Parsons in the early 1900s.

Along with the new and accepted terminology of "school

counselor" will be the redefinition of the position that will not only define the importance of the school counselor, but also clarify implicit and explicit assumptions about the role and function of the job. As a result, principals, teachers, parents, and community personnel of the future will be clear about what a counselor does and how those activities contribute to the educational mission of the school. It is my belief that this clarification will be essential in defining the responsibility and role of school counselors within the context of transforming schools and attaining educational goals. In fact, school counselors of the future will be moving toward assuming leadership roles in their assigned CLCs and schools. They will be responsible for educating teachers, administrators, and parents about issues such as child development, mental health as it relates to academic achievement, cultural learning styles, career development and opportunities, college placement, course tracking, group process and relationships, community relations, and family dynamics as they relate to school performance.

Child Development

Child development will play an important role in education in 2021. Teaching will be more closely linked to research on child development, which will transform some aspects of the transmission of knowledge. School counselors will be the experts in this area, informing teachers and administrators how to apply to the CLCs the most recent knowledge based on scientific study. The capacities, abilities, and potential of students will be far more realized by this linkage of theory to practice. School counselors will be the primary resource in this area, providing information through workshops and technological communication to teachers, parents, and administrators about expected areas of growth and development, anticipated problems and developmental strategies to address those problems, and the relationship of academic achievement to emotional and behavioral problems.

Mental Health

Oftentimes, the school system does not understand or creatively utilize school counselors. Their skills, training, and abilities may go unrecognized and misunderstood within the educational milieu. The future will find a better linkage between the school counselors' expertise and the overall educational goals of public schools, particularly as these areas are interwoven with mental health. School counselors will become leaders in defining how psychological and social problems interfere with learning and academic performance. This goes far beyond the contemporary school culture in which behavioral interventions are frequently aimed at "quick fixes" without consideration for the deeper underlying mental health needs that interfere with school climate and classroom performance. Sadly, the failure of schools and systems with quick fixes leads to high dropout rates, failure, violence, and disruption in schools. The future school counselor will provide consultation and insight to teachers, parents, and administrators about students and children from a mental health perspective that is linked to, rather than segregated from, the overall educational goals. Identified mental health issues will be referred to community agencies and teams of professionals, who will be working within schools as part of an interface between agencies and schools. To facilitate this process, school counselors will assume the leadership of mental health teams that include personnel from all areas of the school as well as community agencies. This has been shown to be effective in fostering healthier school environments and student mental health (Comer & Woodruff, 1998; Haynes & Comer, 1996). The future work in this area will promote and cultivate healthier school cultures in both the larger school and the CLCs.

Cultural Learning Styles

The teachers of the future will look toward school counselors as the experts on multiculturalism. School counselors will have immersed themselves in understanding differences in culture, especially as the population moves to a society with a minority of Whites (Bemak & Chung, in press). Race relations, discrimination, racism, cultural differences, and cultural learning styles will be areas of intensive study and expertise for school counselors. These areas will be introduced into the schools by the counselors, who will be consultants regarding how the school culture is affected by cultural differences, as well as assistants in understanding students' behavior and response to certain styles of teaching and the school environment. The counselor will be an essential bridge between culture and school practices and norms.

Career Development and Opportunities

In the future, counselors will utilize technology to a far greater extent to facilitate career counseling. There will be easy-to-use career programs developed with clear and dynamic examples of job opportunities, job placement, requirements for colleges, internship site-placement opportunities, required training for different levels of specific employment, and so forth. Students, with the guidance of the counselor, will be able to visit work sites, interact with the employees about their jobs on and off sites, access extensive reviews of different types of employment, speak with professionals online, enter chat rooms set up by their counselors, and experience a virtual reality job to explore their interests. School counselors will facilitate and process these technological and off-site "immersions" by students, helping them to understand and critique their job options and interests.

With the assistance of technology, school counselors will be able to spend significantly more time in person and online with each student, and ascertain specific in-depth plans and steps necessary for students to accomplish their career goals. A clear pathway of courses, grades, and test scores using data and records will delineate career options for each student.

College and Work Options

School counselors will guide students' futures more intensely. Current data are conclusive in finding that low-income and minority students are counseled toward technical schools and community colleges with far greater frequency than their higher income and White peers, despite equal grades (The Education Trust, 1998). Technology should have a major impact on tracking, course placement, and college recommendations for all students. School counselors will have a responsibility to track students into appropriate and challenging educational paths using a monitoring and counseling process during students' public school years. There will be far more interaction between counselor and student regarding college and work options, using technology and on-site programs to provide more thoughtful and applicable choices for students.

Course Tracking

Course tracking has been done on the basis of individualized records, to the detriment of many students, especially low-income and minority students (The Education Trust, 1998). The future school counselor will use far more sophisticated, technologically advanced means to determine the academic trajectory of all students. This usage of data, and compilation of information based on more rounded and developed information than just testing scores, will provide many more minority students (who will be majority students in 2021) and low-income students with greater opportunities to achieve their potential. Using the data, counselors will consult with teachers about the performance of all students and keep administrators informed about overall classroom and teacher effectiveness. An important aspect of course tracking will be the school counselor using the data to advocate for students using objective information rather than subjective beliefs (Bemak, 2000).

School Counselors as Guides

Today's school counselor assumes many different responsibilities and tasks, based on particular needs at a given time in a school or schools. One vision of the future school counselor includes having a definitive and established role instead of a "catch-all" role that tries to fill system gaps rather than contribute to better academic achievement for all students through regulated and systematic school counseling plans and activities. In this vision, the future school counselor will be acting as a guide for students, teachers, parents, administrators, and community members, rather than as an expert who has all the answers. This would relate to more extensive consultation training, an emphasis on the collaborative process, and a newly developed skill area that provides the tools for school counselors to be guides and facilitators of process rather than content experts. This guidance will be in line with the teacher's redefined role and concurrent with the philosophical values, beliefs, and practices of school systems that aim to guide students in their academic, psychological, and social development rather than teach "at them." Counselors will have a leadership role in this process, coming from a discipline that encourages facilitation and accentuates process. These basic areas will be modified to meet the needs of the school of 2021, and will place the school counselor in a role as one of the lead guides.

Academic Achievement

Academic achievement as it relates to counseling has been a neglected area for many school counselors. This is in direct contradiction to the goals of public education, which are increasingly emphasizing academic advancement and performance. In 2021, school counselors will be more consistent in their attempts to be central team members focusing on academic achievement. Counseling activities, such as guiding the wide array of professionals, students, family members, and associated contributors to the school goals; developing prevention programs; and so forth, will all be geared toward the primary goal of schools, that is, improving academic performance. Counselors will have a clear understanding of this and be able to articulate how their job description, the mission of the school, and their activities coincide.

Partnership with Parents
School counselors will be the liaison with parents. This will be done through technology, outreach, and in-school meetings. Technological advances will allow counselors regularly to communicate with parents, distributing assignments, students' notes on performance, upcoming activities, and questions and recommendations for parents at any given time. In turn, parents may also receive consultation and advice on a regular basis from school counselors via technology. This enhanced communication will provide an important linkage with families in a critical step toward improving family-school partnerships, with an aim toward better academic performance. In addition, school counselors will work flexible hours that accommodate outreach to students' homes on a needed basis. Being in the community is particularly important for some families that are afraid of or resistant to visiting the school. This move to integrate the community by bringing the school counselor to the community is an important step, especially for students who are identified as being at risk. Finally, ongoing in-school meetings will continue between counselors and parents or groups of parents that will offer prevention programs as well as individual consultations.

Partnership with the Community
It has been found that community and parental involvement enhance student performance (Eccles & Harold, 1996; Keys, Bemak, Carpenter, & King-Sears, 1998). Linkages with communities through technology, visits to community sites that are relevant to educational studies, and visits by community representatives will grow significantly by 2021. School counselors will have a major role in coordinating these activities and be responsible for developing new and innovative programs for teachers, parents, and students. The result of these partnerships will be the establishment of a greater "open door" policy in schools: Community agencies and businesses will have greater

access to schools, and, simultaneously, schools will have greater access to community agencies and businesses, who will offer facilities for schools.

School Reform

The school reform movement has been forging ahead without the input or participation of school counselors (Bemak, 2000). I suggest that in 2021, school counselors will be major players in this process, contributing a unique and critical aspect to the continuing development and growth of schools. They will participate in examining school culture and environment, multiculturalism within schools, social and behavioral problems, career counseling, psychological issues, and child development as contributing forces to academic performance.

Teachers as Partners

In 2021, there will be more merging and less differentiation of roles as counselors and teachers assume roles as guides and mentors. This will create more partnerships between counselors and teachers, who will cooperate within and outside the classroom with the common aim of working toward the goals of the school. School counselors will work with teachers to develop prevention programs that they will jointly present in the CLCs and in the larger school. Furthermore, there will be far less division into distinct roles, beginning with graduate training, where counselors, teachers, and administrators will experience collaborative classes and projects. This collaborative spirit will carry over into schools.

Management Councils

Administrative structures of schools will change dramatically by 2021. Rather than a principal having full authority to dictate policies and practices, management councils will be established within schools. Participation in the governance of the school will be equal. School counselors will have an important role in this process, because they may be the only professionals on the management council that are trained in group process. Therefore, they will assume a leadership role in assisting with group dynamics and process, in support of this very different leadership structure.

Conclusion

The school of the future will look very different and will require major role transformations of staff. The future school counselor will undergo a major shift and assume key leadership roles in school reform, creating healthy school climates, and serving as an essential resource for teachers, parents, community personnel, and administrators. This will result in school counselors participating in the management and administration of the overall school and the Community Learning Centers (or a similar system). Furthermore, the school counselor will be the guardian of mental health within the school, linking this closely to academic achievement and growth, career development, and higher education and training. The counselor will also have expertise in the usage of data to guide and support decisions about course enrollment and college options as well as be versatile in technology that can be applied to these functions. Counselors will be more mobile and spend flexible time in schools, as well as in communities and students' homes where linkages will be critical to academic success. No longer will there be questions about what purpose or utility school counselors have within schools; they will have essential roles in making the schools of 2021 work.

References

Bemak, F. (2000). Transforming the role of the school counselor to provide leadership in educational reform through collaboration. *Professional School Counseling, 3* (5), 323–331.

Bemak, F., & Chung, R. C-Y. (in press). Immigrant students: Issues and recommendations for multicultural school counselors. In P. Pedersen & J. C. Carey (Eds.). *Multicultural counseling in schools: A practical handbook* (Vol. II). Boston, MA: Allyn & Bacon.

Carlson, C. (1996). Changing the school culture toward integrated services. In R. Illback & C. Nelson (Eds.). *Emerging school-based approaches for children with emotional and behavioral problems* (pp. 225–249). New York: Haworth Press.

Comer, J. P., & Woodruff, D. W. (1998). Mental health in schools. *Child and Adolescent Psychiatric Clinics of North America, 7*(3), 499–513.

Dryfoos, J. (1990). *Adolescents at risk: Prevalence and prevention.* New York: Oxford University Press.

Eccles, J. S., & Harold, R. D. (1996). Family involvement in children's and adolescents' schooling. In A. Booth & J. F. Dunn (Eds.), *Family school links: How do they affect educational outcomes?* (pp. 3–34). Mahwah, NJ: Lawrence Erlbaum Associates.

The Education Trust (1998). *Education watch 1998: The Education Trust state and national data book* (Vol. 2). Washington DC: Author

Gonzalez, J. M., & Darling-Hammond, L. (1997). *New concepts for new challenges: Professional development for teachers of immigrant youth.* Washington DC: Center for Applied Linguistics.

Haynes, N. M., & Comer, J. P. (1996). Integrating schools, families, and communities through successful school reform: The school development program. *School Psychology Review, 25*(4), 501–506.

Keys, S., Bemak, F., Carpenter, S., & King-Sears, M. (1998). Collaborative consultant: A new role for counselors serving at-risk youth. *Journal of Counseling and Development, 76,* 123–133.

Kirst, M. (1991). Improving children's services: Overcoming barriers, creating new opportunities. *Phi Delta Kappan, 72,* 615–618.

U.S. Department of Education (1998). *Violence and discipline problems in U.S. public schools* (NCES Publication No. 98-030, pp. 15–17). Washington DC: Counseling 2021.

About the Author

Fred Bemak is currently a professor and program coordinator for the Counseling and Development Program in the Graduate School of Education at George Mason University. He has previously held appointments as the chair of the Department of Counseling and Development at Johns Hopkins University and section head of counselor education, school psychology, and rehabilitation services at Ohio State University. Dr. Bemak was a recipient of a Dewitt Wallace-Reader's Digest Fund grant to transform school counseling and has consulted extensively nationally and internationally in more than 30 countries, giving lectures, presentations, workshops and seminars on working cross-culturally with youth populations identified as being at risk. He has directed several federal and state programs including Upward Bound and the Massachusetts Department of Mental Health Region I Adolescent Treatment Program, has held numerous grants focusing on addressing problems faced by today's youth, and has published extensively in this area. Dr. Bemak is a former Fulbright Scholar, a Kellogg International Fellow, and a recipient of the International Exchange of Experts and Research Fellowship through the World Rehabilitation Fund. He continues to work in schools and communities with marginalized and disenfranchised youth and families.

Chapter Four

Counseling in Community Myth or Reality?

Jackie Allen

Thinking in the Future Tense, as James (1996) so aptly named her book, may not be as easy a task as one might think. A child born in the twenty-first century, the year 2003, will graduate in 2021; how can we imagine what life might be like 20 years from now? Is it really possible to see into a crystal ball, to be futurists? Can we leap from the secure present into the unknown, where nobody has gone before, without having some doubts of our personal capabilities as soothsayers?

Thinking about the future, I am reminded of my experience many years ago as a freshman student at the University of Redlands. Before attending freshman orientation, all new students to the university were sent special instructions and two or three books to read. One of those books was Orwell's *1984,* which I found to be an unimaginable look at the future that as a freshman I was awed to contemplate, let alone explore. I read that book with amazement, wondering what would happen not only in the history of the world, but also in my immediate future in college. I was 17 years old when I read Orwell's book, and most of his predictions by now have come true. It is my turn now to think in the future tense. What an awesome responsibility! With that responsibility comes a challenge—to dare to move forward, to be a changer, to be a reformer, to break new ground, to ask those questions that will lead to a better future. Is there really any choice after all? For in reality, not to move forward is to die.

Death or Life?

During the 1960s, there was a new development in theology called the *death of God* movement. The death-of-God theologians claimed that God was really dead and the world existed in a nihilistic aftermath without purpose, goals, or foundational beliefs. This movement caused me, a seminary student at the time, to answer for myself an existential question: Did I believe that God was really dead? Was it possible that a group of believers had turned their backs on the possibility of a future with God and were abandoning their former faith and looking elsewhere for a new god in which to believe and follow? Each believer had a choice: to confirm his or her belief in God or to abandon hope, moving into the realm of the unknown. The fact that a decision had to be made and a path chosen caused the believer to pause from the mundane occurrences of daily life and contemplate the future; for to be alive was to have faith in tomorrow, to move forward, to anticipate what tomorrow might bring, and to envision a future that had meaning in which to place one's faith.

Some have said that counseling has no future, that it is meaningless, that its effectiveness cannot be proven. Others argue that it is not a science and are equally skeptical about its being an art form. If there is no future, surely counseling will die on the pyre of unbelief and skepticism, ridicule and doubt, never again to rise from the ashes of a bleak grave. To abandon faith in counseling is to lack direction in our profession and to wander in disbelief looking everywhere for a new discipline in which to put our faith. To abandon the possibility of a future, although it may look different than the present, is to sign the death warrant of counseling.

The Myths of Counseling
The storyteller takes tales from the past and retells them, making them relevant to the future. To gain a proper perspective on the profession of counseling, it is necessary to look first to the past and then retell the stories, applying their lessons to the future. Joseph Campbell (1991) has written about the power of myths in our daily lives and how humans create their own myths. What are the myths we have grown up with in the twentieth century? What stories do we tell about counseling and guidance for the twenty-first century? Because counseling and guidance is a relatively new field compared with history and philosophy, fewer myths have been created. Having begun my personal counseling career in the early 1970s, and having worked in the counseling field through the 1980s and 1990s, I would like to propose a myth for each decade to help us understand our past.

The myth of the 1970s must be described as the *hero myth*. Carl Rogers' unconditional positive regard was the counseling theory of the decade. Counseling was often explained as the outgrowth of an older discipline, psychology; counselors put into practice psychological theories as they worked with their counselees. The practice of working with clients was considered an art form. Counseling became the knight in shining armor. In private practice, in churches, in schools, and in industry, counseling theories and practice flourished. Counselors were out to save the world. The world quickly became overwhelming, and the 1970s might be seen as the last positive decade for counseling.

Then came the 1980s, a more skeptical time in which counseling was no longer a knight in shining armor, rescuing those with problems and troubles, but a battle-worn warrior, soon to be replaced by the next savior. Starting in California, and soon spreading to many other parts of the United States, counseling quickly fell prey to the *victim myth* in the face of public voter referendums such as Proposition 13, from which education lost and property owners gained. And when the schools lost funding, counseling resources were cut and morale plummeted. The stories told were of reduced services, counselors being reassigned to classrooms, and, in some cases, entire programs being cut. Loss and despair were common tales and the storytellers began to ask audiences if counseling would survive. Was this the death knell of counseling? Was this young profession, not yet an adolescent, gone too soon to really establish itself in the world, make its contribution, and know what life was really about?

But alas, as the storytellers began to tell their stories of counseling and guidance in the 1990s, the victim myth changed to the *stepchild myth*: a Cinderella story of sorts, in which the stepchild did not have the full rights and privileges of other members in the family. Counselors were asked to work very hard, like Cinderella, as the other professionals went to the ball and got the funding prize. Managed care and budget cuts in schools reduced salaries and opportunities for counselors to offer their programs and services. Many counselors retired and were not replaced as their remaining colleagues were asked to do more and more. Counselors in private practice competed with school counselors, and counselors in general competed with other mental health professionals and educators for jobs that would pay a decent salary. New specialties were born and many counselors of the 1960s and 1970s found themselves retraining in career, gerontological, and multicultural counseling to compete in a niche market for the remaining jobs.

A Paradigm Change

In the last three decades, the counseling stories that were told were not exactly supportive of a flourishing profession. Are these myths a proper legacy for the twenty-first century? If counseling is to survive in the twenty-first century, the new myth must not be naive, nor must it be negative. The twenty-first-century story of counseling can be none other than *counseling in community*. Together the counselors across the United States can join with mental health professionals, career development specialists, and educators to write the story of the twenty-first century—the story of working together, not in competition but in collaboration, to transform counseling for the future. Creation of a myth for the future, a legacy for the twenty-first century, a program plan for the graduate in 2021, will require a new paradigm for counseling.

Joel Barker (1992) explained in *The Future Edge* the characteristics of a paradigm. Paradigms are common and must be functional; they provide the rules for the direction and development of the organization. When the paradigm changes, the paradigm, in effect, reverses the common-sense relationship between seeing and believing and builds a new perception of how things are or might be. When old paradigms are adhered to very strongly, lacking flexibility, paradigm paralysis, a terminal disease of certainty, may result. The best paradigm characteristic, according to Barker, is that human beings can choose to change their paradigms. Will counselors be able to change their paradigm and envision a new future?

Looking back on the world of the twentieth century and into the future of the twenty-first century, what paradigm of counseling will be possible, probable, and visionary? The best strategy for a counseling paradigm is paradigm pliancy— divergent thinking, brainstorm planning, and creative envisioning. In order to construct a functional paradigm for the year 2021, some basic premises must be established. First, the paradigm must take into account the economics of the century; economic power in the educational, political, and social structures must be acknowledged. The global nature of economics must also be understood (Flowers, 1996). The human rights of all peoples in microsociety in a specific country and in the larger macrosociety of the world must be considered. The diversity of various cultures, races, and nationalities must not be ignored. The interconnection of systems will be an essential element. Technology will grow and flourish and will continue to provide new means of communication. The paradigm must be amenable to change, use the best techniques and methodologies to facilitate that change, be flexible enough to take the energy of the age and flow with that energy, and employ the very best leaders to light the way.

Counseling in Community

Counseling in community will be the myth and the paradigm for the twenty-first century. The community will be a global community in which the emphasis will be on the health and wholeness of all persons in society; the foundations will be spiritual; the methodology will be technological, utilizing the techniques of virtual reality; organizations will change in structure and ideology; and the leadership will be synergistic.

Global Community

Diversity and multiculturalism will begin to fuse into a true understanding of inclusiveness—the underprivileged will no longer be on the fringe. Integration of mind and body will promote wholeness and wellness. A philosophy of oneness and collaboration in community will supersede individualism. Cultures, races, and nationalities will discuss common problems of personhood, somewhat oblivious to ethnocentric experiences, with the true desire of tackling the indigenous problems of all nations and nationalities.

Spiritual Foundations

Spirituality will become the foundation of counseling. Inner stability, strength, and connectedness with the source of one's being and the free-flowing energy of the universe will be emphasized in theory. Spirituality will be integrated into counseling through such techniques as the experiential focusing method employed by Elfie Hinterkopf (1998). Self-knowledge, self-sufficiency, and spirituality will be the goals of therapeutic interventions. Spirituality will infuse the experience of the home, the workplace, and the nature of oneness in the world.

Counseling Methodology

Counseling will be done in cyberspace; virtual reality counseling will be a popular methodology. Counselor access and client understanding will improve through the use of new technological methods. Virtual laboratories of all cultures, philosophies, and theories will be at the learner's fingertips. Simulations with indices of possible solutions will stimulate minds to reach inward to personal strength and creativity to solve exterior problems. Person and machine will struggle together to bring meaning to existence, dignity to personhood, and unity within and between global communities. Technology may become a viable force for social action (Casey, 1998). Research not only will adequately support practice, but also will initiate new methods of practice. Technological developments will enhance the knowledge base for counseling research and speed up the process through the use of counseling in cyberspace. Prevention and intervention will fuse into a third "vention," "self-vention," by which the individual, through spirituality and self-realization, will enhance self-knowledge, self-sufficiency, and self-actualization. Barriers among and within groups will begin to diminish as the sense of community grows.

Organizational Structure
Unity of national and state organizations may no longer be an issue, as international entities will grow in popularity and effectiveness. Operations will no longer be defined by the wall of a building or the geographical location on a map; only the capabilities of technology and communication will limit outreach and growth. Specialties may diminish and the concept of general practitioner return as the counselor uses a large technological support system to assist in the counseling process. Turf issues may decrease as the world of counseling professionals seeks to effectively collaborate on working with the patient's health and wholeness in body, mind, and spirit. The issue of accreditation standards and accrediting bodies will continue, but the client will be more interested in the counselor's history of effective interventions, which by then may be readily available on the Internet. Training programs will continue to use distance teaching and learning methods to reach prospective counselors in their homes, regardless of country. As technology breaks down the physical walls, unity of philosophy and oneness of purpose will break down the walls of dissension and prejudice.

Leadership
Strong synergistic leadership will develop to guide the counselors of the twenty-first century. The vision to change the profession must come from within the profession, and within

the individual counselor, and develop into a collective synchronicity of purpose and commitment to community (Jaworski, 1998). These new leaders will lead from inner strength, a sense of mission, and an understanding of the collective evolution of community. The evolution of a new paradigm, the development of the concept of community, will emanate from the heart of counseling to encompass those who may not be of like mind and will reach beyond to unify all in global cyberspace.

Conclusion

The concept of community will encompass counseling in the new millennium. Counseling will increase in popularity and growth around the world as small nations and third world countries continue to work with large nations and world leaders in developing a global theory of counseling. Counseling will be alive in the twenty-first century, but its metamorphosis may challenge the comfort level and stretch the imagination of the twentieth-century counselor. Franklin Delano Roosevelt, in an undelivered address prepared for Jefferson Day, April 13, 1945, said: "The only limit to our realization of tomorrow will be our doubts of today. Let us move forward with strong and active faith."

These thoughts and musings about the future are both a glimpse and a hope that as counseling evolves in the twenty-first century, it will be a force for unity and a paradigm of community. By the time the neophytes of the twenty-first century graduate in the year 2021, some of these changes may have taken place, whereas others may take many more years. Nevertheless, we can move the profession and the practice forward by making the myth of the twenty-first century—counseling in community—become a reality.

References

Barker, J. A. (1992). *The Future edge: Discovering the new paradigms of success.* New York: William Morrow & Co.

Campbell, J., & Moyers, B. (1991). *The power of myth.* New York: Anchor Books.

Casey, J. A. (1998). Technology: A force for social action. In C. C. Lee and G. R. Walz (Eds.), *Social action: A mandate for counselors* (pp. 199–211). Alexandria, VA: American Counseling Association, and Greensboro, NC: ERIC Counseling and Student Services Clearinghouse.

Flowers, B. S. (1996). *Creating the future.* (Cassette Recording No. 2-96113). Alexandria, VA: Association of Supervision and Curriculum Development.

Gardner, H. (1995). *Leading minds: An anatomy of leadership.* New York: Basic Books.

Hinterkopf, E. (1998). *Integrating spirituality in counseling.* Alexandria, VA: American Counseling Association.

James, J. (1996). *Thinking in the future tense: Leadership skills for a new age.* New York: Simon and Schuster.

Jaworski, Joseph (1998). *Synchronicity: The inner path of leadership.* San Francisco: Berrett-Koehler Publishers.

Orwell, G. (1992). *1984.* New York: Knopf.

Roosevelt, F. D. (Undelivered address prepared for Jefferson Day, April 13, 1945).

About the Author

Jackie M. Allen is an education programs consultant with the Student Support Services and Programs unit of the California Department of Education. She received her doctorate in education at the University of San Francisco in 1990. Her primary research interests are counseling and the special needs student, assessment and accountability of student support services, and counseling and the human brain. The editor of *School Counseling: New Perspectives and Practices,* Allen has also authored numerous articles on counseling and student support services. She is a past president of the American School Counselor Association, has served two terms on the American Counseling Association Governing Council, and has received the California Association of Counseling and Development Clarion Modell Distinguished Service Award.

Chapter Five

Counselors and the Community

Ron Anderson

Over the last quarter of the twentieth century, the counselor role moved substantially from one that focused primarily on remediation (kids struggling) to one that focused on prevention (kids at risk of struggling). While some talk has occurred about a third role shift to a developmental focus, movement toward this framework has been limited. The shift to a developmental perspective rests on the premise that we need to provide emotional and social support so that all children succeed. Counselors have been constantly fighting the battle of what to do with children who need serious and significant help to succeed at school.

The other factor negatively affecting a movement to a developmental framework is the scope of the task. How can we really affect the total development of a child? Although schools clearly have an impact on children, many other factors also come into play. Clearly, if counselors and schools are going to have this expanded impact, new roles and structures will have to be created, tested, and promoted. In this chapter, the community involvement model for developmental guidance is offered for consideration, using data from the Search Institute's 40 developmental assets to present a model of mobilizing a community effort to meet the developmental needs of children (Benson, 1997). The model includes role changes for schools and school counselors.

One national movement that addresses development is character education. Character education programs have mushroomed across the country and "fill the void" of academics only. "To educate a total individual, we need to educate the mind and the morals" is the rationale often given for the establishment of character education programs. A closer look at character education reveals a striking similarity to developmental guidance programs. The goal of character education is to help children develop the social and emotional skills to get along and to be successful in the world. Some character education initiatives stress the importance of the community. After all, where does character (social skills, emotional health) come from? To assume that schools can be primarily responsible for this development is to ignore the obvious—character and social skills develop within families and communities in diverse and complex ways. Although some communities have taken on an expanded role in the planned development of character and social skills, most have not. What if schools and counselors resisted the temptation to take this role on for all children and parents who "struggle" and looked instead to how they could assist the community in expanding its role to help children develop into healthy, responsible citizens?

A model for mobilizing communities to meet developmental needs has been developed and implemented in more than 900 communities under the Healthy Communities/ Healthy Youth initiative of the Search Institute (Benson, 1997). Beginning with the premise that there are 40 research-based, key internal and external factors that support healthy development, the Search Institute has endeavored to measure these factors (called assets). By correlating them with thriving and risk-taking behavior, the Search Institute has laid a solid foundation for assessing the developmental needs of the children in a community. Table 1 shows the 1997 national sample of results from student responses to the Search Institute survey regarding external assets. Figures 1, 2, and 3 illustrate the correlation of assets (or lack thereof) with risk-taking behavior.

The 40 assets show a strong resemblance to a guidance-program set of goals and objectives. The external assets of support, empowerment, boundaries and expectations, and constructive use of time represent outcomes counselors seek for students in different ways.

For example, when counselors start a peer helper program, they are building the following assets: (The numbers refer to the number of the asset from the larger group of 40.)

5. (caring school climate),
7. (community values youth),
8. (youth as resources),
9. (service to others), and
15. (positive peer influence).

Table 1: External Assets

Asset Type	Asset Name	Definition	Percent
Support	1. Family support	Family life provides high levels of love and support.	76
	2. Positive family communication	Young person and his or her parent(s) communicate positively, and young person is willing to seek parent(s') advice and counsel.	37
	3. Other adult relationships	Young person receives support from three or more non-parent adults.	51
	4. Caring neighborhood	Young person experiences caring neighbors.	47
	5. Caring school climate	School provides a caring, encouraging environment.	34
	6. Parent involvement in schooling	Parent(s) are actively involved in helping young person succeed in school.	37
Empowerment	7. Community values youth	Young person perceives that adults in the community value youth.	32
	8. Youth as resources	Young people are given useful roles in the community.	33
	9. Service to others	Young person serves in the community one hour or more per week.	54
	10. Safety	Young person feels safe at home, school, and in the neighborhood.	51
Boundaries and Expectations	11. Family boundaries	Family has clear rules and consequences. and monitors the young person's whereabouts.	54
	12. School boundaries	School provides clear rules and consequences.	60
	13. Neighborhood boundaries	Neighbors take responsibility for monitoring young people's behavior.	52
	14. Adult role models	Parent(s) and other adults model positive, responsible behavior.	37
	15. Positive peer influence	Young person's best friends model responsible behavior.	73
	16. High expectations	Both parent(s) and teachers encourage the young person to do well.	55
Constructive Use of Time	17. Creative activities	Young person spends three or more hours per week in lessons or practice in music, theatre or other arts.	24
	18. Youth programs	Young person spends three or more hours per week in sports, clubs. or organizations at school and/or in community organizations.	58
	19. Religious community	Young person spends one or more hours per week in activities in a religious institution.	70
	20. Time at home	Young person is out with friends "with nothing special to do" two or fewer nights per week.	59

When counselors speak to parents at a PTA meeting about listening skills or discipline practices, they are building these assets:

1. (family support),
2. (positive family communication), and
11. (family boundaries).

The internal assets identified by the Search Institute (see Table 2) are related to developmental tasks that counselors seek in their programs. These are the skills, competencies, and values that children need in order to be successful and healthy individuals.

For example, when counselors teach lessons on handling anger, they help students develop the following assets:

32. (planning and decision making),
33. (interpersonal competence), and
36. (peaceful conflict resolution).

Table 2: Internal Assets

Percent of Your Youth Reporting Each of 20 Internal Assets			
Asset Type	Asset Name	Definition	Percent
Commitment to Learning	21. Achievement motivation	Young person is motivated to do well in school.	74
	22. School engagement	Young person is actively engaged in learning.	61
	23. Homework	Young person reports doing at least one hour of homework every school day.	68
	24. Bonding to school	Young person cares about his or her school.	54
	25. Reading for pleasure	Young person reads for pleasure three or more hours per week.	24
Positive Values	26. Caring	Young person places high value on helping other people.	55
	27. Equality and social justice	Young person places high value on promoting equality and reducing hunger and poverty.	56
	28. Integrity	Young person acts on convictions and stands up for his or her beliefs.	69
	29. Honesty	Young person tells the truth even when it is not easy.	70
	30. Responsibility	Young person accepts and takes personal responsibility.	64
	31. Restraint	Young person believes it is important not to be sexually active or to use alcohol or other drugs.	56
Social Competencies	32. Planning and decision-making	Young person knows how to plan ahead and make choices.	31
	33. Interpersonal competence	Young person has empathy, sensitivity, and friendship skills.	51
	34. Cultural competence	Young person has knowledge of and comfort with people of different cultural/racial/ethnic backgrounds.	47
	35. Resistance skills	Young person can resist negative peer pressure and dangerous situations.	48
Positive Identity	36. Peaceful conflict resolution	Young person seeks to resolve conflict nonviolently.	50
	37. Personal power	Young person feels he or she has control over "things that happen to me."	49
	38. Self-esteem	Young person reports having a high self-esteem.	58
	39. Sense of purpose	Young person reports that "my life has a purpose."	65
	40. Positive view of personal future	Young person is optimistic about his or her personal future.	76

When counselors help students evaluate the results of a career interest survey, they are helping students develop these assets:

39. (sense of purpose) and
40. (positive view of personal future).

The 40 assets represent a comprehensive framework that correlates successfully with most guidance objectives. As counselors help structure the environment of students to build assets, they focus on healthy development and associated behaviors, such as school success. When the Search Institute correlated self-reported student assets with risk-taking behavior, they found strong and dramatic connections (see Figures 1, 2,

Figure 1: School Problems

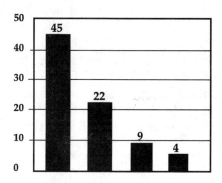

Skipped school two or more days in last 4 weeks and/or has below C average

ASSETS PROTECT CHLDREN BY HELPING THEM SUCCEED IN SCHOOL

Figure 2: Use of Alcohol

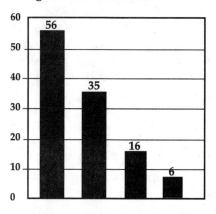

Used alcohol once or more in last 30 days

ASSETS PROTECT CHLDREN FROM ALCOHOL USE

Figure 3: Violence

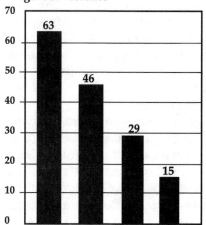

Hit someone one or more times in last 12 months

ASSETS PROTECT CHLDREN FROM VIOLENT ACTS

and 3).

Whereas the 40 developmental assets model lays out a strong rationale for a developmental guidance program, the Search Institute has taken this information to the community-organizing level. In his book *All Kids Are Our Kids*, Peter Benson (1997), president of the Search Institute, has detailed a plan for communities to rebuild their developmental infrastructure for children. It is Dr. Benson's contention that the entire community must become engaged to raise the average number of assets in the children in that community. In more than 900 communities that have embraced the Search Institute's asset model, efforts are being made to get adults to interact with children and youth in new, asset-building ways.

Increasing intergenerational relations is at the heart of asset building. Children learn from adults and grow from the caring, supportive relations they have with them. In many ways this is what counselors do with students with whom they work. A good counselor helps a student through their relationship. This relationship is special and powerful. The more of these asset-building relationships a student has, the more likely he or she is to succeed in school and other areas of life. Many counselors have used this information to mobilize other adults in their schools to build relationships that build assets. Such guidance programs as advising, academic coaching, mentoring, and career shadowing all use the intergenerational model. Counselors who have chosen to organize their programs in this manner have had a greater effect on students than those offering traditional individual and small group counseling. Just as classroom guidance reached more students than previous methods did, developing intergenerational support structures at school has reached even more students in meaningful ways. Most schools with successful adviser-advisee programs also see better academic performance because of the correlation between assets and student performance. A child who has an adult (in this case an adviser) who cares, takes time, and builds assets is at strong "risk" of success.

Benson and the communities that used the asset approach found that the greatest impact assets can have on children lies in the community as a whole. When parents, neighbors, civic and religious leaders, employers, police, human service staff, and the general public collaborate to build assets, the potential for large-scale change is powerful. Their efforts generally center on community awareness about the developmental nature of assets and their power to protect students from risk-taking behavior. While many counselors could see this activity as well beyond their scope or abilities, others have embraced the idea of a guidance program that helps children grow in healthy ways and also leads to academic success through community engagement.

In Wake County, North Carolina, counselors are taking a leadership role in this movement and transforming their guidance programs. By being partly focused on the community, these programs reach more students than traditional approaches do. A community-based guidance program could have some of the following features:

Parental involvement and education: As parents are the first and most important asset builders in a child's life, counselors could reach out to PTAs to educate parents about their influence on the 40 assets. Through presentations, workshops, and newsletters, parents' involvement and education would be a key to success. Even unusual outreach efforts to involve parents who are traditionally hard to reach can be employed.

Community involvement and education: To build assets in communities and neighborhoods, counselors could speak to civic and neighborhood groups about the power of building developmental assets. When neighbors agree to "look out" for each other's children, children feel safer and learn that community has some degree of consensus about what is acceptable and expected. The community could also reward service, effort, and resistance to risk taking. Such a supportive community would surround all children with both opportunities and safe alternatives. An example of this occurs each year as the graduates of Raleigh schools attend a gala graduation party that is alcohol and drug free.

Emphasis on life skills: To protect children from harm, counselors could work closely with community and religious groups to emphasize "life skills" that are asset based (decision making, anger and behavior control, socialization, helping others, and so forth). Such groups as YMCA, recreation programs, camping programs, community sports programs, scouting programs, boys' and girls' clubs, youth groups in religious institutions, and many other groups that serve youth are working with counselors and community leaders to build assets by teaching life skills as well as providing supportive, nurturing environments.

Career development: In a community-based guidance

program, counselors and other educators could work closely with employers to advance career development for youth. The asset approach to career development focuses on more than job training, however; students would learn with community adults in a manner that fosters intergenerational sharing and nurturing. Career shadowing, career mentoring, and emphasizing the importance of life skills as outlined in the assets would also differentiate this approach from the minimal job-training approach. Counselors in Wake County are reaching out to employers to teach them about assets and to help them view themselves as asset builders.

Conclusion

Although the potential benefits of a community-based guidance program grounded in an assets approach are relatively clear, the challenges are significant. To get out of the traditional office and into the community is the biggest paradigm shift. Counselors and guidance-program designers can learn much from the Cities in Schools (CIS) programs that gained popularity and support during the 1990s. This outreach program utilizes school staff as community outreach workers. The CIS coordinators recruit mentors, talk to employers, and reach out to parents and others in the community to help students who or at risk of dropping out of school. The paradigm these coordinators have is one of connecting community members to at-risk youth. To accomplish this, they spend large amounts of time in the community. If counselors adopted this model, they would also go into the community to recruit and educate citizens. A guidance program that is community based would tie all support activities to school success in new and exciting ways. Counselors would gain new respect among students and peers for their work on behalf of all students. Whether recruiting study buddies or matching career mentors to students, counselors would be proactively altering the opportunities students have to increase the number of developmental assets in their lives. Those who question the sense of this new design need only refer back to Figures 1, 2, and 3.

References

Benson, P. (1997). *All kids are our kids*. San Francisco: Jossey-Bass.

The Search Institute. (1999, November). *Profiles of student life*. Report 80059, prepared for Wake County Schools. Minneapolis, MN: Author.

About the Author

Ron Anderson, Ph.D., is the current senior director of the Safe Schools/Healthy Students Grant for Wake County Schools. Previously, he served as the director of guidance and social work for Wake County, a school system of 100,000 students. He is also adjunct professor in Counselor Education at North Carolina State University. Anderson has presented extensively on topics such as the 40 Developmental Asset Framework as a model for school counseling, accountability for school counselors, and play therapy. Dr. Anderson has been a school counselor in Gainesville, Florida, an assistant professor of Counselor Education at Northern Illinois University, and guidance consultant for the North Carolina Department of Public Instruction. a former president of the North Carolina Counseling Association, he is currently the chair of the Duke Endowment funded Building Youth Assets initiative in Raleigh, North Carolina.

Section 2:

Counseling for Employability

Chapter Six

Taking Comprehensive Competency-Based Guidance to Business and Industry

Tina K. Ammon

While state supervisor of guidance and counseling at the Arizona Department of Education (1985–1994), and in conjunction with a Guidance and Counseling State Task Force recommendation, I helped develop the Arizona Comprehensive Competency-Based Guidance (CCBG) program model, which was piloted in six Arizona schools in 1986 in order to create a set of CCBG videotapes modeling CCBG program prototypes in large urban high schools, midsize suburban high schools, and small rural high schools. The pilots were successful and there was consensus of the stakeholders to take the Arizona CCBG program model statewide through an annual counselors' academy.

The National Career Development Guidelines were piloted for the career domain of curriculum competencies in the Arizona CCBG program. From 1986 to 1994, various Arizona schools developed curricula to deliver the National Career Development Guidelines competencies.

The Arizona CCBG program model is being delivered in Arizona schools today and has proven to be a highly successful model. Whether the template used for CCBG program design is Johnson's Competency-Based Guidance Model or Gysbers' Missouri Comprehensive Program Model, the program structure and curriculum competencies of both models provide all students with the knowledge, attitudes, and skills they need to be successful in school and the world of work (Bloom, 1994).

As a career consultant for Motorola, Inc., in Phoenix, Arizona, I set out to deliver the adult National Career Development Guidelines competencies to Motorola employees. At the corporate career center in Phoenix, I initiated a project to pilot the National Occupational Information Coordinating

Committee (NOICC) Adult Career Portfolio to find out how viable the portfolio was in business and industry.

The NOICC Adult Career Portfolio Project

Business and industry employees ranging in age from 17 to 70 participated in the NOICC portfolio project. Ten employees interested in their career development were just handed the portfolio to use in order for us to see how viable the portfolio was as a self-directed tool. Other employees were scheduled for two different small-group guidance sessions. One group was to use the portfolio for career development planning and the other group for educational planning. Each group session was planned for four hours, using basically the same pages from the portfolio in each session. A sample agenda for career planning appears on the next page.

Participant evaluations of the group sessions were consistently positive. For the next four years, the NOICC Adult Career Portfolio was used in several career centers at Motorola as a career guidance and counseling tool.

The 10 employees given the portfolio as a self-directed tool thought the portfolio looked interesting but they "hadn't found the time" to actually use it. The group session was a superior method because employees were permitted time to work on portfolio sections and were offered counselor guidance and input. Completing sections of the portfolio requires extensive introspection, which employees found tedious. The pages that required the user to identify skills and then write information on how he or she demonstrated those skills on the job were excellent for developing a performance-style resume, a style template available through a software program used in the career centers.

NOICC Adult Career Portfolio:
Paradigms for Future Guidance Programs

After years working with high school students in job placement (co-op) and career counseling, I wasn't surprised to find that youth lacked initiative related to their own career guidance. I *was* surprised to find that business and industry adults who were considered high-powered employees were unable to find the time and initiative to use the NOICC Adult Career Portfolio as a self-directed tool.

Portfolio for Career-Planning Group Session

Time	Agenda Item
1:00–1:15 p.m.	Introductions and overview
1:15–1:45 p.m.	True Colors (cards and vocabulary test) Closure: pages 1-3 of the portfolio
1:45–2:15 p.m.	Participants complete pages 11-16 of the portfolio
2:15–2:45 p.m.	Group debrief of portfolio pages 11-16
2:45–3:00 p.m.	Participants complete Transferable Skills Checklist in the Motorola University Catalog in order to identify training gaps
3:00–3:45 p.m.	Job-O A career assessment administered
3:45–4:00 p.m.	Closure: portfolio pages 18-20
4:00–4:45 p.m.	Tentative career plan
4:45–5:00 p.m.	Informational interviewing resources
5:00 p.m.	Evaluation of group session
Workshop follow-up	Follow-up: Participant completes portfolio sections Deciding and Planning, and Acting, in preparation for his or her one-hour follow-up visit (30 days later) with counselor to finalize career plan.

Later, as the manager of a highly computerized career center, I developed an eight-hour self-directed career-planning program using CD-ROM career guidance tools, such as Repacking Your Bags. This software program guides the user in developing a dialogue with his or her significant other using a series of topics and postcards for decision making regarding changing to employment in another geographic area. Few people (five) requested these highly advertised self-directed tools. Employees in business and industry preferred career development activities such as panels, counselor-led classes, and one-on-one counseling.

When it comes to the topic of "What will I be when I grow up?" human beings of all ages seem to want to be directed, even to the point of wanting the career counselor to help them figure out what personal information to include on their resumes. In contrast to client need, business and industry continues to offer online self-directed career development tools. It was evident from attending various business and industry conferences, such as the Summit on Linking Career Development with the New Corporate Agenda (Various Corporate Sessions, 1998) that only 50% of corporations are offering career services to employees. The corporate trend is to provide online career development information. At Motorola, employees would access the online information if they had Internet access, but they still came to the career center for one-on-one counselor interaction. My experiences with youth in education and adults in business and industry led me to the conclusion that the human need for counselor interaction related to career development will persist into 2021. Whether business and industry or education will meet that client need is another question.

Career Decidedness Study

The Career Decidedness Study, involving business and industry employees, was developed to improve counseling skills and the services offered to employees seeking career counseling at the Motorola Mesa Career Management Center (Mesa CMC). I prepared an extensive write-up of the Career Decidedness Study and presented it at the Second Motorola Worldwide Research Conference (Ammon, 1997). What follows are salient points related to the study and its implications for career guidance in 2021.

Selection and Definition of the Research Problem
Career counseling is interactive, and, optimally, client need determines the counseling intervention. The Mesa CMC counseling staff used multiple career guidance interventions: for example, one-on-one counseling intervention using the World of Work Inventory (one-on-one WOWI); the portfolio group session using the NOICC Adult Career Portfolio, coupled with the Job-O A career assessment instrument and other business- and industry-developed materials; an eight-hour career development class (module); as well as various self-directed CD-ROM career-planning programs. The business and industry

thrust for these career guidance interventions was the Individual Dignity Entitlement (IDE) corporate initiative, specifically question number four of the initiative: "Do you have a personal career plan, and is it exciting, achievable, and being acted upon?" Developing a personal career plan requires a certain level of career decidedness. "Employees are 'career decided' if they have established a career goal with which they experience relative certainty and comfort. Employees are 'career undecided' if they have either not established a career goal or established a goal with which they experience substantial uncertainty and discomfort" (Greenhaus, Callahan, & Kaplan, 1995). Career guidance interventions that help employees raise their level of career decidedness would facilitate their completion of a career plan.

One of the measures the Mesa CMC used to address customer satisfaction was a set of five questions on the CMC Participant Information form. Following their four-hour one-on-one counseling experience using the WOWI, employees answered yes or no to the following questions:

The CMC process provided

1. the opportunity to increase self-understanding and self-knowledge

2. information that will assist in locating, evaluating, and interpreting occupational information

3. information regarding relevant education and training programs

4. insight for making appropriate career decisions

5. action steps to begin career planning

During 1995, the Six Sigma result of clients' satisfaction as addressed by these five questions was 6.0 (high). The portfolio group sessions provided participants with evaluation forms to rate the quality and satisfaction of services based on similar questions used on the CMC Participant Information form as previously described. The composite of evaluations from both the portfolio group session and the eight-hour career development class evidenced a high degree of customer satisfaction; employees continued to request those interventions. This evaluation data are consistent with the research findings of Kileen & Kidd (1991), who stated that 90% of the studies regarding career guidance and counseling evidenced at least some positive effects.

Pilot Study

In an effort to be more precise about the effect of the various CMC career guidance interventions, I initiated a pilot study in November 1995. The pilot study served as a feasibility study to determine if client career decidedness was raised by any or all of the guidance interventions offered by CMC; that is, the one-on-one WOWI, portfolio group session, eight-hour career development class (module), and CD-ROM self-directed career-planning programs. I used Osipow's Career Decision Scale (CDS) as the instrument in the pilot study. I administered the CDS as a pretest and readministered it within a 30- to 45-day timeframe during the client follow-up as a post-test. The eight-hour career development class participants were mailed the CDS 30 days after completing the class and were asked to complete and return the CDS post-test via confidential mail. Statistical analysis of the pilot study data conducted by Robert Watkins, Motorola engineering manager, in his initial report of July 24, 1996, confirmed that with samples of at least 75 to 100 employees per guidance intervention, data collected would yield a statistical analysis that showed whether guidance intervention made a significant difference in successful career development.

One of the values of the pilot study was the validation of the Career Decision Scale as a usable instrument with employees accessing CMC services. They were able to read and answer the questions with no instructions other than those appearing on the instrument.

Another value of the pilot study was that it had already led to improvement of the Mesa CMC career management process. Of the 200 participants in the pilot study, 85 completed a usable pretest but only 28 participants returned for their follow-up and completed the CDS as the post-test. In career counseling, clients not returning for their follow-up session is a common problem, and the reasons vary. After the pilot study, the CMC process was refocused so that after employees completed the career guidance intervention of their choice (one-on-one WOWI, portfolio group session, or career development class), they also completed a tentative career plan. The follow-up session was redesigned to review the tentative career plan and make changes based on informational interviews or other information-gathering activities assigned to increase the likelihood of a more defined career plan. Because the IDE initiative called for employees to develop a career plan, this refocusing of the CMC career development process increased the number of employees attaining that outcome.

Also, the training-hour credits were tied to the follow-up session; in other words, the employee did not receive four training hours of credit for the portfolio group session until the follow-up session was completed. Employees who did not show up for the follow-up session were logged into the No-Show Report that went back to their supervisor. This increased the number of employees returning for the follow-up session. During the first quarter of 1997, 40% of participants completed the follow-up session and the CDS as a post-test.

During 1995, there was an effort to develop an online career development program called the *Personal Career Navigator,* which received high visibility as the career tool of the future. During 1999, the *Personal Career Navigator* CD-ROM program was abandoned after an expenditure of millions of dollars. A few pieces of the *Personal Career Navigator* program were salvaged for online Internet users, but business and industry reorganizes so quickly, it was deemed impossible to keep the system up to date regarding company divisions, job titles, and job descriptions. The success of the project was in finding out what didn't work. The *Personal Career Navigator* participants would be an important sample in the 1997 Career Decidedness Study.

Career Decidedness Study Research Methods
The statement of the problem for this study was
How can the Mesa CMC improve the career guidance interventions offered to employees within the framework of corporate initiatives and client expectations?

The purpose of the study was to identify the discriminating factors, including the score levels of Decidedness and Indecision of Osipow's Career Decision Scale (CDS), for selection of employees for the various career guidance interventions at the Mesa CMC.

Null Hypothesis
The null hypothesis of this study was
There is no significant difference between employee mean gain scores on the CDS, one-on-one WOWI sample, portfolio group session sample, eight-hour career development class sample, or CD-ROM career-planning program sample.

Population

The population for the study was Mesa SPS employees at the Dobson and Broadway plant who requested career guidance services from the Mesa CMC. This population consisted of males and females, ranging from 17 to 70 years of age, involved in various types of work, such as manufacturing associates, management, administrative assistants, security guards, engineers, and so forth. They came to the Mesa CMC to complete career or educational plans. They ranged at all levels of career decidedness from totally undecided and exploring options to the more decided, such as an engineer choosing an engineering rotational assignment. Each employee accessing CMC services completed the CMC Participant Information form. Responses to this form provided demographic information and 12 reasons why employees accessed CMC services.

Sample

Only Mesa SPS employees who completed the pretest, a CMC career guidance intervention, and the post-test were used in the sample for statistical analysis. In line with the recommendations related to the pilot study sample and data analysis, a sample of 75 to 100 was required for each career guidance intervention for validity and reliability purposes. This data and sample requirement were collected from September 1996 to October 1998.

Validity Controls

In this study sample, employees completed the CDS as a pretest and post-test. All employees completed the CDS prior to the intervention (that is, the one-on-one WOWI, portfolio group session, career development class, or CD-ROM career-planning programs). All employees completed the post-test after a 30- to 45-day follow-up period to control for the threat of history to internal validity. I or a trained certified career counselor administered all CDS pre- and post-tests to control for the external validity factor of the interaction of testing and intervention. I or the career counselors delivered all four guidance interventions involved in the study.

Study Design

In this study, the career guidance interventions were the independent variables. The dependent variable was the gain scores of the post-test samples on the CDS. The research design used in this study was a pretest/post-test design.

$$O\ X_1\ O$$
$$O\ X_2\ O$$
$$O\ X_3\ O$$
$$O\ X_4\ O$$

O denoted the collection of data (dependent variable) from employees.

X represented the career guidance interventions: X_1 represented CMC employees completing the one-on-one WOWI counseling session. X_2 represented employees completing the portfolio group session. X_3 represented employees completing the eight-hour career development class. X_4 represented employees completing the CD-ROM self-directed career planning programs.

Data-Collection Procedure

1. Mesa plant employees requested services from the Mesa CMC. Employees completed the CMC Participant Information form and CDS as a pretest.

2. Employees completed the career guidance intervention of their choice: one-on-one WOWI, portfolio group session, eight-hour career development class, or the CD-ROM self-directed career-planning programs.

3. Employees returning for their follow-up session (30 to 45 days later) completed the CDS as a post-test. Employees using the CD-ROM self-directed career-planning programs completed a software evaluation form that assessed the effectiveness of the software in meeting their needs.

4. I or a trained certified career counselor collected all CDS pretests and post-tests. I hand scored all tests.

Data Analysis: Pilot Study

I hand-scored the 28 CDS pre- and post-test samples and used "Appendix C: Adults Seeking Continuing Education" of the *CDS Interpretation Manual* (Osipow, 1987) to grossly evaluate pilot study data. Robert Watkins, engineering manager, analyzed the pilot study data using a paired t-test and Wilcoxon Signed-Rank Test. With regard to the certainty scale, pilot study data analyzed for the eight-hour career development class sample did support the rejection of the null hypothesis. However, data were too sparse to make any other comparisons.

Data Analysis: Career Decidedness Study

As I continued to gather and hand-score CDS data, reaching a sample of at least 200, it became clear that the one-on-one WOWI counseling session was the intervention that consistently raised career decidedness on the CDS. The portfolio group session data analysis revealed that it did not raise career decidedness on the CDS but was excellent for adults wanting a career exploration activity. The eight-hour career development class was discontinued in 1997, so the sample and data, other than pilot study data, were inconclusive. (With the downturn in the semiconductor industry in 1997 and 1998, factory managers did not support any eight-hour career guidance intervention. Production needed to be increased and factory employees to be on-task.) The CD-ROM self-directed career-planning programs, even though well advertised, were not requested enough over the two years to provided a sample.

Study Conclusions

The review of literature regarding increasing employee career decidedness concurs with the intent of the study. "Research indicates that vigilant career decision making produces positive work attitudes and the least stress" (Greenhaus et al., 1995). Positive work attitudes would result in lower absenteeism, greater job satisfaction, and a more "on-task" employee. Having knowledge of career guidance interventions that raise career decidedness is significant for the career counselor, especially within a corporate environment with a corporate initiative requiring a career plan. In a rapidly changing workplace, perhaps the only security an employee has is a viable career plan with at least two good options for future employment toward which he or she can train and network.

Hornak and Gillingham (1980), in their journal article "Career Indecision: A Self-Defeating Behavior," list the prices of career indecision as follows: increased anxieties and possible depression; psychosomatic illness; unnecessary expenditure of money, energy, and time in school; disapproval of significant others; feelings of discouragement and inadequacy compared to peers who make firm decisions; inability to capitalize on collegiate opportunities; erosion of self-confidence; and poor grades because of lack of purpose.

To summarize, when one compares the benefits of raising career decidedness against the costs of indecision, the quest for career guidance interventions that raise career decidedness are worthy of research efforts.

Career Decidedness Study: Paradigms
for Future Guidance Programs

Problems that plague counselors in an educational setting are similar to those in business and industry: for example, the importance of professional credentials. Our profession believes that a master's degree in educational counseling and coursework in career guidance are necessary in order to work with students in developing educational and career plans; this emphasis on credentials is further supported by State Department certification requirements for counseling. However, vocational teachers and uncredentialed part-time employees work in career centers involved in career counseling. In business and industry, career counseling is found in the human resources (HR) department. Because the number of HR specialists is greater than the number of career counselors (200 to 1, respectively), the human resources degree is preferred, and the leadership for employee career development rests with human resources specialists and managers. Furthermore, business and industry uses professional outplacement firms for downsizing; these firms offer career planning, and their staff members generally have a bachelor's in business management or psychology. There are some exceptions: There is usually one "token" certified career counselor on staff. Our profession of counseling works for professional credential recognition and the right to exercise career development leadership in both arenas: education and business and industry.

One vehicle that lends credibility to a profession is professional research.

The purpose of the Career Decidedness Study was to improve the delivery of career development interventions for employees and to improve the counselor's performance. Research in business and industry is just as difficult to conduct as it is in education. The research deals with human beings, so getting clients to return for a follow-up session and complete a usable post-test is difficult. During my four and a half years of employment at Motorola, there were two major reorganizations, resulting in my moving from a corporate career center to managing a plant career center and finally to orchestrating regional career services. Just as in education, where an election can mean a new state superintendent of public instruction and a "new regime" with a "new thrust," every business and industry reorganization leads to a new CEO and a new regime with a new thrust. A research project started one year might or might not survive the next, so long-term research (two to five years) is difficult to accomplish. This trend of constant business and industry reorganization and elections of new state superintendents will persist to the year 2021. Research will continue to be difficult to accomplish, but it is worth our efforts to continue to establish the counseling profession and recognition of professional counseling credentials.

Implementing the National
Career Development Guidelines

The services of the Mesa CMC were provided in response to the corporate Individual Dignity Entitlement (IDE) initiative; question number four of that initiative (as previously stated) served as the cornerstone of the IDE mission statement. All CMC career services revolved around the nine adult National Career Development Guidelines competencies.

There is no career guidance program model in business and industry similar to the CCBG program model. Career services offered to employees are developed in response to the corporate career development initiative and the knowledge and talent of individuals delivering those career services. One of the business and industry trends for organizing career development interventions is the concept of "career resilience; i.e., the ability to adapt to changing work circumstances, even when the circumstances are discouraging or disruptive" (Collard, 1994). According to Collard, the four elements of career resilience are self-confidence, the need for achievement, the willingness to take risks, and the ability to act independently and cooperatively, depending on the situation. One of the documents developed to work with organizational clients was the Career Resilience Self-Assessment packet using the concept of career resilience and the employee's report of the proficiency of the adult National Career Development Guidelines competencies to determine needed career development training. The immediate response of employees completing the self-assessment packet was, "Were the National Career Development Guidelines customized to our business?" and the response was yes. A presentation and document I developed, entitled "The Answer," is an in-depth customization of the adult National Career Development

Guidelines in response to the corporate IDE initiative. The adult National Career Development Guidelines are usable in business and industry but need to be updated to reflect business and industry trends, such as project work.

A serious problem that confounds career guidance in education and business and industry is the constantly changing nature of work and job titles; this problem will continue into 2021. Bill Bridges's (1995) predictions in *Job Shift* regarding project work are a reality in business and industry now. The big thrust in training in business and industry is certification in project management. Job titles constantly change. The State of Arizona Occupational Information System (OIS) lists occupational information for computer scientist and computer operator, but there are myriad computer-work job titles and descriptions in business and industry that are not found in the OIS, such as network administrator. An example of a job title change in human resources is a change from human resource specialist to human resources performance consultant. In-house training to become the human resources performance consultant is short term and leads to a certificate. There is no committee or training organization determining job title changes; rather, it is the work of "high potentials," employees (30 to 40 years of age) who are bright and Internet savvy, creating job titles as they move through the world of work. Their resumes and chat room conversations are the source of knowledge about new job titles.

Paradigms for Future Guidance Programs

It is true that what drives business and industry and the work done there is global competition. Business and industry constantly changes its focus in career development for employees. In 1994, the focus at Motorola was the family concept: "The company will take care of you and provide you the training needed to have a job with the company." Later that year, the IDE was rolled out as the new corporate career development strategy: "It is your responsibility to develop a career plan and remain viable in the company; we will provide the training for you to do that." In 1998, the corporate career development thrust changed again: "You need to work with your manager to see if you still fit with the company's new direction and have the skills needed for that next job. Take time to talk with your manager about a future career direction." In other words, career development and skills attainment are the responsibility of the employee, and the employee's manager is the key to that employee's future. Bill Bridges predicted that the future of employees in the world of work was to find a successful manager and move with that manager and organization to the next project. That is a good scenario for 2021 students to understand. Certainly the concept of career resilience as described in Betsy Collard's "Career Self-Reliance" would be valuable to students entering the world of work in future years. A good activity for high school students might be to explore various job titles in their top three occupational clusters and plan sample paths of possibilities, listing a series of acceptable job titles or project work that would interest them.

Schools and school counselors will find a CCBG program still viable in future years if they work with business and industry advisory council members to understand project work and new job titles, and to build into their models the concept of career resilience as related to the career and educational domains. A new set of competencies related to marketing oneself needs to be added to the high school and adult career development competencies, most likely under the National Career Development Guidelines. Counselors need to understand the urgency of career development guidance and to continue to strive to make sure that every student has attained the National Career Development Competencies by grade 12. Business and industry does not want to spend its money or training time doing that job. The youth who has mastered the National Career Development Competencies and who knows how to develop a tentative career plan for the next three years has the basics needed to begin in the world of work.

Online and CD-ROM career development programs will be valuable for information, reinforcement, and additional practice of competencies, but it is evident from having operated a state-of-the-art computerized career center that people want the personal guidance of a counselor, and time will not change that human need.

Counselors and education in general need to come to a demystified understanding of business and industry. A representative of a particular business or industry has expertise in that industry just as the teachers and counselors of the educational community have expertise in education. Million dollar mistakes are made each year in business and industry, such as the *Personal Career Navigator* CD-ROM program, and there is little consequence. Industries think nothing of requiring employees to work 12-hour shifts that interfere with family life and increase stress. Educators and counselors cannot afford to make mistakes with youth because youth are not expendable. Education and, particularly, counselors are held to a higher standard than business and industry when it comes to performance in relationship to human beings and their nurturing and growth. We need to keep business and industry as our partners to keep up with the changing world of work, but educators and counselors need to remain the providers of career and educational competencies and the experts in educational direction.

References

Ammon, T. K. (1997, May). *Career decidedness study.* Paper presented at the Second Motorola Worldwide Research Conference, Tempe, AZ.

Bloom, J. W. (1994). Competency-based comprehensive guidance programs: A review of evaluation models and outcome studies. *Arizona Counseling Journal, 19,* 11–18.

Bridges, W. (1995). *Job shift: How to prosper in a workplace without jobs.* 2nd. ed. Reading, MA: Addison-Wesley.

Collard, B. A. (1994). *Career self-reliance.* White paper presented at the 1998 Linking Career Development with the New Corporate Agenda summit.

Greenhaus, J. H., Callahan, G. A., & Kaplan, E. (1995). The role of goal setting in career management. *The International Journal of Management Development, 14*(10), 48–63.

Hornak, J., & Gillingham B. (1980). Career indecision: A self-defeating behavior. *Personnel and Guidance Journal, 59,* 252–253.

Kileen, J., & Kidd, J. (1991) *Learning outcomes of guidance: A review of recent research.* London, England: National Institute for Career Education and Counseling.

National Occupational Information Coordinating Committee. (1995). *Adult career portfolio.* Stillwater: Oklahoma Department of Vocational and Technical Education.

National Occupational Information Coordinating Committee. (1996). *National career development guidelines*. Stillwater: Oklahoma Department of Vocational and Technical Education.

Osipow, S. H. (1987). *Manual for the Career Decision Scale* (2nd. ed.) Odessa, FL: Psychological Assessment Resources.

Various Corporate Sessions. (1998, January). The 1998 summit on linking career development with the new corporate agenda, New Orleans, LA.

About the Author

Tina K. Ammon, Ed.D., NCC, NCCC is currently a faculty member with the University of Phoenix teaching in the Masters of Educational Counseling program and providing career and personal counseling for individuals referred from business and industry (Motorola) and Arizona State University. She received her doctorate in Secondary Education from Arizona State University in 1988. Her published dissertation is *Measuring the Effectiveness of a Career Placement Document in Lowering Vocational Indecision.* In 1993–94, she served as the president of the National Association of State Supervisors of Guidance. She received the AZSCA Supervisor/Administrator of the Year Award (1993) for her leadership role as the state supervisor of guidance and counseling at the Arizona Department of Education. The video she produced and edited, *Entrepreneurship: An Application for Student Job Placement* won the 1985 Award of Excellence from the National Child Labor Committee. Published articles include "Arizona Continues its Move Toward Implementing Competency-Based Guidance Programs"(*National Career Guidance News*). In her employment history with Motorola (1994–2001), Phoenix, AZ, Dr. Ammon was a career counselor and the regional manager of career centers

Paradigms for Future Guidance Programs: A Longitudinal Approach to Preparing Youth for Employability

Conrad F. Toepfer, Jr.

Will Rogers reportedly once quipped, "Things aren't as good as they used to be, but then they never were!" However, it would seem that the goal to educate all the children of our nation at public expense was more achievable in the past. Levels of learning required by the masses early in the twentieth century were far lower than what present and emerging needs require. Urban industrialization was beginning to encroach on a largely agrarian society. There was little scholarship opportunity for bright but impoverished students. Those who completed high school usually possessed both the intellectual ability to complete high school and the financial ability to enter a college or university.

Those who had the first but lacked the second of those qualifications usually dropped out of school to enter the workforce. Learning targets beyond basic ciphering and literacy were largely reserved for affluent students. Prestigious private colleges and universities accommodated able upper-class students. Unskilled labor needs, not academic success, afforded less affluent students with opportunity to achieve economic self-sufficiency and a better quality of life.

In 1900, approximately 25% of American youth entered ninth grade and as few as 12% completed high school. The economic need for unskilled labor easily accommodated such dropout casualties. While concerns for better educated masses gradually increased, the 40% of Americans not completing high school in 1950 still posed no problems in post–World War II America. However, the shifting world economy since then has reversed that situation. The disappearance of well-paying unskilled work and the inability of schools to assist less able students to achieve economic self-sufficiency now risks creating a virtual impoverished caste.

Today, schools are criticized for failing to achieve universal high school completion of increasingly rigorous post-secondary preparatory curricula. Yet efforts to do so are being attempted within the same school model from which large percentages of students dropped out earlier this century. The prospects for this model preparing virtually all students for the demands of life in the twenty-first century are not encouraging.

In defending the difficulty of that challenge, some say, "We have different kids today." What is the nature of those differences from students in the early twentieth century? Both were children of poor immigrants, but earlier immigrants were predominantly from European backgrounds. However, most of today's "new Americans" are from Africa, Asia, and Latin America. Their cultures, mores, and customs differ greatly from those of the largely White earlier European immigrants.

Aside from dissimilar geographic origins and cultural backgrounds, the critical difference may be in the circumstances faced by today's new Americans. Earlier immigrants arrived when unskilled labor needs allowed them to achieve elevated economic status for themselves and their families. Their children were motivated to complete public school and enter college, and their grandchildren are among the best of today's public school students. Today's immigrants lack that opportunity to move their children to middle-class circumstances.

With 20/20 hindsight, descendants of earlier European immigrants may extol "the good old days" and the accomplishments of their parents and grandparents. The experiences of diverse Americans, however, particularly Native Americans and Americans of African descent whose grandparents were already here when the waves of earlier European immigrants arrived, gave them a different hindsight.

Their legacy was one of unequal access to employment opportunities, lack of equal protection under laws, no access to common public facilities, and denial of voting franchise. Those conditions persisted into the second half of the twentieth century. Many of today's immigrants and their children learn that history from the ghettoes in which they now live. These and other societal changes pose critical challenges to our nation's schools.

Educational Standards: Tilting at Another Windmill

As adults, today's students will have to deal with emerging problems societal changes are creating. Improving public education for all of the children of all of the people will require educational reform that better accommodates under-served American youth. Educational policy seeks to accomplish that for the mass of United States students through higher assessments and exit standards implemented at fixed times in schools.

The educational standards movement assumes that virtually all learners can achieve those benchmarks through assessments at set points in the elementary- and secondary-school continuum. Most states "cap" that with high-stakes testing near the conclusion of high school. This chapter will address the approach in New York state as an example of what is occurring across the nation.

In accordance with New York State Education Commissioner Richard P. Mills' recommendations, the Board of Regents has enacted fourth, eighth, and eleventh grade standards for students at large. The late architect Frank Lloyd Wright stressed the need for "form to follow function." The "function" of educational standards reform is for schools to enable students at large to achieve those higher learning standards.

Lacking the "form" of a school model designed to accomplish that, how will merely raising standards help those students presently unable to meet existing ones? Such an expectation could be as hazardous as expecting propeller-driven aircraft to perform better using fuel developed for jet engines.

A study just released by the Consortium for Policy Research in Education identifies serious concerns about New York state's educational standards initiative. The study was developed by educational specialists familiar with the details of reform plans in New York and elsewhere. Simon (1999) summarized their concerns as follows.

Senior Research Fellow and former President of the Association of Public Policy Analysis and Management Richard E. Elmore stated: "Pretty soon, there's going to be a very large backlog of kids who have failed one or another of the required exams. We need to face the fact that teachers and schools are being asked to do something they don't know how to do" (p. A22). Harvard researcher Gary Orfield cautioned: "It's going to ruin a lot of students' lives and not have substantial benefits. If you have just one standard, you're eventually going to find the inner city schools with high concentrations of poverty and identify them as failures" (p. A22).

As adults, today's students will undoubtedly need skills and knowledge beyond those achieved by past generations. However, the present school model was not designed to accomplish that for the masses within a common time frame. The naiveté of assuming that it can could doom possibilities for students at large achieving higher learning standards.

Accommodating the learning needs of all the nation's youth will necessitate shifting from an instructional to a learning paradigm. Lasley (1998) noted:

> Most teachers and a majority of administrators focus on the instructional paradigm. That is not their espoused theory, but it does emerge as their theory-in-use. They and the larger community they serve (parents and a variety of significant others) want to see students looking busy and getting their work done.
>
> Far fewer teachers embrace the learning paradigm. Teachers who are oriented in this way function very differently in their role as facilitators of learning. They are constantly "reading" the students to determine how to create a better atmosphere for student growth. Learning paradigm teachers get outside themselves and get inside the *needs of students.* They continually ask, How do they learn? How do they construct knowledge? How do they make sense of the world? How can I, the teacher, participate in the learning process with students?
>
> The classroom that operates according to the learning paradigm is emotionally and intellectually demanding. The demands on a teacher who seeks to foster a learner-centered classroom are numerous. More time is needed to plan lessons, more effort is needed to reach the students, and less teacher control can be used to force students to conform to the will of the teacher.
>
> The learning paradigm teacher takes more

personal risks and creates more administrative challenges. The curriculum of a learning paradigm teacher is a guide, not a dictate, and, as a consequence, the sequence of learning often conflicts with the prescribed learning paradigm of the school. (pp. 84–85)

Rather than pursuing a learning paradigm, current reform has chosen to increase singular educational standards for the vast majority of students. Moving toward universal high school graduation will entail more than tinkering with yesterday's education model. A "zero-defect" education model needs to provide the masses with improved skills for continued learning.

What Educational Standards Can and Cannot Do

Classroom teachers have been largely excluded from planning educational standards initiatives, which are primarily defined by other stakeholders. As Wood (1999) noted:

> This school year, Massachusetts fourth graders will spend close to 15 hours over the course of two weeks practicing and taking standardized assessments to measure their proficiencies against state curriculum standards. It is a scene repeated across the nation, as the "accountability" approach continues to grow stronger in the powerful educational establishment, which consists of state school boards, national policy groups, politicians, and the "trade" media of education. It is a sad fact that teachers, who often have the clearest insights about children and the most direct contact with them, are seldom included in this powerful group. (p. 38)

Paul Houston (1997), executive director of the American Association of School Administrators and the first spokesperson of a national educational association to voice caution about the educational standards movement noted:

> Standards, higher standards. World-class standards. Standards have become the mantra of school reform. They have replaced apple pie and motherhood as the one thing no educator can be against. We do need to

improve what we are doing, though, and improve it dramatically, because incremental improvement will not suffice in an exponential environment. Expectations for all children have skyrocketed against the past, and we have not kept up with those expectations. So, improvement is needed, but not for the reasons the critics assume. And if we have misdiagnosed the problem, we are likely to prescribe the wrong treatment; a blind call for higher standards without examining what children need to know how to meet. (p. 44)

Dewey (1917) commented that "when shooting at the target, not the target, but hitting the target is the end in view" (p. 123). From that perspective, Tanner (1997) identified "tunnel vision" possibilities in the educational standards movement:

In effect, the formulation of standards without the means serves to perpetuate a dualism between ends and means that is counter-productive for education. To conceive of knowledge as merely results as measured by "standards" neglects the processes or means through which the learner is to become increasingly knowledge/able (the capacity of putting knowledge into use). For the processes or means is the truly significant aspect of giving meaning to experience and the outcomes of the educational journey. (p. 120)

The fourth and eighth grade assessments being implemented in New York state are of particular concern here. Integrated language arts examinations were instituted at those levels before new curricula were fully developed and teachers prepared to implement them. What was served by the "ready, aim, fire" administration of new assessments before students experienced the new curricula and teaching strategies? Considering children grow up, not down, shouldn't educational standards be raised in a bottom-up sequence?

As educational standards initiatives are being implemented, they may increase the success of many motivated, high ability, and some average ability students. However, the challenge persists to help less able or unmotivated students with whom schools have never had substantial success. The latter will require extended time to meet higher standards, something that the current model of American public schools was not designed to provide.

What about students who score poorly on those assessments in high-performing suburban schools? They risk being overlooked or passed by in the context of successful and superior performance by the majority of more able or more affluent students in those communities. Clearly, the schedule for meeting higher standards needs to provide flexibility of time, which individuals with varying capacities shall require in order to achieve the standards.

In view of the notion that all students can meet common standards, Gran's concerns (1970) about the varying capacities of the masses persist: "Amazing, how we go about clucking that the modern school respects the dignity of the individual, then march all the individuals into some sterile central spot, slap a standardized test before them, snap on the stopwatch, and complacently sort and classify children by percentiles, grade placements, deciles, stanines, and other e bins and boxes contrived to house individuals" (p. 53).

> Consider the physician who would require all his patients to undergo a tonsillectomy at age 6.6, since this is the age established as readiness for tonsillectomies. Or imagine a lawyer who tells you that today everyone will be tried for petty larceny, for this is the day he has decided to offer that particular experience—even though what you want is help with your income tax. Absurd? Then why are teachers asked to hammer and tong children into reading at age 6.6? Why is Grade 5 the right time—the only time—for Book 5 in Arithmetic? (p. 53)

Today one might ask why must *all* students take the fourth and eighth grade assessments at the end of those school years? If some require longer to master that content, why couldn't they be allowed to take the first in 5th or even 6th grade if that is when they reach those levels? Again, Gran (1970) gibes about the expectations of everyone meeting common standards at the same time.

> Next time you shop for shoes, insist on the standard size for your age and the number of years you have worn shoes. If the miserable things pinch, don't complain. If you don't like the style, keep still. After

all, the shoes are standard and right for your age and period of non-bare-footed-ness. The problem is not the shoes; it's your feet. Anyway, eventually your feet will become so numb you won't notice them or even care about the shoes. Eventually, they'll take on some kind of bizarre shape that fits the shoe. The shoe is the important thing. Adjustment is up to the individual. Standardization is the key. Above the median is the place to be. (p. 54)

European and Asian educational systems provide substantial educational opportunity in technical and vocational areas for students with the interests and abilities to study and develop employability skills for such careers. However, in the United States, lower public esteem for both technical-vocational education and occupations often encourages students with such talents and interests to pursue college preparatory programs, regardless of their potential for success. All students will need improved academic skills, but standards also need to be defined for those who will pursue post-secondary vocational study and careers. Light (1999) noted, "Not all students are academically oriented but many can do well in vocational schools and a separate set of standards. There is a great need for students in skilled trades and these students must not be abandoned" (p. H2).

The singular focus on academic standards risks creating (a) a surplus of overqualified people for employment opportunities requiring academic preparation, and (b) a substantial population of others unable to achieve those standards who have not developed other employability skills. More than preparing rocket scientists, our society needs to provide all students with basic technological literacy. Mishodek (1999) makes a strong case for the latter.

Imagine every child's being successful in the current American model of education. All children would graduate from high school and go to college, preparing for professional careers. A vision of heaven? Think again. Who would repair our plumbing, fix the car, hang the signs over our stores? Who would enter data in our computers, style our hair, paint our houses? Our world would be in utter chaos without people in these careers; indeed all societies are built on a solid base of manual labor, agricultural jobs, and trades. We would not survive without them. But politicians and cultural attitudes would have us think otherwise. Academic standards are being raised all the time to produce college-grade high school graduates. And what parent today brags vociferously, "My son is a welder!"

I *do* have a welder for a son, and am exceedingly proud. He does his job well. I know what he does is as important as designing a new freeway overpass, or splicing genes. But I have been anguished watching him falter through school, as I have seen so many other students do, with little interest in what is being taught. He is a "hands-on" guy, but schools are not set up for those kinds of students. Generally absent from today's schools are courses like shop and home economics. But over and over, I have seen students who slowly lose interest merely because they are forced to sit without any kind of physical engagement. It's a perfect setup, for some, for behavioral problems. Yet, these same students have shared with me how they built their own bikes or computers, created beautiful drawings, learned how to get a cranky VCR to work. Why not offer more classes—or tailor existing ones—to appeal to *their* talents and skills? Are we not supposed to educate every child and help them all become fully actualized?

I propose that our reform efforts include *all students* by offering more options to serve individual needs: a return of truly hands-on classes, such as industrial arts; academic classes tailored to support vocational education training; and more apprentice-style programs, such as are envisioned in the school-to-work model. These reforms should begin in middle and junior high school. Why? As a teacher, I know that too many students in the bloom of adolescence give up on school because it doesn't meet their needs, talents, and interests. At an age when they are trying to "find themselves" as individuals, what a crime it is to impose a one-way ticket for their education. (p. 37)

Should not public education be obliged to help all students develop skills for continued learning in school, the workplace, and adult life? The United States needs an educational system that can help all students (a) discover who and what they want to and can become; (b) learn as quickly or slowly as they are able; and (c) meet higher standards appropriate to their individual needs and interests.

Light (1999) endorsed the need to compromise on the current timetable for implementing the New York state education standards initiative.

> What is overlooked, however, is that not all are created equal. Some have lesser intellectual capacity than others. Some from disadvantaged social backgrounds are not as prepared as others for the challenges of learning. What do these new standards do to these youngsters? In New York state alone, about 28,000 students drop out of school each year. It's almost a certainty that with new tougher standards, the number will increase significantly. That's not a goal anyone should consider desirable. (p. H2)

Dropping out is not a high school problem in itself. Students drop out in high school because that is when most reach legal school-leaving age. Many reveal that they made the emotional decision to drop out in their middle and even elementary school years. Not being able to keep up with "one-size-fits-all" learning schedules, many simply gave up. Feeling it useless to continue trying to achieve what they could not do in the time given to do it, many developed a sense of learned helplessness. Unless they experience subsequent success in learning, their self-concepts as learners will not improve.

Often, a slower pace can bring beginning success to such defeated learners, causing them to believe they *can* learn. Schedules for assessing the progress of such students toward meeting higher educational standards can be formulated based on their demonstrated improvement in learning. People from all sectors need to coalesce in trying to persuade Commissioner Mills and the New York State Regents to put aside the current one-size-fits-all schedule for meeting higher standards. Light (1999) concluded, "There is no shame in setting standards designed to meet the needs of all students. What is in place now is unfair to too many" (H2).

Raising educational standards in itself will only exacerbate the achievement gap between high ability and other students. It is suggested that developing zero-defect schools will help virtually all students achieve appropriately higher learning standards, something the current American public school paradigm is ill equipped to do.

Taking Time out of a Bottle

Systemic reform that markedly increases school achievement by the masses will require long-term effort. Reville (1999) reported the failure of a promising idea that was too much, too soon:

> Several years ago, I chaired the Massachusetts Commission on Time and Learning, which was charged with guiding the commonwealth in re-designing the structure of classroom time. Taking our cue from the national commission, which called for a "new paradigm" in the nation's approach to educational time, our commission urged the development of an educational system that ensured each student the amount of instructional time that he or she needed in order to master a certain standard of performance. School time in such a system would not necessarily be the same for everyone, as in our current system, but rather would be "consumer-" or need-driven. Students would get as much time as they needed in order to achieve mastery. The goal would be to ensure that each and every student leaves school capable of the educational equivalent of that reasonably competent game of chess. (p. 39)

As Reville noted, public and community orientation to, involvement in, and education about this dramatic shift was insufficient and too hurried:

> The pressure to stick with the status quo is enormous and has resulted in nearly uniform and highly ineffective school practices across virtually all school jurisdictions in the United States. Our commission's failure to prompt the "paradigm shift" in Massachusetts and elsewhere mirrors the failure of similar efforts around the country, and demonstrates just how hard it is to achieve dramatic changes within a system that has amassed decades of inertia. (p. 39)

That inertia continues to hinder attempts to alter or replace the persisting American public school model. Eventually, those efforts regress to the mean of existing practice. Although adult society embraces advances such as online Internet shopping, satellite television, and cellular telephones, it fiercely guards efforts to change and improve schools. "If it was good enough for me, it's good enough for my children" reflects parental wishes to retain what they feel was adequate for their own educational needs. Were he to awaken from his lengthy sleep today, schools would be among the few things the legendary Rip Van Winkle would probably recognize in our nation.

The critical task is to help parents and adult society understand the need to make changes in schools to better meet the educational challenges facing today's youth. As the core of general education and common knowledge needed by almost all students continues to increase, the success of students in adult life will depend upon how well they learn and master those skills and that information. It must also be recognized that not all students can learn and master that core in the same amount of time.

To succeed in continued learning in the workplace and in adult life, some students will require more time to learn, master, and apply what they have learned. Thirty years from now it won't matter if individuals took a year or two longer to complete school. It will matter if they did not have the time they required to gain the background necessary for success in their adult lives. Parental understanding and support of that reality is central to developing a zero-defect education model that can significantly assist American youth at large.

Referring to the course on which chariot races were held in Roman civilization, *curriculum* is defined as the "course to be covered." The idea of covering or completing school courses has persisted in educational practice with students who "finish first" being considered as "the winners." In motor racing, vehicles with similar power compete together within particular classifications. A Honda Civic, for example, takes longer to complete the same course than a high-powered automobile does. Yet schools expect virtually all students, despite their varying intellectual abilities, to achieve success on standardized assessments in a single time frame. Shouldn't it be obvious that students with lesser "intellectual horsepower" may need extended time to complete the same course than higher ability learners require?

To help all students become "winners," American public

education might better adapt the long-distance marathon paradigm. After runners cross the finish line, wheelchair competitors are celebrated as they complete the same distance. In like manner, our schools need to help all students stay and complete the course as their abilities allow.

Furthermore, should it matter whether an individual takes a particular course (e.g., algebra) in seventh or tenth grade? That should depend on when the student develops the necessary background and demonstrated readiness to take that course. Again, flexibility of time for students to learn and progress, as best they can, is essential. The extremes might be that some can complete a course in 20 weeks while others may require as many as 60 weeks. Current New York state education law allows students to remain in high school until age 21. Thirty years from now it won't matter whether some students required two or three additional years to complete school successfully. However, it will matter if they did so earlier but, in barely scraping by, failed to develop the skills they needed for continued learning and achieving personal and economic self-sufficiency.

In the present school model, time is the constant. To make learning the constant, time needs to become a flexible variable that enables students to learn at the rates they are able. To meet the needs of the masses, educational standards should appropriately encourage students to learn and master necessary skills and information as quickly as they can or *as slowly as they must*, at rates that do not violate their abilities and readiness for particular educational challenges.

Improving Learning for All

Today's graded-school model cannot provide the time flexibility necessary for students at large to achieve proposed higher standards for high school graduation. Goodlad and Anderson (1959) defined a flexible-time continuous-progress model that still surpasses the limited graded-school model.

That flexibility will be essential in zero-defect schools for the masses. Students with more intellectual abilities will be able to progress in adaptations of today's educational paradigm. Others, however, will require multi-age, continuous-progress settings that provide the additional time they require to learn and master specific skills, concepts, and information. Such approaches have been in place in some schools for as long as 40 years. Their success is reflected in the fact that significantly higher numbers have completed high school, even though some students needed extended time to complete required curricula. Dropout statistics have also decreased in these schools.

Eliminating single school-grade learning quotas enables individuals to progress as their abilities allow. In the continuous-progress model, students with similar current achievement and learning needs work together. Individuals move on and regroup with others in terms of their achievement progress and readiness. That genuine success overcomes social promotion of individuals who know they have neither learned nor can do what other age-mates have achieved.

Cohen (1989a, 1989b) examined the success of schools using continuous-progress, multi-age approaches. Contrasted with students in graded schools attempting to memorize information to pass year-end tests, student progress in continuous-progress schools is based on what they learn and can apply. In reviewing the results in multi-age, continuous-progress schools since 1969, Cohen (1989a) noted:

> To proponents of ungraded or mixed age classrooms, letting pupils develop at their own pace helps those at differing ability levels push and pull each other along. Programs built on such a philosophy shun the restriction of individual grade levels. They offer, instead, flexible groupings that encompass a two- to four-year span, allowing movement between levels for those pupils ready to advance or needing more help in decades of inertia. (p. 9)
>
> Lilian G. Katz, director of the ERIC Clearinghouse on Elementary and Early Childhood Education at the University of Illinois, says the arrangement is "emerging as a possible trend for a number of reasons." Conventional grading, she explains, assumes "that if you put children with the same age group, you can teach them all the same thing, at the same time, and on the same day, and that's an error. We're missing a bet by trying to educate children in litters," Katz argues. (p. 1)

In a companion article, Cohen (1989b) discussed the success of such efforts in two K–6 elementary schools, one in Lake George, New York, and the other in Brooklyn, New York.

On the surface, the Lake George (NY) Elementary School and the Walter F. White Elementary School in the Brownsville section of Brooklyn are a study in contrasts. One is set in a striking one-level building on a wooded road in a quiet resort town. Its pupils are predominately white and middle class. The other is housed in a three-level structure bordered by factories and housing projects on a stark urban street. Most of its pupils are low-income Blacks and Hispanics. Inside, however, the schools share a common philosophy that officials say has reaped promising results.

Their operative principle is that children's development does not always match their grade level—and that they learn best when allowed to develop at their own pace. While neither school has spurned standard grades completely, both cluster children by age groups and allow movement between levels for pupils ready to advance or needing more time in a given subject. And both try to individualize learning, so that a child entering a new age group can proceed from where he or she left off at the last level. (p. 1)

Cohen further noted:

Because the [Lake George] school allows movement among the age levels for children ready to accelerate or needing more time on a concept, about 6 percent of its pupils join older or younger groupings for some subjects, Mr. Ross [the principal] said. A small number may remain in a grouping for more than two years, but others have moved into junior-high work by 6th grade.

The local junior high school has worked with the elementary school to accommodate pupils of varying progress levels, Mr. Ross said. Faculty members sometimes keep a child in an accelerated program rather than send him to junior high early, he noted, or promote a child of junior-high age they feel would not benefit from retention in elementary school. To foster a climate in which the "youngsters are not threatened by comparison," Mr. Ross said, the school has no "pecking order that awards kids responsibility because of age, there is no graduation or special privilege by age." (p. 1)

The Walter F. White school, also known as Public School 41, served 561 of the school's 925 K–5 pupils through its "core" project. The project organized "cores" of classrooms serving children in age groups five and six, six and seven, seven and eight, and eight and nine. Each day, core teachers shared lunch and preparation periods together.

> PS 41 teachers also coordinate instruction around common themes and share information, so that "a child who needs more help or enrichment in a subject can be moved around within the core," said Principal Herbert Ross, who is not related to Mr. Ross of Lake George. The school also has committees to help make decisions on pupils' movement between age groups and some ability grouping in the cores. (Cohen, 1989b, p. 10)

Movement toward a continuous-progress model must be initiated from the bottom up, beginning at the earliest programs in the school district. Plans to replace the graded-school model in district middle-level and high schools should be designed upon results of student progress through such earlier school programs.

In contrast, educational standards initiatives set top-down fourth and eighth grade and high school achievement standards and assessments. The keystone should be defining realistic expectations in the early school years for developing school practices that help students achieve those benchmarks. Standards at later school levels should be formulated upon student progress at earlier levels.

Parents and their children perennially breathe sighs of relief when the latter either "pass" year-end tests or "make" honor rolls. However, the nature of students' persisting deficiencies is often not scrutinized. Assessment results should be used to identify the following:

1. In what specific areas do students have persisting serious deficits?
2. What do students and their parents or guardians need to know regarding those deficits?
3. What experiences will students require during the next school year to overcome those deficits?
4. What information do teachers receiving students the

next school year need in order to plan learning experiences to help them overcome those deficits?

Few people with a serious health problem would be satisfied if their physicians told them, "Well, the test shows you are a 65. That's a D- but don't worry, you passed." Most patients would press to know as much as possible about their specific problem, their progress, and what needs to be done to overcome that condition. However, similar attention is seldom given to students' persisting learning needs.

For example, one student scores 63% in a final examination or final average in a subject and repeats the course. Another scores 65% on the same test or final average and is promoted to the next grade in that subject. Despite the closeness of their scores, each student probably has critical needs in differing areas of that subject. The present school model seldom identifies those needs for students, their parents or guardians, or those who will teach them either in a repeat course or in the next grade level. As a result, neither student will probably receive the focused intervention he or she needs.

Rather than repeat the entire course, students who almost pass might better repeat and focus on those areas in which they have critical deficiencies. Such focused intervention will help develop the background necessary for success in later study in that subject. Likewise, students who barely pass the course probably have similar critical deficiencies in different areas of that subject. They also need focused intervention in those areas after promotion to the next grade.

Either-or options in both situations will not help students learn the skills and content necessary for continued school success. Common lock-step exit assessments in the graded-school model make that success virtually impossible for the masses. In light of the new educational standards assessments facing students, significant progress toward the goal of universal high school graduation seems unlikely.

The goal for all students should be to conceptualize and learn skills, processes, and information, and be able to apply them in subsequent situations as best they can. That will require teachers to develop individual and group experiences in response to specific learning needs of the students coming to them.

Moving toward zero-defect schools will require that testing and other assessment procedures include the following:

1. Review student test data to identify students' demonstrated proficiency and persisting learning needs

in specific skill and information areas.

2. Apprise parents and students of those learning needs to be pursued in the following school year.
3. Inform teachers of incoming students' persisting learning needs.
4. Provide time for teachers who are sending and receiving students to discuss how best to deal with those individual needs in the coming school year.

In a lifelong learning society, zero-defect schools need to accommodate all of the children of all of the people. The goal to become lifelong learners through school, in the workplace, and in adult life will require invitational learning experiences that assist students in achieving their maximum potential as their abilities allow.

Consider the turn-around in the nation's automotive industry since 1965. Then, many Ford, Chrysler, and General Motors vehicles left production sites with serious defects. Purchasers had no alternative but to return to dealer agencies for corrections under warranty programs. Eventually, consumers refused to accept that corrections could not always be fully made.

Conversely, purchasers of Toyota and Honda vehicles found they seldom had to return to dealer agencies to correct production errors. As Japanese and other foreign automobile producers approached zero-defect production, sales of American-built vehicles declined severely and, by 1976, the Chrysler corporation was on the verge of bankruptcy.

Since then, the American "big three" automobile producers have regained a share of their market by emulating the foreign zero-defect production paradigm. The General Motors Saturn has been particularly successful. Accordingly, many people still believe that Americans cannot equal the zero-defect production of, for example, Toyota and Honda vehicles. However, it is American workers in Ohio, Kentucky, and Georgia Toyota and Honda production plants who now produce vehicles for both American and foreign markets.

The primary factor was a new automotive-production paradigm that required changes in the roles of workers. In like manner, American schools need to negotiate a paradigm shift toward a zero-defect model that prepares students to access increasing quality of life as adults. Our society can no longer tolerate the student casualties that were acceptable earlier in the twentieth century.

Conclusion

Wood (1999) reminds us: "The Greek word for the word 'school' is 'scoleri,' which literally translated as 'leisure.' Consider how far we've moved from our educational roots. Teachers who want to dedicate themselves and their classrooms to a pace that encourages investigation, contemplation, and community must struggle with social and educational influences that force them in the opposite direction" (p. 36).

American schools have taken on broader societal responsibilities that require teachers' time and energy. As Stevenson (1998) notes:

> Teachers in the United States consistently suggest that one of the biggest constraints on the rate and success of education reform is their lack of time for professional activities other than the direct instruction of students. Instruction and the host of other chores required for the smooth running of their classrooms leave few opportunities for the other challenging aspects of educational reform. How, they ask, can they engage in thoughtful planning when no sustained blocks of time are available and work must be accomplished in short bursts of intense effort, and often alone? (p. 40)

Because the success of Japanese and European schools continues to be lionized, the professional responsibilities of their teachers with those of American teachers merit comparison (Stevenson, 1998):

> Only about half of the Japanese teachers' daily eight or nine school hours are actually spent instructing students. In contrast, instruction typically occupies more than two-thirds of the school day of German and American teachers. But German students and teachers are generally through with school shortly after noon, while U.S. children and teachers remain much longer.
>
> The short instructional day in Germany leaves teachers with ample amounts of self-directed time. Although Japanese teachers remain in school longer, their greater amounts of non-instructional time and opportunities to have sustained periods when they are

not teaching leave nearly half their non-instructional time for interacting with their fellow teachers and students, preparing lessons, planning, and grading papers. (p. 40)

Changes in the current American school model must accommodate the "difference-of-kind" educational demands faced as we enter a new century and millennium. The goal for all American students to achieve higher standards will require a school paradigm that is, in some respects, similar to those in Germany and Japan. American teachers need extended time and opportunity to plan instructional means that increase success across the range of their students. Our task is to make the journey to school completion one that captures students' interest and excites them to work at maximizing their talents and abilities. Let us develop a model that assists the mass of students in achieving appropriately higher standards as quickly as they can, or as slowly as they must.

References

Cohen, D. (1989a, December 6). First stirrings of a new trend: Multi-age classrooms gain favor. *Education Week, 4*(9), 1, 9.

Cohen, D. (1989b, December 6). 'Living laboratories' let pupils develop at their own pace. *Education Week, 4*(9), 1, 10.

Dewey, J. (1917). *Democracy and education.* New York: Macmillan.

Goodlad J., & Anderson, R. (1959). *The nongraded elementary school.* New York: Harcourt Brace & World.

Gran, E. W. (1970, May). If I have but one life to live, let me live it above the median. *The National Elementary Principal, 49,* 54.

Houston, P. (1997, June 4). Raising the caution flag on the standards movement. *Education Week, 15*(36), 44.

Lasley, T. (1998, September). Paradigm shifts in the classroom. *Phi Delta Kappan, 80*(1), 84–86.

Light, M. B. (1999, November 14) New regents standards are unfair to many students. *The Buffalo News,* p. H2.

Mishodek, S. (1999, December 1). Talents unrecognized: The case for making vocational education part of our school reform plans. *Education Week, 19*(14), 34–37.

Precious, T. (1999, November 5). Legislators seek to put off new Regents standards. *The Buffalo News,* pp. C1, C12.

Reville, S. P. (1999, May 5). Breaking out of the 'prison of time.' *Education Week, 18*(1), 39.

Simon, P. (1999, December 26). State aiming too high, school experts say. *The Buffalo News,* pp. A1, A22.

Stevenson, H. (1998, September 16). Guarding teachers' time, *Education Week, 18*(6), 39–40.

Tanner, D. (1997, Spring). Standards, standards: High and low. *Educational Horizons, 75*(3), 115–120.

Toepfer, C., Jr. (1997–98, Winter). New York state's standards initiative: A Trojan horse for middle-level education? *In Transition: Journal of the New York State Association, 15*(1), 15–19.

Wood C, (1999, October 13). Time and reform. *Education Week, 19*(7), 36–38.

About the Author

Conrad F. Toepfer, Jr., is professor emeritus in the Department of Learning and Instruction, State University of New York at Buffalo. He was a junior high school teacher and public school administrator before moving to the university in 1965. Past President of the National Middle School Association, he chaired the National Association of Secondary Principals Middle Level Education Council from 1981 to 1993. He is a member of the Advisory Council for the National Resource Center for Middle Grades Education, and of the National Advisory Board of EPIC (Every Person Influences Children). He has worked with middle schools throughout North America and abroad, addressed several European Middle School League Conferences, and worked with middle-level schools in Austria, Belgium, Germany, the Netherlands, and Switzerland. Dr. Toepfer has written thirty-five books and monographs, published more than 150 articles in major professional journals in the curriculum and middle level educational literature. In addition to being awarded the Most Distinguished Professor Award, he has been the recipient of honors by numerous professional associations, universities and honor societies.

Section 3:

Considering Multicultural Issues

Chapter Eight

The Counselor as a Member of a Culturally Proficient School Leadership Team

Randall B. Lindsey, Kikanza Nuri Robins, & Delores B. Lindsey

The paradigm presented in this chapter is predicated on certain assumptions about the future of schools and schooling as well as the role of the school counselor (Lindsey, Robins, & Terrell, 1999):

- The cultural and demographic profile of school counselors will continue to be different from the profile of students. In California, 80% of educators are White, but the statewide profile of students of color is higher than 50%. In urban areas, the proportion of students of color is even higher.
- The role of the counselor will evolve so that a larger portion of time will be devoted to coaching teachers, administrators, students, and families on guidance-relevant matters. The counselor will have an ever-present role in school leadership teams.
- The traditional comprehensive high school will continue; however, alternative programs will proliferate. The cultural proficiency model presented in this chapter will work in either setting.
- The counselor will have career, personal, and civic functions, and the cultural proficiency model will be inextricably interlinked with these functions.

Through a successful diversity program, counselors will play an ever-important role in improving staff and student morale by improving the effectiveness of communication, reducing complaints, and creating a more comfortable and pleasing climate for persons in the school. As educational leaders, counselors, along with other members of the school leadership team, will learn concepts and skills that can be translated into new initiatives, curricula, programs, and activities that will enrich school life for all students and staff. As greater awareness and understanding develops in schools, so, too, will grow awareness and understanding of the larger community. We believe that very few of us actually intend to hurt other people. Diversity programs provide all of us with the information and skills we need to help us avoid unintentional slights or hurts and to improve the quality of life for our school and home communities.

Cultural Proficiency: What Can It Be?

Clearly, counseling educators need some means of addressing cultural diversity. As the United States continues into the twenty-first century, the need for addressing issues of diversity is going to grow. In our experience, the most effective and productive approach to addressing cultural diversity within schools is a model known as *cultural proficiency*. In a culturally proficient school, the educators and students will know they are valued, and they will involve community members in the school to facilitate their own cultural understanding. The culture of the school will promote inclusiveness and will institutionalize processes for learning about differences and for responding appropriately to differences. Rather than lamenting, "Why can't *they* be like *us*?" teachers and students will welcome and create opportunities to better understand who they are as individuals, while learning how to interact positively with people who differ from themselves.

The cultural proficiency model uses an inside-out approach, which focuses first on those of us who are insiders to the school, encouraging us to reflect on our own individual understandings and values. It thereby relieves those identified as outsiders, the members of historically excluded and new groups, from the responsibility of doing all the adapting. The cultural proficiency approach to diversity surprises many people who expect a diversity program to teach them about other people, not about themselves. This inside-out approach acknowledges and validates the current values and feelings of people, encouraging change without threatening people's feelings of worth.

The cultural proficiency approach prizes individuals but focuses chiefly on the school's culture, which has a life force beyond the individuals within the school. This focus removes the need to place blame on individuals or to induce feelings of guilt. The process is to involve all members of the school community in determining how to align policies, practices, and procedures in order to achieve cultural proficiency. Because all of the participants will be deeply involved in the developmental process, there will be a broader base of ownership, making it easier to commit to change. This approach attacks at a systemic level the problems that often arise from the diversification of students, faculty, and staff.

Building cultural proficiency will require informed and dedicated faculty and staff, committed and involved leadership, and time. Counselors and other educators cannot be sent to training for two days and be expected to return with solutions to all of the equity issues in their school. For instance, this model does *not* involve the use of simple checklists for identifying culturally significant characteristics of individuals, which may be politically appropriate, but is socially and educationally meaningless. The transformation to cultural proficiency requires time to think, reflect, assess, decide, and change. To become culturally proficient, educators must participate actively in work sessions, contributing their distinctive ideas, beliefs, feelings, and perceptions. Consequently, their contributions will involve them deeply in the process and make it easier for them to commit to change.

What Are the Points on the
Cultural Proficiency Continuum?

Cultural proficiency represents either the policies, practices, and procedures of a school, or the values and behaviors of an individual, which will enable that school or person to interact effectively in a culturally diverse environment. Cultural proficiency will be reflected in the way a school treats its faculty and staff, its students, and its surrounding community. The culturally proficient person will not claim to—or perhaps even attempt to—know everything there is to know about all cultural groups. Rather, a culturally proficient person will know how to learn about cultures and respond effectively to specific groups and situations.

Cultural proficiency is the endpoint on a continuum, the point at which educators and the school environment will optimally facilitate effective cross-cultural interaction. There are six points along the cultural proficiency continuum, which indicate unique ways of seeing and responding to differences (see figure 1). The points on the cultural proficiency continuum reflect a progression for dealing with persons who are different, which schools have tended to follow.

Figure 1. The Cultural Proficiency Continuum

Cultural destructiveness		Cultural blindness		Cultural competence	
	Cultural incapacity		Cultural precompetence		Cultural proficiency

The continuum provides a perspective for examining policies, practices, and procedures in a school by giving reference points and a common language for describing historical or current situations. For instance, it is easy to apply the cultural proficiency continuum to events that have resulted in people being murdered, maimed, or exploited by dominant and destructive groups. More subtle outcomes, however, may be more difficult to categorize. Therefore, educators will need various opportunities to practice using the continuum in order to identify how students' opportunities have been preempted, denied, limited, or enhanced.

As you read the following section, view the continuum using two trains of thought. First, read the material, creating your own illustrations of how groups of people have been affected at various times in history. Second, use the continuum to learn to examine how students have been—and are currently being—affected by practices in your school that either limit or enhance their opportunities.

Cultural Destructiveness

The easiest to detect and the most negative end of the continuum *(cultural destructiveness)* is represented by attitudes, policies, and practices destructive to cultures and consequently to the individuals within the culture. Extreme examples include cultural genocide, such as the U.S. system of enslaving African captives and the North American westward expansion that resulted in the near extinction of many Native American nations. Other examples of cultural destructiveness are the many Bureau of Indian Affairs educational programs that took young people from their families and tribes and placed them in boarding schools—where the goal was to eradicate their language and culture—and the mass exterminations of many peoples that have occurred throughout the twentieth century. The twentieth century has been witness to the Nazi extermination of Jews, Gypsies, gay men, and lesbians, as well as others viewed as less than desirable by occupying forces. Other destructive acts have included the pogroms of Russia, the Turkish extermination of Armenians, the killing fields of Southeast Asia, and the "ethnic cleansing" that occurred in the Hutu–Tutsi wars of central Africa and in the former Yugoslav Republic.

Elementary and high schools historically have been places where students were socialized to become U.S. citizens and to learn basic skills for functioning in the workplace. In the nineteenth and early twentieth centuries, this process of acculturation involved socializing people from all parts of Europe into an emerging dominant Anglo culture. This melting-pot approach to public school education was seen by some as relatively effective within two to three generations for the European immigrants. Over the past 50 years, compulsory attendance requirements have brought into schools increasing numbers of Latinos, African Americans, Native Americans, immigrants from Southeast Asia, and indigenous European Americans from low socioeconomic groups. There are no indications of this trend reversing. Although members of these groups have had striking successes in education, their acquisition of English proficiency and middle-class mores did not necessarily ensure their access either to higher education or to middle-class lifestyles. The cultural destructiveness that these groups experienced in schools often resulted in markedly lower achievement, higher dropout rates, and lower social mobility. Specific examples of cultural destructiveness in schools have included:

- "English only" policies and the elimination of bilingual education programs so that children are essentially prohibited from using their native language at school, and
- policies that provide no acceptable options for girls who must not wear shorts or who must cover their heads at all times because their culture dictates a modest dress code.

Cultural Incapacity
Another point on the continuum *(cultural incapacity)*

describes a school or individuals who show extreme bias, believe in the superiority of the dominant group, and assume a paternal posture toward so-called lesser groups. These systems or individuals are often characterized by ignorance, as well as by either a dislike or an unrealistic fear of people who differ from the dominant group. Cultural incapacity virtually guarantees limited opportunities and can lead to *learned helplessness,* people's belief that they are powerless to help themselves because of their repeated experiences of powerlessness.

Historical examples include restrictive immigration laws targeting Asians and Pacific Islanders (such as the Oriental Exclusion Acts) and the Jim Crow laws, which denied African Americans basic human rights. Other examples include discriminatory hiring practices, generally lower expectations of performance for minority-group members, and subtle messages to people who are not members of the dominant group, conveying that they are not valued or welcomed. Specific examples of cultural incapacity in schools have included:

- assuming that all African American families experience poverty,
- believing that it is inherently better to be heterosexual than homosexual,
- announcing that a new Latina has been hired to be a role model for Latinas, without recognizing that all children can benefit from having role models from their own and other cultural groups.

Cultural Blindness

The third point is the most vexing point on the continuum. *Cultural blindness* is the belief that color and culture make no difference and that all people are the same. For many educators, that is the goal of a diversity program. The values and behaviors of the dominant culture are presumed to be universally applicable and beneficial. The intention of the culturally blind educator is to avoid discriminating—that is, to avoid making an issue of the differences manifested among the students. Culturally blind educators have too often viewed students' cultural differences to be indications of disobedience, noncompliance, or other deficiency. They assume that members of minority cultures do not meet the cultural expectations of the dominant group because they lack either the cultural traditions of the dominant culture (i.e., they're culturally deficient) or the desire to achieve (i.e., they're morally deficient). In reality, the system works only for the most highly assimilated minority groups. As a result of many educators' blindness to the differences among students, too many students are left feeling discounted or invisible in school.

In our conversations with educators who prize their own cultural blindness, they are always painfully unaware of how their behavior affects their students. When confronted with the inappropriateness of cultural blindness, they initially retreat into the defensive position that they never intended to discriminate. It is difficult for good people who are committed to fairness to believe that they sometimes hurt their students. It is important not to focus on intentions, but to become aware of the impact that educator behavior can have on students.

Counselors need to recognize that students from nondominant groups view their differences as important aspects of their identity. Their differences also affect how they are viewed both within their respective communities and in the larger society. These counselors are surprised to learn that Black children would not choose to be anything other than Black, that Cambodian children are proud of their language, and that the child in the wheelchair does not feel disadvantaged. Culturally proficient educators are aware of the importance of their students' cultures, the impact of students' experiences with cultural epithets, and the invisibility of many students in much of the school curricula.

Culturally blind counselors and other educators may teach that Abraham Lincoln is a hero to all African Americans, assume that Cinco de Mayo is a Latin American holiday, and believe that girls are predisposed toward the arts rather than the sciences.

Other examples of cultural blindness in schools include
- leadership training that fails to address issues of diversity
- lack of awareness that each school has its own unique culture and that each group experiences it differently
- inability or failure to articulate the school's cultural expectations to all students, staff, and faculty members

Cultural Precompetence

Cultural precompetence is an awareness of limitations in cross-cultural communication and outreach. While the culturally precompetent person wants to provide fair and equitable treatment with appropriate cultural sensitivity, this desire is accompanied by the frustration of not knowing exactly what is possible or how to proceed. An example is the belief that the accomplishment of a single goal or activity fulfills any perceived obligation toward minority groups; as a result, culturally precompetent educators will point with pride to the hiring of one disabled person, or the serving of a soul food meal during Black History month, as proof of a school's cultural proficiency. Other examples include:

- recruiting members of underrepresented groups but not providing them support or making any adaptation to the differences they bring to the workplace;
- dismissing as overly sensitive anyone who complains about culturally inappropriate comments;
- failing to hold accountable any members of minority groups who are not performing well; and
- making rules against hate speech instead of having a curriculum that teaches the cherishing of history, cultures, and languages that are different.

Cultural Competence

At the point of *cultural competence,* schools and counselors and other educators will accept and respect differences, carefully attend to the dynamics of difference, continually assess their own cultural knowledge and beliefs, continuously expand their cultural knowledge and resources, and make various adaptations of their own belief systems, policies, and practices. This is the first point on the continuum that fully addresses the needs of diverse student populations. Culturally competent educators will:

- incorporate culturally appropriate behavior in performance appraisals;
- model culturally inclusive behaviors (e.g., learning to speak Spanish in a predominantly Latino community);
- speak on issues facing handicapped persons, gay men, and lesbians, even when the individuals themselves are not visibly present;
- advocate for changes in policies, practices, and procedures throughout the school and community;
- teach communication strategies that lead to understanding of other people's views; and
- teach cultural variables in conflict resolution.

Cultural Proficiency

Cultural proficiency is more than the esteeming of culture.

Whereas culturally competent counselors and other educators will function effectively in several different cultural contexts, the culturally proficient counselor will know how to learn about culture. Confronted with the challenges of a new cultural setting, culturally proficient counselors will know how to find out what they need to know in a nonoffensive manner. The culturally proficient leader will seek to add to the knowledge base of culturally proficient practices by conducting research, developing new approaches based on culture, and taking every available opportunity to formally and informally increase the awareness level and knowledge base of others about culture and about the dynamics of difference. Culturally proficient leaders will:

- unabashedly advocate for culturally proficient practices in all arenas;
- actively interact with the larger school community by visiting families and providing communities with information and resources that will insure inclusion for student and school life;
- help to develop curriculum based on what is known about multiple intelligences;
- take advantage of teachable moments to learn of and teach their colleagues about culturally proficient practices.

What Is Culturally Proficient Behavior?

The cultural proficiency continuum takes a broad look at the range of behaviors and attitudes that address the issues of diversity. This section describes the specific behaviors that need to be present within your school and yourself, as a counselor or other educator, for you and your school to be culturally proficient. We call these behaviors the five essential elements of cultural proficiency: (a) value diversity; (b) assess your culture; (c) manage the dynamics of difference; (d) institutionalize cultural knowledge; and (e) adapt to diversity (see figure 2).

Value Diversity
As a culturally proficient counselor, you will be proactive in involving a wide variety of people from all areas of the school. You will demonstrate that you value diversity by openly addressing the need to effectively serve all persons who are different, and you will accept that cultures vary, evoking different feelings and behaviors. You will be actively engaged as a member

Figure 2. The Five Essential Elements of Cultural Proficiency

1. Value Diversity: *Name the Differences*
- Celebrate and encourage the presence of a variety of peoples in all activities.
- Recognize difference as diversity rather than inappropriate responses to the environment.
- Accept that each culture finds some values and behaviors more important than others.

2. Assess Your Culture: *Claim Your Identity*
- Describe your own culture and the cultural norms of your organization.
- Recognize how your culture affects others.
- Understand how the culture of your organization affects those whose culture is different.

3. Manage the Dynamics of Difference: *Frame the Conflicts*
- Learn effective strategies for resolving conflict among people whose cultural backgrounds and values may be different from yours.
- Understand the effect that historical distrust has on present day interactions.
- Realize that you may misjudge others' actions based on learned expectations.

4. Institutionalize Cultural Knowledge: *Train about Diversity*
- Integrate into systems for staff development and education information and skills that enable everyone to interact effectively in a variety of cross-cultural situations.
- Incorporate cultural knowledge into the mainstream of the organization.
- Teach origins of stereotypes and prejudices.

5. Adapt to Diversity: *Change for Diversity*
- Change past ways of doing things to acknowledge the differences that are present in the staff, students, and community.
- Develop cross-cultural communication skills.
- Institutionalize cultural interventions for conflicts and confusion caused by the dynamics of difference.

of the school community and viewed as a respected school leader. As a culturally proficient school counselor and community leader, you will provide leadership in developing policy statements on diversity or ensuring that the school's and district's missions and goal statements include the concept of diversity. You will take these statements and act on them by communicating inclusion to marginalized groups and by directing human and financial resources into curriculum, training, and other school endeavors to proactively address diversity.

As a culturally proficient school leader, you will celebrate and encourage value for diversity in all activities by:

- ensuring that all stakeholders in the school community are involved in the process;
- recognizing difference as diversity rather than as inappropriate responses to the school setting;
- accepting that each culture finds some values and behavior more important than other values and behavior.

Assess Your Culture

To assess your culture, you will analyze yourself and your environment so that you will have a palpable sense of your own culture and the culture of your school. The purpose of assessing your culture directly relates to the inside-out approach of the cultural proficiency model. For example, as a culturally proficient educator, you will start with yourself and your own school. You will not assume that everyone will share your values, nor will you assume that everyone knows what behaviors are expected and affirmed in a culturally proficient school; in fact, most persons will be simply unaware. Therefore, you will understand how the culture of your school and district affects those whose culture is different. You will state and explain the cultural norms of each classroom, school, or district so that people whose cultural norms differ will know how they must adapt to the new environment. By recognizing how the school's culture affects other people, you will gain the data you need to make adjustments in style or processes so that all people feel comfortable and welcomed. As a culturally proficient leader, you will:

- understand how the culture of your school affects those whose culture is different;
- describe you own culture and the cultural norms of your school;

• recognize how your school's culture affects others.

Manage the Dynamics of Difference

A school that values diversity will not be without conflict. As a culturally proficient counselor, you will acknowledge that conflict is a natural state of affairs, and you will develop effective, culturally proficient strategies for managing the conflict that occurs. Your skills will be put to use by counseling and coaching individual students as well as groups of students, parents, and educators. Once you have embraced the value of diversity and have begun to articulate the cultural expectations of your school or classroom, the differences among the school's community members will be more apparent. You will be ready for this situation by providing an opportunity for everyone in the school community to learn effective strategies for resolving conflict among people whose backgrounds differ. As a leader, you will provide training sessions and facilitate group discussions so that people will understand the effect of historical distrust on present day interactions. You will realize that the actions of others may be misjudged based on learned expectations, and you will implement programs and processes that create new cultural expectations for the culturally proficient community. As a culturally proficient leader, you will:

> • learn effective strategies for resolving conflict among people whose cultural backgrounds and values may differ from yours;
> • understand how historical distrust affects present day interactions;
> • realize that you may misjudge other people's actions based on learned expectations.

Institutionalize Cultural Knowledge

As a culturally proficient school leader, you will prize ongoing staff development that promotes a commitment to lifelong learning. You will clearly understand that information and technology continue to evolve at an ever-quickening pace, thereby dictating the need for continuous upgrading of knowledge and skills. Similarly, as our society continues increasingly to appreciate its multicultural nature and its intimate interconnections with the wider world, you will recognize the increasing importance of cultural proficiency. You will readily integrate into systems of staff development and education the information and skills that enable educators and students to interact effectively in a variety of cross-cultural situations. You will affirm the importance of cultural knowledge, not only for the climate of the school or district, but also as a knowledge base on which all students will continue to build throughout their lives.

As a culturally proficient leader, you will realize that students need knowledge about the cultural practices of different people and groups, the experiences that many of these people and groups have had with stereotyping and prejudices, and how stereotypes are developed and maintained in society. You will help students and colleagues to develop skills for eliminating prejudices through various human interactions, curricula, and instructional programs in schools. As a culturally proficient leader, you will:

- integrate into the educational system the information and skills needed for effective interaction in a variety of cross-cultural situations;
- incorporate cultural knowledge into the mainstream of the school;
- take advantage of evolving classroom interactions that arise related to issues of differences, and use those teachable moments and other opportunities to learn from or to teach to one another.

Adapt to Diversity

To understand adversity you need to understand that all of us are constantly undergoing change. In traditional approaches to diversity, such as throwing everyone into the melting pot, the groups that were not a part of the dominant culture were expected to change and to adapt to the culture of the dominant group. The culturally proficient approach to diversity invites and encourages everyone to change. Once you make the commitment to cultural proficiency, you will help all aspects of the school community to adapt. You will help the host groups change by becoming more conscious of cultural norms that deny the value of diversity and the goal of cultural proficiency. You will encourage the newer or less dominant groups to change because they will know clearly the cultural expectations of the school. You will enable the school or district to change by using culturally proficient behaviors as the standards for performance appraisal and as the basis for analyzing and revising school and district policies. As a culturally proficient leader, you will:

- change the way things are done by acknowledging the differences that are present in the faculty, staff, students, and community;

- examine policies and practices that may convey benign discrimination;
- institutionalize cultural interventions that address the conflict and confusion caused by the dynamics of difference.

What Are the Principles That Guide Culturally Proficient Practice?

By deliberately and systematically implementing the behavior outlined in the preceding five essential elements of cultural proficiency, you will achieve cultural proficiency for yourself and for your school. To carry out this ambitious task, you will need a firm value base. With such a base, you will transform a daunting challenge into an opportunity that brings all people together to create a culturally proficient school community. The cultural proficiency model includes five principles that may help to guide you as you work toward cultural proficiency (see figure 3). This section describes the guiding principles.

Culture Is Ever Present
Your culture is a defining aspect of your humanity. It is the predominant force in shaping values and behaviors. Occasionally, you may be inclined to take offense at behaviors that differ from yours, but as a culturally proficient leader, you will remind yourself that offensive behavior may not be personal; it may be cultural. You will recognize that members of so-called minority populations have to be at least bicultural, and this creates its own set of issues, problems, and possible conflicts. All people who are not part of the dominant group have already gained competence in one culture before they began to learn standard English or dominant U.S. cultural norms. Therefore, when members of nondominant cultures resist or hesitate in using the language or cultural norms of the dominant culture, they are not necessarily ignorant or incompetent; rather, they may be simply using language or cultural behaviors with which they are more familiar or more comfortable.

Culturally proficient counselors and other educators will recognize that what they experience as normal or regular is part of their culture. This may tempt them to feel a sense of entitlement, but by recognizing these feelings, they will then acknowledge and appreciate the subtle cultural differences among members of the dominant culture. Rarely do European Americans experience the process of acquiring another language or a new set of values, norms, or behaviors. They also less seldom need to seek appropriate and accepted places for using their first language and culture. This lack of experience often leads to misunderstanding and an ignorance of what it means to be perceived as different on a day-by-day basis. It also insulates members of the dominant culture from the negative judgments ascribed to people because of their linguistic and cultural differences. As we come to understand, somehow, the reality of exclusion experienced by members of minority groups, then it will become possible to turn such understanding into a value of diversity.

Figure 3. The Guiding Principles of Cultural Proficiency

Culture Is Ever Present
Acknowledge culture as a predominant force in shaping behaviors, values, and institutions. Although you may be inclined to take offense at behaviors that differ from yours, remind yourself that it may not be personal; it may be cultural.

People Are Served to Varying Degrees by the Dominant Culture
What works well in organizations and in the community for you, and others who are like you, may work against members of other cultural groups. Failure to make such an acknowledgment puts the burden for change on one group.

People Have Group Identities and Personal Identities
Although it is important to treat all people as individuals, it is also important to acknowledge the group identity of individuals. Actions must be taken with the awareness that the dignity of a person is not guaranteed unless the dignity of his or her people is also preserved.

Diversity within Cultures Is Important
Because diversity within cultures is as important as diversity between cultures, it is important to learn about cultural groups not as monoliths, such as Asians, Hispanics, Gay Men and Women, but as the complex and diverse groups that they are. Often, because of the class differences in the United States, there will be more in common across cultural lines than within them.

Each Group Has Unique Cultural Needs
Each cultural group has unique needs that cannot be met within the boundaries of the dominant culture. Expressions of one group's cultural identity do not imply a disrespect for yours. Make room in your organization for several paths that lead to the same goal.

People Are Served to Varying Degrees by the Dominant Culture

Culturally proficient counselors and other educators will adjust their behaviors and values to accommodate the full range of diversity represented by their school populations. They will recognize that some individuals from minority cultures find success in varying degrees in schools where only the dominant culture may profit from such a setting. Some members of some nondominant groups may do well despite such a setting, but many other students and educators may find such an atmosphere stifling and limiting. Such an imbalance of power puts the total burden for change on one person or group. Culturally proficient leaders will see the need to ensure that the responsibility for change is shared by members of dominant groups, historically oppressed groups, and new cultural groups.

People Have Group Identities and Personal Identities

It will continue to be important to treat all people as individuals, as well as to acknowledge each group's identity. It demeans and insults individuals and their cultures to single out particularly assimilated members of ethnic groups and to tell them that they differ from members of their own group, implying that being different somehow makes them better, or more acceptable, in the eyes of the dominant group. Culturally proficient leaders know that to guarantee the dignity of each person, they must also preserve the dignity of each person's culture.

Often, so-called personality problems are actually problems of cultural differences. Culturally proficient leaders address these problems. They will recognize that cultural differences in thought patterns (e.g., those of non-Western, non-European people versus those of Westerners) reflect differing but equally valid ways of viewing and solving problems. No cultural group will appear to use just one approach exclusively for processing information and solving problems, although some cultures will be traditionally associated with one approach more than others. One approach will not be held to be superior to the other across all situations. Culturally proficient leaders will recognize these and other cultural differences, and they will use this knowledge to promote effective communication among diverse people.

Diversity within Cultures Is Important

Because diversity within cultures is as important as diversity between cultures, it will be increasingly important to learn about ethnic groups not as monoliths (e.g., Asians, Latinos, or Whites), but as the complex and diverse groups we will continue to be. Within each major ethnic group are many distinct subgroups. Often, because of the class differences in the United States, there will be more in common across ethnic lines than within them. For example, upper-middle-class U.S. citizens of European, African, and Japanese descent will be more likely to share values and a similar worldview than will members of any one ethnic group who come from varying socioeconomic backgrounds, from working class to upper class. Culturally proficient schools will recognize these intracultural differences and will provide their faculty, staff, students, and parents with access to information about people who are not like themselves in various ways. These schools will create an environment that fosters trust, safety, and enhancement of self for the people who work and learn in them.

Each Group Has Unique Cultural Needs

European Americans have been able assume that a public school in this country will have information about the history and culture of their people in the United States, as well as about their countries of origin. Other U.S. citizens and U.S. immigrants cannot make such assumptions. The culturally proficient educator will teach and encourage colleagues who are members of the dominant culture to make the necessary adaptations in how schools provide educational services, so that all people will have access to the same benefits and privileges as members of the dominant group in society. The culturally proficient counselor will be instrumental in creating these settings.

One of the barriers to cultural proficiency is lack of awareness of the need to adapt. The first step toward removing that barrier will be to recognize that highlighting the aspects of all people represented in the community enhances the capacity of everyone. As educators in a school try to develop their cultural proficiency by increasing their value for diversity, assessing the school's culture, and institutionalizing cultural knowledge, they will increase people's awareness of the need to adapt, as well as people's respect for the unique cultural needs of diverse populations.

Concluding Comments

It can be argued that the purpose of schools and schooling will continue to be debated throughout much of this century.

Twenty years from now we may still be unsettled over whether the purpose of schools is to create a literate citizenry for a democratic society or to mold and shape workers and employees for the unknown jobs and careers of the future. We view these points of view as worthy of discussion but too often dead-ended into false dichotomies. It is our belief that we can do both. The use of the cultural proficiency model is one way to do this. This model recognizes the basic value of humanity and equips educators with the knowledge and skills to educate all children and youth. Counselors and other educational leaders are faced with challenges and opportunities to transform the schools of today into schools for the future. By actively implementing policies, practices, and procedures that value, include, and engage all members of school communities, educators will embrace the responsibilities and opportunities for educating all learners.

References

Lindsey, R., Robins, K. N., & Terrell, R. D. (1999). *Culturally proficient schools.* Thousand Oaks, CA: Corwin Press.

About the Authors

Randall B. Lindsey teaches in the Graduate School of Education and Psychology at Pepperdine University and has a practice centered on educational consulting on issues related to diversity. He has served as a junior high school and high school teacher, as an administrator in charge of school desegregation efforts, as executive director of a nonprofit corporation, and recently as chair of the Education Department at the University of Redlands. Prior to that he served for seventeen years at California State University, Los Angeles, in the Division of Administration and Counseling. His Ph.D. is in educational leadership from Georgia State University, his M.A. in teaching is in history education from the University of Illinois. All of Randy's experiences have been in working with diverse populations and his area of study is the behavior of White people in multicultural settings. Randy serves as a consultant and facilitator on issues related to diversity and equity, as well as on topics of leadership, problem solving, long-range planning, and conflict resolution. With co-authors Kikanza Nuri Robins and Raymond Terrell, he recently published *Cultural Proficiency: A Manual for School Leaders. Culturally Proficient Instruction: A Guide for People Who Teach* (with Kikanza Nuri Robins, Delores B. Lindsey, and Raymond D. Terrell) in August 2001.

Kikanza Nuri Robins has been interested in language, culture, and learning her entire life. She has addressed these interests professionally through her work as an organizational development consultant. Over the past twenty-five years, Dr. Nuri Robins has focused on working with a variety of not-for-profit organizations in health, education, criminal justice, and religion, helping them with such issues as strategic planning, conflict resolution, and cultural competence. Her clients range from the New York Public Schools and Marriage Encounter to the National AIDS Fund and the Make-A-Wish Foundation. She is a trustee of the San Francisco Theological Seminary and serves on the board of the Southern California Foster Family Agency. She is an avid designer, a talented seamstress, and the author of many articles and two books: *Unspoken Visions* and *Cultural Proficiency.*

Delores Lindsey earned her Ph.D. in educational leadership from the Claremont Graduate University. She believes that the culture of an organization or team is best reflected by the language and stories used within the organization. She captures many of these stories in her writing and speaking. As director of the California School Leadership Academy (CSLA) in Orange County, California, Delores leads and coaches organizations using "strategic visioning," team development strategies, and leadership standards for excellence. Drawing from her Southern heritage, Delores shares her personal stories as a student, classroom teacher, middle school principal, and staff developer. Audiences and workshop participants appreciate her refreshing look at life within an organization as reflected in the stories and language of its members.

Chapter Nine

School Counseling in the Twenty-First Century: A Systemic Multicultural Approach

Shari Tarver Behring

As school counseling educators and practitioners, we frequently find ourselves so focused on the daily activities of serving our schools that rarely do we have the luxury of considering a long-term and large-scale vision for our profession. Yet a vision that anticipates the future needs of school counseling in a proactive manner is just what our profession must develop in order to survive, prosper, and be truly effective. I do have dreams about ideal school counseling services. These dreams seem unattainable to me at times; nonetheless, they are dreams of a systemic multicultural approach by the field of school counseling in the twenty-first century.

A Systems Worldview

As a graduate student in educational psychology at the University of Wisconsin at Madison, I was profoundly affected by the systems theory taught in family therapy, school consultation, and educational curriculum and reform. For the first time, I learned how to look at a situation from a bigger context and from many different perspectives. I also learned to consider structure as well as process issues, which are sometimes hidden, when understanding how and why family systems and school systems function as they do. I began to understand all professional activities as taking place inside of systems. Some are smaller systems, such as an individual school, and some bigger systems, such as the surrounding community, the local school district, the state department of education, and the federal branch of education.

Sarason (1971) was one of the first in the fields of education and counseling to identify the culture of school systems and some associated characteristics: communication patterns linked to the school, leadership styles of principals, implicit school rules, morale issues of teachers, power and who controls it, various school professional roles, and the challenge of teaching diverse learners. He also described the rigid and often competitive subsystems and roles of teachers, administrators, specialists, custodians, and other staff in schools. Sarason noted how the school organization dictates school structure, resources, and job definitions. The organization of the school, in turn, is a reflection of the beliefs and influence of the surrounding community; current educational politics; funding; and local, state, and federal educational governing bodies.

Many of Sarason's observations about the problem of change in schools still remain true: rigidity of roles among school professionals; entrenched school structures not set up to truly meet the educational needs of diverse student bodies; and larger political and educational governing systems that dictate policy, which in turn makes local school change next to impossible to accomplish. However, school counselors have increased their awareness of what is needed for improvement of professional services. We now are better able to understand our role as school counselors in the context of the larger educational environment, composed of the school organization, parents, students, and the surrounding community. Beyond counseling services, we see our jobs as having a direct relationship to educational areas, such as curriculum and placement, that lead to academic success. We have begun to understand the importance of data-driven goals for change, and measured outcomes that demonstrate programs that promote student success, even though we do not always have time to apply these measures.

Despite these advances, the primary focus of school counselors often continues to be handling academic programming, discipline, and attendance in a rigidly defined role, separate from others who are integral for the counseling program to succeed at the school (parents, teachers, administrators, and community). To make things worse, school counselors are sometimes ostracized by others who resent someone who can sit in an office and work individually with students. Ironically, individual student contact by school counselors is often bureaucratic in nature and frequently not rewarding, because the counselor's activities do not address the full potential of students due to the structure of the counselor advising process, which restricts creative, individualized educational services. The administration frequently pressures school counselors to maintain behavioral control and academic performance levels through advisement and programming, often blaming the counselor for problems in these areas, problems that are more often due to a restrictive, rigid, and even prejudicial structure of the school, as well as other outside systems that contribute to student problems but are not interlinked with school services, such as dysfunctional families, economic hardships, racism, and so forth.

Change is possible only when the greater system is understood and confronted as a part of the change process. School counselors must assess the political and cultural climate that surrounds a school by gathering information from all sources. These should include school personnel at all levels, students, parents, community, and state and federal educational and political governing agencies. A historical understanding of the school and the people within it can reveal the origin of current practices and suggest changes that avoid past mistakes. For example, an ineffective school counselor, or a principal who did not support counseling services in the past, could lead to a small and rather powerless counseling program at that school in the present. Each school has a unique culture that can be understood by looking at the larger system and its history. Leadership, morale, power, hidden rules, communication patterns, and student and community needs all need to be assessed. Each school will then be understood as a unique, dynamic system interconnected to other systems.

School counselors can use their understanding of the school system to assess what is working and what is not. This type of service is very different from the current activities of school counselors and has been called *organizational change, social advocacy, industrial psychology,* and *systemic intervention.* It requires understanding and agreement from all constituencies involved. Change then will occur in a broad-based, planned, and very powerful manner.

What would this type of activity do to the current role of school counselors? It would definitely change our current job responsibilities! Our systems analysis would reveal different, and much more effective, activities for us to do. Each systemic analysis would yield its own unique school counseling job description. We would continue to use our counseling competencies to promote individual and school success and adjustment, but we would now share our role and activities with others (teachers, specialists, parents, community members) connected to the school who also have skills and resources to create change that promotes school success, and who would join us in a systematic, collective change effort. Thus, our work and roles would become much less defined and much more fluid and collaborative in order to increase the effectiveness of services and avoid waste of time and resources.

Meanwhile, back at the institutions of higher learning, school counseling educators would do well to note the systemic analyses of surrounding schools and could, through a similar structural analysis, discover that their own universities and colleges suffer from role rigidity and stagnation as well. The combined data from all educational levels would be used by school counseling training programs along with other teacher and administrator training programs to restructure the higher educational institution to support and contribute to the needs of the larger system of education, community, and political climate of which the institution is a part. Departments might dissolve in favor of collaborative educational initiatives across educational areas. Classes could be team taught at public school sites where systemic change was being implemented while students learned about it.

As systemic change agents, all members of the systems in which we operate educationally (community; family; school; college; local, state and federal educational boards; and the greater political arena) would interact and change one another while moving toward the most effective conditions for school success. Think for a moment how different this would be from the much less connected way school counselors and these various constituents operate now.

Why would anyone in their right mind agree to the systemic approach just described? Because many of our urban schools are in crisis, and nothing else seems to be working. We are overwhelmed by the diversity of learners and the inability of our antiquated system to meet the students' educational and adjustment needs. Programs are developed in response to problems, rather than proactively, and in isolation of understanding or involving the larger system that surrounds schools and that must be addressed for change to occur. We often are unaware of duplicate programs, relevant data about the problems and proven solutions, and forces that might help or, conversely, work against, our efforts. School counseling, and the educational field as a whole, must move to an integrated, systemic approach in order to truly attain large-scale, effective, and long-lasting educational and personal success for all students.

Multicultural School Systems

Another systemic characteristic that has had a profound impact on schools and school counselors is the cultural background of those who are connected to the school. Here, culture has a broad meaning in comparison to the school culture as described by Sarason. Culture is defined in terms of membership in subgroups based on gender, ethnicity, socioeconomic status, religion, sexual orientation, and handicapping conditions; each group has values, beliefs, norms, traditions, language, and other features that are distinct and that define the group (Tarver Behring, Cabello, Kushida, & Murguia, 2000; Tarver Behring & Gelinas, 1996; Tarver Behring, Gelinas, Peyton, & Munoz, 1995). Culture is a multifaceted component that includes individual identity, group identity, cognition, communication, and behavioral patterns. Further, there exist multiple cultural group memberships for any one person, rendering culture a broad definition with much variation within groups as well as between them (Ponterotto & Pedersen, 1993; Sue & Sue, 1990).

Within school settings, children and educators have cultural backgrounds; the school structure and the greater systems that surround it, as outlined previously, also have unique cultural characteristics. There is a growing recognition of how a dominant European American male worldview influences the manner in which the school system operates (Harris, 1996). European Americans, who make up the mainstream culture in the United States, may be the least aware of the way their culture influences their behavior and interactions, most likely due to the dominance of their culture and the absence of a perceived need to acknowledge diversity among non–European Americans (Lynch & Hanson, 1992). Lack of awareness of one's own culture and that of others can create a mismatch of educational and counseling services (Hall, 1997).

Understanding one's own culture in relationship to other cultures is a necessary prerequisite to culturally sensitive school services (Tarver Behring & Ingraham, 1998). Cultural awareness at the beginning of the helping relationship has been found to play a significant role in the process and outcome of counseling when the counselor and client are from different backgrounds (Sue & Sue, 1990). The identification of characteristics of one's own cultural beliefs is especially important for European Americans because of the tendency of European American groups to view culture in an ethnocentric manner—the European American culture as the primary or prevailing culture (Lynch & Hanson, 1992). This belief system inhibits awareness for and acceptance of ethnically different cultures and could lead to a misconception that educational and counseling approaches, as they currently exist, are sensitive and effective for all cultures.

By developing a multiplistic cultural self-identity, that is, developing an awareness that each person holds membership in multiple groups with associated privilege or prejudice, counselors can move beyond an ethnocentric worldview (Tarver Behring & Ingraham, 1998). As educators, counselors, and consultants from all possible cultural backgrounds develop self-awareness of diversity and how it differs from others, they take the necessary first step in moving toward an understanding of conscious, culturally appropriate services in the public schools.

If we return to the previous discussion of the school as a system, we might think for a moment about the huge impact of culture on the structure and activities of the school system. The predominant culture in general in our country is European American; therefore, it follows that the beliefs and values by which our public schools are set up are also European American. Some examples of European American values in contrast with those of certain Latino cultures include emphasis on individual versus group achievement, competition versus cooperation in earning grades, and analytical or scientific versus holistic learning approaches (Dana, 1993). (For a more detailed examination of European American culture, see Dana, 1993; Katz, 1985; and Sue & Sue, 1990.)

School counseling programs for students are also culturally loaded with European American values, as is the field of psychotherapy. Yoder and Kahn (1993) describe how the fields of counseling and psychology in the United States often reflect European American privileged male standards without recognizing that differences from these standards exist and are equally valid. Others have discussed the cultural biases of theory and practice in the fields of counseling and psychology (Hall, 1997; Harris, 1996; Pedersen, 1997; Sue & Sue, 1990; Sue & Zane,

1987). Because school counseling services occur in a European American school system, programs also reflect approaches best suited for European Americans. There is little information in the school counseling literature about how to adjust school counseling approaches for work with specific cultural groups. Our theories and approaches about how to build relationships, promote goals, and intervene are based on research with European Americans for European Americans.

What happens when the students attending a European American–based school system are not themselves European American? Harris (1996) has noted that "there will be a lack of mutual goals, frustration and disappointment" (p. 3) when cultural differences are not addressed. In Los Angeles, the high dropout rates, academic failure, and crime on campus are likely related to the negative reactions of students within culturally foreign schools and counseling programs. As systemic and culturally multiplistic thinkers, school counselors can work with those within an existing ethnocentric school system to develop greater cultural awareness and acceptance through systemic self-study, and then to set goals toward a multicultural system that is truly reflective of and responsive to the diversity of *all* of those who are in it, and those who surround it.

Changing school systems to be responsive to multiple cultures does not mean lowering educational standards. It does, however, mean changing the process of achieving these standards to increase the potential for success for the diversity of learners within the system. The school counselor could work with administrators, teachers, parents, and community members in a multitude of ways. These include helping school staff to understand multiple cultures and develop cultural self-awareness and awareness of others; setting inclusive academic goals that are fairly measured using qualitative and quantitative culture-fair achievement measures; collaborating with others in the school and community to offer multiple language-based programs and curricula that are appropriate for diverse learning styles; offering equity in advisement and academic programming to ensure the same high educational outcome for all students regardless of culture (such as completing high school and entering post-secondary institution of their choice); providing culturally appropriate counseling programs that are integrally linked to other aspects of the system, such as the classroom, parents, community, the educational mission, and so forth; linking the above efforts with those of people who are working in a similar manner at the elementary through college levels for consistent system-wide change; organizing school and community representatives and political lobbyists to interact with the larger governing systems surrounding the school, in order to encourage these other systems to engage in the systemic process toward collaborative educational change efforts; demonstrating permanent, successful systemic outcomes through system-wide, data-based measurement.

What might multiculturally inclusive school counseling services look like in the twenty-first century? Here are just a few examples. A school counselor might oversee paraprofessionals who use technology, such as computers, to program all students into college prep classes; create on-site training for parent groups from diverse backgrounds to learn the same curriculum as the students, with input from teaching staff, and in native languages; review language-based programs and consult personnel in order to provide effective bilingual education; team teach a school-site-based graduate class with school personnel and parents who are representative of, and share knowledge and skills about, the diversity and associated worldview and needs of the surrounding community; advocate with school administrators for culturally appropriate curricula and programs; coordinate a system-wide cultural awareness program for students, teachers, administrators, school counselors, special educational staff, and parents; organize a representative governing body (teachers, parents, students, administrators) that engages in collaborative decision making about culturally appropriate educational assessment, curricula, and support services at each culturally unique school; create a mentoring program for all students, not just those at risk, to provide educational support and advisement and to promote attendance and retention; coordinate on-site community services for health, education, employment, and counseling; provide K–12 student courses and create student portfolios for college selection, admission procedures, post-college job application, and financial aid; conduct and publish research about the successful multicultural approaches in the school as a model for others to follow.

Once ethnocentrism in American education and the harm it causes to non–European American students are understood, a multicultural systemic change effort clearly becomes the right thing to do. Certainly, some of those who have enjoyed the privileges of membership in the dominant culture will resist giving up the associated benefits of privilege rather than helping to create a more equitable situation. However, allowing inequitable standards to be learned by students, regardless of cultural background, is a disservice to all students; the rich benefits to the entire system of developing multiple educational approaches that are reflective of educational diversity more than outweigh the costs of change.

In the next century, I look forward to the time when a multicultural worldview is infused into all aspects of the educational system, so that we no longer need to use the word *multicultural* to describe specific services. I believe in the continual moral evolution of the fields of school counseling and education as a whole and the integrity in each of us to promote an inclusive school environment where each student truly experiences equity in educational and counseling services within a school system created for all students.

References

Dana, R. H. (1993). *Multicultural assessment perspectives for professional psychology*. Boston: Allyn & Bacon.

Hall, C. (1997). Cultural malpractice: The growing obsolescence of psychology with the changing U.S. population. *American Psychologist, 52*(6), 642–651.

Harris, K. C. (1996). Collaboration within a multicultural society. *Remedial and Special Education, 17*, 2–10.

Katz, J. H. (1985). The sociopolitical nature of counseling. *The Counseling Psychologist, 13*, 613–624.

Lynch, E. W., & Hanson, N. J. (Eds.) (1992). *Developing cross-cultural competence: A guide for working with young children and their families*. Baltimore, MD: Paul H. Brookes.

Pedersen, P. (1997, March). *Learning to hear the voices as a cross-cultural competency*. Keynote presentation at the Cross-Cultural Competencies for Interactive Diversity Western regional conference of the Association for Multicultural Counseling and Development, San Diego, CA.

Ponterotto, J. G., & Pedersen, P. B. (1993). *Preventing prejudice*. Newbury Park, CA: Sage Publications.

Sarason, S. B. (1971). *The culture of the school and the problem of change*. Boston, MA: Allyn & Bacon.

Sue, D. W., & Sue, D. (1990). *Counseling the culturally different: Theory and practice*. New York: John Wiley & Sons.

Sue, S., & Zane, N. (1987). The role of culture and cultural techniques in psychotherapy: A critique and reformation. *American Psychologist, 42,* 37–45.

Tarver Behring, S., Cabello, B., Kushida, D., & Murguia, A. (2000). Cultural modifications to current school-based consultation approaches reported by culturally diverse beginning consultants. *School Psychology Review, 29*(3), 354–367.

Tarver Behring, S., & Gelinas, R.T. (1996). School consultation with Asian American children and families. *The California School Psychologist, 1,* 13–20.

Tarver Behring, S., Gelinas, R. T., Peyton, T., & Munoz, A. (1995). *Multicultural consultation training manual: School consultation with Asian American, African American and Hispanic American students and families*. Northridge, CA: Author.

Tarver Behring, S., & Ingraham, C. L. (1998). Culture as a central component of consultation: A call to the field. *Journal of Educational and Psychological Consultation, 9,* 57–72.

Yoder, J. D., & Kahn, A. S. (1993). Working toward an inclusive psychology of women. *American Psychologist, 48*(7), 846–850.

About the Author

Shari Tarver Behring, Ph.D., is an associate professor and program coordinator of the School Counseling Program in the Department of Educational Psychology and Counseling, California State University, Northridge. She earned a master of science degree in clinical psychology from Marquette University in 1981 and a doctorate in educational psychology with a specialization in school psychology from the University of Wisconsin at Madison in 1986. She is a licensed psychologist and holds credentials in school psychology and school counseling in California. Her research interests include multicultural school consultation, full inclusion for children with special educational needs, and organizational change efforts to promote educational equity in schools.

Section 4:

Staying the Course

Chapter Ten

Comprehensive School Guidance Programs in the Future: Staying the Course

Norman C. Gysbers

At the beginning of the twentieth century, guidance in the schools emerged in response to the dramatic changes that had occurred in the industrial, occupational, educational, and social structures and institutions of that time. It was called *vocational guidance* and was loosely organized around a position titled *vocational counselor*. Most often the position was filled by teachers who were given lists of tasks to do with little or no released time from their teaching duties in which to do them (Ginn, 1924).

In the 1920s and 1930s, in response to the lack of an organized approach to guidance, the service model of guidance become popular as a way to guide the work of individuals who held the position of school counselor. Various services were identified as necessary, including individual inventory service, information service, counseling service, placement service, and follow-up service (Smith, 1951). By this time, too, the traditional way of describing guidance as having three aspects—vocational, educational, and personal-social—had emerged. Vocational guidance, instead of being guidance, had become one part of guidance (Gysbers & Henderson, 2000).

From the 1920s to the 1980s, the position orientation to guidance dominated professional training and practice in our schools. The focus was on the position of school counselor, not on the program of guidance. Administratively, the position of school counselor was included in pupil personnel services (today often called student services), along with such other positions as attendance worker; social worker; school psychologist; and speech and hearing, nursing, and medical personnel (Eckerson & Smith, 1996).

Because of the position orientation of school counselors, guidance in the schools during this time was often seen as an ancillary support service in the eyes of many people. Unfortunately, this view of guidance placed school counselors mainly in remedial-reactive roles—roles not seen as mainstream in education. What was worse, the position orientation reinforced the practice of school counselors performing many administrative, clerical, and fill-in duties because these duties could be defended as being of service to somebody.

As a result of its position orientation, guidance in the schools became known as the add-on profession. School counselors were seen as the "you-might-as-well" group ("While you are doing this task, you might as well do this one, too"). Because of the absence of an organizational structure and an institutional district policy for guidance, it was easy to assign new duties to school counselors. After all, they had flexible schedules and, because time was not a consideration, there was no need to worry about removing old duties when adding new ones. The list of tasks to be done by school counselors simply became longer. The lack of an organizational structure and an institutional district policy for guidance in the schools left guidance undefined. As a result, guidance in the schools became fragmented. It was neither comprehensive nor cumulative.

Beginning in the 1960s, but particularly in the 1970s, the concept of guidance as a developmental program emerged. During this period, the call came to reorient guidance from what had become an ancillary set of services delivered by a person in a position (the school counselor) to a comprehensive developmental program. The call for reorientation came from diverse sources, including a renewed interest in vocational-career guidance (and its theoretical base, career development), a renewed interest in developmental guidance, concern about the efficacy of the prevailing position approach to guidance in the school, and concern about accountability and evaluation.

The work of putting comprehensive guidance programs into place in the schools continued in the 1990s. Increasingly, comprehensive programs were being implemented in the schools, and as we neared the close of the 1990s, comprehensive guidance programs were rapidly replacing the position orientation to guidance. Comprehensive guidance programs are becoming the major way of organizing and managing guidance in schools across the country.

A Model for Comprehensive Guidance Programs

This chapter briefly describes a model for comprehensive guidance programs developed originally by Gysbers and Moore (1974, 1981) and later refined and updated by Gysbers and Henderson (2000). It is presented here as an example of a current and widely used student-centered program in the schools that is specifically designed to facilitate students' personal, career, and academic development with strong support from and in collaboration with parents, teachers, administrators, and community members, including personnel in the business and labor communities. The model contains three major elements: content, organizational framework, and resources. Figure 1 provides a visual representation of the model.

Content
The content element of the model identifies student competencies considered important by the school district for students to master as a result of their participation in the district's comprehensive guidance program. The competencies are often organized around areas or domains such as career, educational, and personal-social. They are grouped in various ways, including by specific grades or grade-level groupings.

Organizational Framework
The organizational framework element of the model contains structural components and program components. The structural components define the program, provide a rationale for it, and list basic assumptions that undergird the program. The program components identify the four parts of the delivery system that organize the program's guidance activities and interventions. The program components are guidance curriculum, individual planning, responsive services, and system support.

The curriculum component was chosen because a curriculum provides a vehicle with which to impart guidance content to all students in a systematic way. Individual planning was included as part of the model because of the increasing need for all students to systematically plan, monitor, and manage their development and to consider and take action on their next steps personally, educationally, and occupationally. The responsive services component was included because of the need to respond to the direct, immediate concerns of students, whether these

Comprehensive Guidance Program Elements

| Content | Organizational Framework, Activities & Time | | Resources |

Competencies	**Structural Components**	**Program Components and Sample Processes**	**Resources**
Student competencies grouped by domains	Definition Assumptions Rationale	Guidance Curriculum Structured groups Classroom presentations	Human Financial Political
		Individual Planning Advisement Assessment Placement & follow-up	
		Responsive Services Individual counseling Small group counseling Consultation Referral	
		System Support Management activities Consultation Community outreach Public relations	

Suggested Distribution of Total Counselor Time

Percentage Rate

	Elementary School	Middle/Junior High School	High School
Guidance Curriculum	35–45	25–35	15–25
Individual Planning	5–10	15–25	25–35
Responsive Services	30–40	30–40	25–35
System Support	10–15	10–15	15–20
	100	100	100

concerns involve crisis counseling, referral, or consultation with parents, teachers, or other specialists. Finally, the system support component was included because if the other guidance processes are to be effective, a variety of support activities, such as staff development, research, and curriculum development, are required. Also, system support encompasses the need for the guidance programs to provide appropriate support to other programs in a school, including school counselors assuming "fair share" tasks that all faculty may do from time to time in operating the school.

These components serve as organizers for the many guidance methods, techniques, and resources required in a comprehensive guidance program. A program is not comprehensive unless school counselors are providing activities to students, parents, and staff in all four program components.

School counselors' professional time is a critical element in the model. How should they spend their time? How should their time be spread across all four components of the total program? In this model, the four program components provide the structure for making judgments about appropriate allocations of school counselors' time. One criterion to be used in making such judgments is the concept of program balance. The assumption is that school counselors' time should be spread across all program components, but particularly the first three. The rule of 80-20 is used. Eighty percent of school counselors' time should be spread across the first three components, the direct service to students components of the program. The remaining 20% is devoted to the indirect component of the program, system support.

Another criterion is the differing needs of grade levels: Different grade levels require different allocations of counselor time across the program components. For example, at the elementary level, more school counselor time is spent working in the curriculum with less time spent in the individual planning. In a high school, these time allocations are reversed.

How school counselors in a school plan and allocate their time depends on the needs of their students and their community. Once chosen, time allocations are not fixed forever. The purpose for making them is to provide direction to the program and to the administrators and school counselors involved.

Since the comprehensive guidance program model is a "100% program," 100% of school counselors' time must be spread across the four program components. Time allocations are changed as new needs arise, but nothing new can be added unless something else is removed. The assumption is that school counselors spend 100% of their time on task, implementing the guidance program.

Resources

Human resources for the guidance program include school counselors, teachers, administrators, parents, students, community members, and business and labor personnel. All have roles to play in the guidance program. Although the counselors are the main providers of guidance and counseling services and are the coordinators of the program, the involvement, cooperation, and support of teachers and administrators are critical for the program to be successful. The involvement, cooperation, and support of parents, community members, and business and labor personnel are also critical. A school-community advisory committee is recommended for the guidance program to bring together the talent and energy of school and community personnel.

Adequate financial resources are required if a comprehensive guidance program is to be successful. Examples of financial resources include materials, equipment, and facilities. The model highlights the need for these resources through its focus on the physical space and equipment required to conduct a comprehensive program in a school district. To make the guidance curriculum, individual planning, responsive services, and system support components function effectively, adequate guidance facilities are required.

The mobilization of the political resources in a school district is also key to a successful guidance program. Full endorsement of the guidance program by the board of education of the school district as a "program of studies of the district" is one example of mobilizing political resources. Another example is the adoption of a clear and concise school district policy that highlights the integral and central nature of the district-wide comprehensive guidance program to the overall educational program of the district.

The Power of a Common Language for the Structure of Guidance Programs

To be effective, guidance programs require consistency and logical coherence in their organizational structures and continuity in their functioning without interruption throughout grades K–12. The model just presented was designed with the meanings of these words (consistency, logical coherence, and continuity) in mind. With this model, a common language for guidance is established in a school district that is marked by the orderly and logical relation of the three elements of a comprehensive guidance program, which afford easy comprehension and recognition by laypersons and professionals alike.

Why is a common language important for the structure of guidance programs now and further into the twenty-first century? A common language for the structure of guidance programs enables school counselors, administrators, teachers, and parents to "coordinate their work and multiply the power of their intellects" (American College Testing Program [ACT], 1998, p. 9). In addition, a common language for the structure of guidance programs allows these "individuals to communicate and replicate" (ACT, 1998, p. 9) guidance program activities. Finally, a common language for the structure of guidance programs provides the basis for program, personnel, and results evaluation across a school district and grades K–12.

Does the use of a common language for the structure of guidance programs mean that all school counselors in the district must carry out the same tasks, in the same way, for the entire school year? The answer is no. School buildings and grade levels in districts differ in their needs. School counselors' expertise differs. Thus, while the common language of the structure of the guidance program is a constant, school counselors' time allocations, the tasks they do, and the activities and interventions they use within the program structure to work with students, parents, and teachers may vary by school building and grade level. Differentiated staffing using the professional expertise of the personnel involved often is a necessity (Henderson & Gysbers, 1998).

Staying the Course

Once a common language for the structure of a school guidance program has been adopted, the task of putting it into place in a school district begins. In fact, preliminary work on preparing the district and the personnel involved should have occurred prior to the adoption of a program structure. The specifics of the process of putting a guidance program into place so that it can function fully have been described in detail elsewhere (Gysbers & Henderson, 2000), so the specifics of this process will not be repeated here. It is important to know and remember, however, that the process takes time to take hold. We are excited about doing something for the first time. Unfortunately, we are less excited about follow-through—staying the course. But follow-through is obligatory if we are to obtain the student results we expect.

Staying the course in the change from position to program requires perseverance. Why perseverance? Because definitions of perseverance include such words and phrases as "steadfastness," "remaining constant in the face of obstacles or discouragement," "having continuing strength or patience in dealing with difficulty," and "adherence to a goal in face of opposition." Why perseverance? Because to accomplish the transition from position to program requires time. Why steadfastness? Because those who want to change must overcome the inertia of others and the resistance of those who want to maintain the status quo.

Staying the course with a common-language guidance-program structure to make sure that it is fully implemented and functioning the way it should is important, too, because it takes time for guidance programs to show student results. Although some student results may appear early, most occur only after the program has been fully operational for a period of time. This is best illustrated by the results of two studies, one from Missouri and one from Utah. Missouri has been involved in a statewide implementation since 1984; Utah began the statewide implementation process in 1989. In the Missouri study, Lapan, Gysbers, and Sun (1997) found that students in schools with more fully implemented guidance programs were more likely to report that they had earned higher grades, their education was better preparing them for their future, their school made more career and college information available to them, and their school had a more positive climate. In Utah, Nelson and Gardner (1998) found that students in schools with more fully implemented guidance programs rated their overall education as better, took more advanced mathematics and science courses, and had higher scores on every area of the ACT.

The Year 2021

Should guidance programs look the same in the year 2021 as they do today? Can a guidance program design from the late

152

twentieth century be responsive to the needs of students, parents, teachers, and the community in 2021? Will needs then be the same needs we see today, or will they be different?

My crystal ball says that the same organizational structure for guidance that works today will work in 2021. I am also certain, however, that some of the guidance activities and procedures that are used today may change, given new individual and societal challenges in the year 2021 and beyond. Professional time allocations will probably change, too. Thus, although the basic organizational structure for guidance will remain, activities, tasks, and time within the organizational structure are flexible, allowing adaptation to change. Staying the course with the basic organizational structure described in this chapter will provide the consistency, continuity, and common language to allow us finally to show the student results we have anticipated for so long in our literature and are beginning to see now as described in the studies from Missouri and Utah.

References

American College Testing Program. (1998, Spring). The power of a common language in workplace development. In *Work Keys U.S.A. 3*, 9.

Eckerson, L. O., & Smith, H. M. (Eds.) (1996). *Scope of pupil personnel services.* Washington, DC: U.S. Government Printing Office.

Ginn, S. J. (1924). Vocational guidance in Boston public schools. *The Vocational Guidance Magazine, 3*, 3–7.

Gysbers, N. C., & Henderson, P. (2000). *Developing and managing your school guidance program* (3rd ed.). Alexandria, VA: American Counseling Association.

Gysbers, N. C., & Moore, E. J. (Eds.) (1974). *Career guidance, counseling, and placement: Elements of an illustrative program guide.* Columbia, MO: University of Missouri.

Gysbers, N. C., & Moore, E. J. (1981). *Improving guidance programs.* Englewood Cliffs, NJ: Prentice Hall.

Henderson, P., & Gysbers, N. C. (1998). *Leading and managing your school guidance program staff*. Alexandria, VA: American Counseling Association.

Lapan, R. T., Gysbers N. C., & Sun, Y. (1997). The impact of more fully implemented guidance programs on the school experiences of high school students: A statewide evaluation study. *Journal of Counseling and Development, 75*, 292–302.

Nelson, D. E., & Gardner, J. L. (1998). *An evaluation of the comprehensive guidance program in Utah public schools*. Salt Lake City: Utah State Office of Education.

Smith, G. E. (1951). *Principles and practices of the guidance program*. New York: Macmillan.

About the Author

Norman C. Gysbers is a professor in the Department of Educational and Counseling Psychology at the University of Missouri–Columbia. He received his M.A. (1959) and Ph.D. (1963) degrees from the University of Michigan. Gysbers' research and teaching interests are in career development; career counseling; and school guidance and counseling program development, management, and evaluation. He is author of 59 articles in 17 different professional journals, 25 chapters in published books, 14 monographs, and 13 books, including *Career Counseling: Process, Issues, and Techniques,* 1998 (with Mary Heppner and Joseph Johnston); *Leading and Managing Your School Guidance Program Staff,* 1998 (with Patricia Henderson); and *Developing and Managing Your School Guidance Program* (3rd. ed.), 2000 (with Patricia Henderson). In 1981 he was awarded the National Vocational Guidance Association National Merit Award and in 1983 the American Counseling Association Distinguished Professional Service Award. In 1989 he received the National Career Development Association Eminent Career Award and in 2000 he received the National Career Development Association Presidents Recognition Award. Currently Gysbers is the editor of the *Journal of Career Development*.

Chapter Eleven

Student Support Programs: 2021

George M. Gazda

Student support programs 20 years hence will most likely be directly related to the configurations of the schools in which they are located. In order to speculate on the nature of the support programs, therefore, it is necessary first to speculate on what types of models our schools will assume. Let us consider some of the more prominent current models that are in practice or under development and some of the major reasons why change is necessary.

The traditional factory model, or graded schools, is still the primary system operating in the vast majority of public and private schools, although there are other models, such as the Montessori schools, Corsini 4-R schools, Paideia schools, the Basic School, shared decision-making (site-based managed) schools, Sizer's Coalition of Essential Schools, Hudson Institute's Modern Red Schoolhouse, the Co-Nect School, Alissi's Outcomes Driven Development model, Glasser's School without Failure model, School–Business Community Partnership schools and variations of these models, among others. Radical changes are rarely possible in the traditional graded school because the model itself forces conformity to its essential concepts. Likewise, most site-based managed schools are warmed-over traditional graded schools with a couple of variations. This is true because the teachers who plan these schools know best what they have been doing, which is following the traditional school model. When site-based (managed) schools become radically different, it is because they have adopted an entirely *new* model that is radically different from the traditional model. (A comprehensive treatment of what is wrong with current traditional schools can be found in Gazda, 1998.)

In September 1993, the Georgia Partnership for Excellence in Education published *The Next Generation School Project*. More than 300 Georgians, myself included, were members of the 10 ad hoc design teams. The publication includes summary reports of each of the following ad hoc teams: (a) Outcomes and Instruction, (b) Readiness to Learn, (c) At-Risk Students, (d) Re-invent Secondary Education, (e) Technology, (f) Quality, (g) Human Resource Development, (h) Intercultural Education, (i) Governance and Leadership, and (j) Seamless Educational Community. I chose to be a member of the Re-invent Secondary Education team because the title suggested this team would be most receptive to radical change proposals, and it was.

Our team chose seven vital change criteria that a school system could use to organize itself differently in order to be more effective. The seven criteria were

- self-paced learning (a student moves as quickly or slowly as he or she is able),
- mastery-based progress (students work on achieving a set level of mastery before progressing to the next level),
- nontracking placement (students will not be placed in classes based on ability or achievement test scores),
- continuous progress (each student progresses at his or her own rate without fear of failure),
- total reorganization commitment (totally reorganize the system to include the vital change criteria),
- external influence (involve parents, businesses, and community volunteers), and
- cooperative learning (students help each other in cooperative learning groups).

Although not listed as one of the seven vital change criteria, options for flexible class scheduling, employment of developing technologies, modification of teacher and staff roles, and the like are encompassed by criterion five.

In order to make the seven vital change criteria operational, school systems and teachers might select methodology that:
1. engages students actively.
2. provides for multiple forms of delivery and evaluation.
3. accommodates varied time frames and settings. The schedule and school year might be flexible; the classroom could be extended to include varied resources within a community.

4. utilizes technology as a means for teaching and learning.
5. emphasizes students' development and use of acquired knowledge and skills.
6. incorporates higher order thinking skills so that students become critical and creative thinkers who can evaluate information, opinions, processes, and outcomes.
7. in all aspects of the curriculum enables students to become effective communicators in oral and written form.
8. includes collaborative learning, allowing students to assume different roles in learning.
9. promotes mastery and self-paced learning whereby students can become independent workers.
10. is be varied for remediation and enrichment.

Administrators, teachers, parents, and students must become aware that different methodologies have different outcomes and lead to varied means of evaluation. Methodologies should be integrated to produce the ultimate in teaching and learning. Time, resources, staff development, and support must be available to ensure an awareness of and competence in different methodologies (Georgia Partnership for Excellence in Education, 1993, pp. G-9–G-10).

Interactive Roles of the Reinvented School and the Community

Schools Reaching Out

The school can reach out to the community in a number of ways. Some examples of these ways are described in *The Next Generation School Project* (Georgia Partnership, 1993, G-10–G-11):

1. Schools can implement transition-to-work programs, such as apprenticeships; cooperative education (offices, retailing, and service occupations); clinical internships (e.g., in medical fields); professional internships in legal and governmental fields; and work-study programs.
2. Community service can be integrated into the school curriculum for credit. Student involvement in community service can lead to the increased sense of civic responsibility and self-esteem that comes from giving to others.
3. Schools can offer advanced placement courses with cooperating colleges, making the transition to college seamless.

4. Tech prep programs can prepare students for entry into technical institutes and technical occupations. These programs can (a) adapt math, science, and English courses to include applied learning; (b) revise vocational education programs to include substantive academic content as it is applied to the workplace; (c) adopt career-focused curricula; (d) articulate with postsecondary institutions; and (e) seek advice and assistance from business and industry representatives.
5. School outreach programs that also serve people beyond K–12 can be adopted; for example, through the creation of family centers.

Parents are the key to the success of their children and must be meaningfully involved with the education of their children. Schools can assist undereducated parents to improve their parenting as well as reading and math skills so that they can better assist their children.

Communities Supporting Schools

Just as the schools reach out to involve the parents and community, the community at-large can support the schools in a variety of ways. *The Next Generation School Project* (Georgia Partnership, 1993, pp. G-11–G-12) lists several options:

1. Adopt-a-school programs and business partnerships can assist particular schools, often as an educational outreach of the chamber of commerce.
2. Mentoring can give the student an adult friend and mentor.
3. Businesses in some school systems can provide part-time teachers for certain topics.
4. Business and industry can have lend-a-manager programs to assist schools in implementing programs and innovations.
5. Parents and businesses can form carefully organized and structured advisory committees. Two examples of these committees in Georgia schools are strategic planning and sex education review.
6. Big Brother and Big Sister programs can provide support and encouragement to many students.
7. Local business equipment can be made available for instructional purposes in school or business settings.
8. Businesses can sponsor staff development sessions, career days, job fairs, and field trips.

9. Culturally diverse role models from the community can volunteer in schools. These role models might include business leaders, religious leaders, entertainers, athletes, or government leaders.
10. Communities and schools can develop collaborative programs to concentrate on keeping students in school, as exemplified by Cities in Schools, the nation's largest nonprofit organization devoted to dropout prevention.
11. School systems can couple service agencies, such as state departments of human resources and education, with families in their schools.
12. The community can become involved in the schools through school renewal site-based decision-making teams. For example, the Southern Association of Colleges and Schools (SACS) has sponsored local decision-making teams for schools that are attempting renewal through some type of site-based management school model.
13. School systems can take advantage of the educational support of certain businesses and industries in their communities, such as Kroger, Pizza Hut, and Domino's.

Assessment

Assessment of student achievement in traditional graded schools is inadequate in many ways. Several of the weaknesses of current practices are described in *The Next Generation School Project* (Georgia Partnership, 1993). Some of these weaknesses are as follows:

1. Most assessment is through short-answer or multiple-choice teacher-made exams. These tests assess mostly recall or recognition of material covered in class, the lowest levels of cognitive learning. Higher order thinking skills and creativity are not assessed. The curriculum and teaching and learning are therefore driven by this low-level assessment practice.
2. Current practices provide no opportunity for student self-assessment, an integral part of the learning and goal-setting process.
3. Behavioral traits and life skills that are necessary for effective living and productivity are minimally assessed (mainly through deportment evaluation in elementary schools).
4. Letter and numerical grading foster competition among

students and lead to winners and losers. Losers (those with less than average grades and scores) lose their incentive to achieve, and winners frequently work just hard enough to achieve A's and then slack off without maximizing their learning abilities.

Because current grading is done on some sort of normal curve standard, it essentially forces one-half of the population to be below average. Being constantly ranked below average is a disincentive to the intrinsic motivation to learn. In order to become and remain motivated, the learner needs to experience repeated success and thus learn to enjoy learning for its own sake. This will not happen when external rewards and punishment through grades is the primary motivational system employed by the schools.

In order to remedy the current prevailing assessment practices, it is recommended that multiple assessment procedures be employed. For example, the development of exhibitions aggregated in a portfolio can be structured to reflect higher order thinking skills and the student's ability to synthesize what he or she has learned. With the employment of a continuous-progress, mastery learning model, assessment can also be accomplished through mastery of "learning units," using a check-off system, with no grades, that simply shows satisfactory mastery for the unit and readiness to move to the next unit. The Corsini 4-R School employs this system very effectively in its nongraded school model.

Teacher Role Changes
In the preceding section of this chapter, numerous changes were outlined for improving the current traditional school model. Embedded in these changes are significant role changes for the teacher. Space does not allow a comprehensive treatment of these changes here, but a more comprehensive treatment can be found in chapter 2 of Gazda et al. (1998), *Human Relations Development: A Manual for Educators.*

Peeler (1992) reports that there seems to be a consensus among leading educators, psychologists, and philosophers that "tomorrow's adults must be prepared for a lifetime of inquiry, analysis, collaborative learning, problem solving, and decision making" and that "these abilities will be the 'basic skills' of the future" (p. 7). According to Peeler, this new definition of learning will require the teacher's role to shift to one more like that of a coach, facilitator, listener, model, guide, and mediator. Peeler believes that the teacher will also need to become computer literate and employ a highly interactive computer system to provide guidance and instruction to students. Koppich, Brown, and Amsler (1990) point out that career ladder programs have added new roles for experienced teachers, including curriculum development and program or staff development, supervision, evaluation, case management, and training.

Firestone and Bader (1991) have observed that "schools are not only expected to solve a great variety of social problems from the drug problem to the AIDS crisis but must also act as sources of day care, entertainment, and community cohesion" (p. 120). Obviously, these expanded services assumed by schools also add new roles for the teacher that are frequently shared with specialists in the school setting, such as counselors, social workers, nurses, and psychologists.

A Projection of the Nature of Student Support Programs: 2021

If the seven vital change criteria described earlier in this chapter are incorporated into models of schools of the future, they will closely resemble the Corsini 4-R School, because it already incorporates these criteria. A description of the school model and locations where it is operational can be found in Evans, Corsini, and Gazda (1990). The school design of the future, with its modified curriculum that includes training in life or social skills as well as the three R's, will require support personnel to provide consultation and training or co-training in life and social skills that is continuous, developmental, and comprehensive throughout the entire preschool through grade 12 sequence and perhaps beyond. Currently, such skills training is being done only in isolated instances and rarely is it comprehensive because support personnel themselves have not been trained systematically in these skills. Skills training provides a preventive mental health model that will become more imperative for the future. (Remedial models are not applicable to preventive mental health interventions.) Health care programs will come to accept the need for preventive models to reduce the cost of health care, both mental and physical.

If school models similar to the model found in the Corsini 4-R School are employed, student learning efficiency will be maximized and there will be time in the curriculum for life and social skills training as well as the 3 R's, the arts, and sports and recreation. The concept of lifelong learning fits this model school system because time limits are not placed on mastery of the curriculum contents. Students will go through the curriculum in a self-paced fashion based on continuous progress, and mastery of knowledge and skills broken into developmental units.

If teachers are going to assume the roles of coach, facilitator, listener, model, guide, and mediator (Peeler, 1992), they will need support personnel to assist them, perhaps even train them, in the skills these roles require. As technology becomes more directly involved in instruction, the teacher's role may shift to allow more time for personal interaction with students, and support personnel roles may shift to more consultation and less hands-on work with students.

Politically, it is popular to advocate for more instructional time for teachers with lower student–teacher class ratios. Chances are that this concept will be pushed to the limit before advocates realize what many already know—class size is not the real culprit in the failure of our schools to produce greater student achievement. New models of schooling will eventually prove to be the real answer to improvement, but it will take many more years for these models to proliferate. In the meantime, the brightest of our students will continue to be siphoned off to private schools where they can handle the traditional school model, and our inner city schools will all become alternative-type schools reaching the status of correctional institutions. The roles of support personnel for these inner city schools will obviously differ significantly from those in private schools and suburban schools on a par with private schools. Instead of preventive mental health interventions, the support personnel in inner city schools will be doing intensive remedial work, individually and in small groups. Much of their time and expertise will be used to deal with the physical condition of the students because of drug-related health problems, child abuse, violence, and teenage pregnancies. More direct work with parents through community family centers will be attempted to allow for earlier interventions and more comprehensive interventions in preparing children for schooling. Child day care and adult education programs will involve support personnel including counselors, psychologists, social workers, nurses, and physician assistants.

In an attempt to expend more dollars on academic instruction, we will likely see a trend, furthered by politicians, to purchase support services from private practitioners in order to reduce long-term costs of retirement pensions and health care insurance. For example, Dykeman (1995) surveyed 253 school district superintendents in Washington state and found that 20% of all counseling in state public schools was contracted to outside providers. Respondents indicated that the present level of privatization would remain steady over the next five years. In the case of both present and projected levels, small districts rely significantly more on contracted services than medium or large districts do. If this strategy prevails, support personnel will likely require a license in their specialty in order to practice in the schools. Social workers may become the primary support personnel left in the schools to provide liaison with governmental human resource agencies.

Multiple education and community service models are likely to emerge in the next 20 years as we search for preferred model(s), a scenario that is already developing. These next 20 years could be a transitional period during which many different options are tried until the more effective models emerge. The most radical experimental models will be found in the public school sector where most of the problems lie. It is not unlikely that the roles of support personnel in the private school sector will remain least changed because the school models will likely retain most of the characteristics of our traditional schools.

Home schooling continues to increase in popularity and this may accelerate as distance learning technology is perfected. The private support personnel contracted by the school system may be employed to assist this growing group of students.

Although multicultural issues have not been singled out thus far, socially and politically they will increase in their effects on schooling. More of the academic curricula and the life and social skills curricula will be devoted to these issues. Support personnel will receive more and more training in understanding and dealing with multicultural-related issues and problems. Bilingual support personnel will be in great demand.

With increasing application of the charter school concept and site-based managed schools, and more opportunity for experimenting with different school models, there is less control over curriculum, school staffing, and so forth, and therefore we are likely to see less regulation of schools and personnel by state and regional accrediting associations. This projected lessening of "standards" could affect the number and quality of support personnel in the schools. If private contracting of support personnel develops, required licensure could potentially ensure quality but not necessarily quantity of support personnel.

Conclusion

I have championed radical changes in the organization and administration of the schools in the United States for the past 15 years. I have encountered intense resistance from virtually all segments of the educational and political arenas, and from parents themselves. It seems that very few are satisfied with the current status of public education, but few are willing to do more than make minor adjustments to a system that long ago outlived its usefulness.

Even as huge sums of money are expended on the public school system, it continues to decline in effectiveness. This condition will only get worse until radical changes outlined in the first part of this chapter are instituted. My experience suggests that it will take 10 to 20 years before the current system reaches its lowest level. In the meantime, a transition period of experimentation with modified school models will occur.

The transition period of the next 20 years will be characterized by multiple roles and models for school support personnel. Their roles in the private schools will not change radically because the system will not change radically inasmuch as the students in private schools will continue to succeed in a traditional school model. Technology, however, will introduce some rather radical changes. More learning and instruction will be enhanced technologically, which will likely lead to more self-instruction.

In the public school system, the suburban schools will resemble the private schools, but the inner city schools will resemble detention centers. Support personnel will be needed to "maintain order" (i.e., to police) and to work for minimal achievement goals, especially of socialization. More medically trained personnel such as physician assistants and nurse practitioners will be required to help manage drug-induced problems and sexually active behavior and its attendant problems of sexually transmitted disease and pregnancy. At the high school levels, counselors will function more like current rehabilitation counselors who work with those with disabilities to help them become employed. Social workers will likely continue to work as liaisons with the students and parents and governmental agencies.

One can only conjecture as to whether the support personnel will be a part of the school staff, work through an agency such as a family center, or be contracted privately. As indicated earlier, schools may very well follow the HMO and PPO models of health care delivery and contract with private practitioners. If they do, counselors, social workers, school psychologists, and nurses may form HMOs and PPOs or become a part of current physician-dominated HMOs and PPOs.

Even though greater effort and political interventions will continue to be made to try to improve the stability and quality of family life, schools or school-related agencies such as family centers will continue to assume roles heretofore assumed by parents. It is quite possible that at some point the state or federal government will pay a parent to stay at home with preschool children (not unlike welfare) rather than seek employment outside the home. In any case, all school support personnel will receive more and more training in working with parents and families and spend more and more of their time in this area.

References

Dykeman, C. (1995). The privatization of school counseling. *School Counselor, 43*(1), 29–34.

Evans, T. D., Corsini, R. J., & Gazda, G. M. (1990, September). Individual Education and the 4 Rs. *Educational Leadership,* 52–56.

Firestone, W. A., & Bader, B. D. (1991). Restructuring teaching: An assessment of frequently considered options. *Educational Policy, 5*(2), 119–136.

Gazda, G. M. (1998). What is really wrong with American education and what to do about it. *The Torch, 71*(3), 11–13ff.

Gazda, G. M., Asbury, F. R., Balzer, F. J., Childers, W. C., Phelps, R. E., & Walters, R. P. (1998). *Human relations development: A manual for educators* (6th ed.). Boston: Allyn & Bacon.

The Georgia Partnership for Excellence in Education (1993). *The next generation school project.* (Available from The Georgia Partnership for Excellence in Education, 233 Peachtree Street, Atlanta, GA 30303).

Koppich, J. E., Brown, P., & Amsler, M. (1990). *Redefining teacher work roles: Prospects and possibilities* (Policy Briefs No. 13). San Francisco, CA: Far West Laboratory for Educational Research and Development. (ERIC Document Reproduction No. ED 326 930)

Peeler, T. H. (1992). *A public-private partnership: South Pointe Elementary School*. (Available from Southeastern Regional Vision for Education, 345 South Magnolia Drive, Suite D-23, Tallahassee, FL 32301-2950)

About the Author

George M. Gazda received his doctorate from the University of Illinois with a major in counseling. Since 1963, he has been associate professor, professor and research professor in the Department of Counseling and Human Development Services, the University of Georgia. Since 1967 he has concurrently held the positions of consulting and now clinical professor in the Department of Psychiatry, Medical College of Georgia. He was associate dean for research, College of Education, the University of Georgia, from 1984 to 1994, when he retired.

Dr. Gazda has been president of the Association of Counselor Education and Supervision, Association for Specialists in Group Work (which he co-founded), American Personnel and Guidance Association (now American Counseling Association), and Division 17 (Counseling Psychology) of the American Psychological Association. Dr. Gazda is a Fellow of the American Psychological Association and the American Society of Group Psychotherapy and Psychodrama. He is a certified trainer of Psychodrama and a licensed psychologist in Georgia. The author, co-author, or editor of 6 books and more than 100 chapters, manuals, articles, and monographs in the professional literature, Dr. Gazda has consulted with numerous organizations and universities both nationally and internationally.

Chapter Twelve

School Counselors Center on Academic Achievement

Charles Hanson

Academic support has long been accepted as a major, if not primary, role of school counselors. Whether mandated by state law or district or school policy, counselors serve in schools to support the learning and academic development of students. Who disputes this? School counselors have accepted this fundamental tenet of school counseling for so long that they no longer question what it means. Of course counselors provide academic support, but how do they do that? The tradition in training school counselors has seen the academic support role served through ancillary functions, such as personal and social counseling, academic advising and programming, and career development. The practice of school counseling further cements these functions as the primary vehicles for academic support. Not only have these roles been fixed in the minds of counselors and school administrators, but teachers, parents, and students themselves view counselors in accordance with these roles.

Traditional roles will not be enough for school counselors in the twenty-first century. Future school counselors will know they cannot meet all of the personal and social needs of students in schools. They will also know that such counseling alone will not make students effective learners. While a child with a troubled mind may struggle to learn, counselors have for too long focused on settling the troubled mind as their first, and often only, level of intervention. The result has been to neglect looking at what it takes for such a child to be successful in school, to learn, and to achieve. Future school counselors will more fully define academic support in terms of building and providing programs and interventions that will directly engage the learning needs of children. School counselors must focus the outcome of their work toward this end if they are to make a difference for children in promoting the academic mission of schools. They must expand their understanding of what academic support means. School counselors and counselor educators must challenge themselves to examine the outcome of all their work in terms of learning and academic outcomes.

Building the School as a Learning Community

How do our schools function as learning communities? Does the school place high value on the learning and success of all students? How do we know? Do teachers, students, administrators, counselors, parents, and community members perceive the school as a place where learning is valued and where success is supported and achieved? Is the school an exciting place to be because learning is the focus? Or is the school seen primarily as a place where teachers and administrators do their job and keep the plant operating, a place where children perform their obligations with lackadaisical interest and slumbering motivation?

These questions and others that focus on how the school functions and is perceived as a learning community will be a critical focus for future school counselors who seek to make academic support the primary target of their work. While school principals and other administrators should have a working concern about the school as a learning community, this is an area of focus for which school counselors are particularly suited. Background and training in systems level thinking, from family systems to school systems, gives the school counselor a base for viewing the school as a working, dynamic system. Counselors potentially have continual contact with all stakeholders in the school, including students, teachers, administrators, parents, and community members. If children are not learning because a teacher is struggling, the school counselor will know. If a child is not learning because of family or personal problems, the counselor is likely to know. If all children are not learning and succeeding at high levels, counselors will know why. Given their perspective on students, families, and the whole school, counselors are well equipped to examine how the school operates as a system and as a learning community. Such examination enables school counselors to bring attention to areas of individual and group need that call for attention and support.

The school counselor of the future will address the school as a learning community through periodic assessments of the learning climate at the school. Such assessments will explore the perceived success of all school stakeholders in promoting learning and achievement. School counselors will use achievement data to shape the outline of the school as a learning community. Survey data will identify the supports students need to become successful learners. Data will also clarify what teachers need in order to assist students to become successful. What supports exist for students beyond classroom instruction? What supports may be needed? Are these addressing the needs of students in a way that is increasing learning and achievement? What supports exist for teachers to assist them in successfully teaching all students in their classrooms? What supports do they need? How do parents perceive the school, and what supports do they need to help their children learn and succeed? How does the school staff address these needs? Future school counselors will not only ask these questions and document their findings, but they will work with teams of teachers, parents, school administrators, and community members to develop programs that fulfill school stakeholder needs, increase student achievement, and positively affect the school as a learning community.

School counselors of the future will further serve as the academic conscience of the school. They will raise the consciousness of school stakeholders about learning and achievement. They will raise the consciousness of the school about what is working and what is not. They will help all stakeholders in the school examine their beliefs about learning and achievement and how these beliefs affect performance. For example, if school staff considers parental support critical to student success, then counselors will work to increase parents' involvement in their children's learning. When parents cannot fill this need, future school counselors will know what educationally supportive parents do for their children and help organize the same supports for children who need them. Counselors of the future will no longer find it acceptable to blame parents or students for inadequate learning or achievement. As advocates for student learning, as messengers of the consciousness of the school as a learning community, they will work to make sure every student learns and achieves success.

Learning Supports

Twenty-first-century counselors will come to schools prepared to organize and implement an array of learning support programs. A major focus for program development at all grade levels will be the teaching of learning and study skills, or the processes and skills that students can employ to learn independently and in classrooms. These skills are neglected in the regular curriculum. Teachers typically instruct students in the content or subject matter to be learned. Specific knowledge is conveyed to students through various teaching and learning methods, and they are expected to follow up on their own, completing homework, writing reports, and studying for tests. Strong students are often those who enter schools with given talents and abilities. These include strong motivation and interest, organizational ability, good memory skills, self-discipline, and self-initiated study skills. These attributes often determine those students who are successful at academic work and those who are not. Although we know these qualities and skills can be critical to learning success, instruction in these areas is neglected. Counselors of the future will not only recognize the need to instruct students in how to learn, but they will consider themselves key members of the school instructional support team to deliver this instruction.

A number of specific qualities and skills are the building blocks to successful learning. These include motivation and interest; goal setting; study organization and climate; time management and task analysis; memory and listening skills; note taking; test taking; strategies, such as cognitive mapping for textbook readings, and writing papers and reports; and knowledge of learning styles and modalities. The following brief overview of these areas will highlight what school counselors can do to support the academic development and achievement of students.

Motivation and Interest

Student motivation and interest form a foundation for all learning. These qualities can be increased through instruction and learning. School counselors are knowledgeable about the relationship between school and work. Their knowledge of career development and the world of work will be valued as a means for increasing student interest and motivation in learning. Students who hold a vision for their future, knowledge of their strengths and attributes, and awareness of their values and interests are already known to be successful in school. Helping students to form a vision of their future and connecting these visions to education and learning is critical. For some, this comes naturally. Others will need to be instructed. Future school counselors will see such instruction as central to their role and the mission of guidance and counseling. Their knowledge of career development programs will enable them to assist students in developing personal dreams and aspirations, and in learning about their interests, values, and personal qualities in relation to the world of work. Future school counselors will insist that this work be started in the elementary grades and refined through secondary schooling.

Goal Setting

Most children know little about goal setting, and most receive no instruction in how to do it. Although it is known that without goals, one seldom accomplishes anything, instruction and guidance in goal setting is typically absent in schooling. Counselors for the new millennium will develop instructional programs to teach this skill. Students will learn to develop goals for classroom and independent learning and receive the assistance of counselors in accomplishing their goals. Long-term goals will be tied to short-term goals, and counselors will assist students in setting goals that are attainable. Successful goal attainment in academic work furthers student motivation in learning. Self-monitoring, evaluation, and goal modification will be part of the package for becoming effective at goal setting and accomplishment.

Learning Environments

Many children, as well as their parents, know nothing about setting up an environment in their homes or communities that is conducive to successful study and learning. They need to be taught how to create an environment in the home that is free from distractions and interruptions, that has good lighting and space for writing, and that supports preferred learning modalities. Many families, particularly poor families, cannot organize such an environment in their homes due to overcrowding, the absence of sufficient furniture, or the inability to eliminate distractions. These children and families need assistance in creating study space in their communities—in libraries, at friends' or other family members' homes, in apartment building rooms, at recreational centers, in churches and temples, or at school. Such instruction appears simple, but it is often lacking. Perhaps the very simplicity of informing students and parents about study environments leads educators to neglect to talk about it. Counselors in the new millennium won't underestimate the need for such instruction. They will provide it. They will also work to ensure that students set up and use the environments they need. They will discuss successful locations with students, request follow-through with notes from parents, talk with peer study groups, and check the work students do until they achieve mastery of this basic skill and need.

Time Management and Task Analysis

Time management and task analysis are skills successful students must master. Few students are taught these skills, and if taught, few master them. Time management involves planning time for doing homework, working on reports and projects, and studying—and then following through on one's plans. Mastery of this skill requires students to reward themselves for task accomplishment along the way or when projects are completed.

For many students, time management is new information. It seems that educators presume students know how to manage time without any instruction, so it is seldom taught as part of regular classroom instruction. It is not surprising, then, that when students learn about time management, they recognize that they can do it—organize their time and accomplish the work they set out to do—and wish they knew this skill much earlier in their educational program.

Future school counselors will recognize the importance of students learning to manage their time and will teach them how to do so. Tied to time management is task analysis. Reading chapters, doing homework, and writing reports and papers are tasks that typically can be broken down into several component parts. Teaching students to break such tasks into their components and organize them on a time line helps them see their work in doable chunks rather than becoming overwhelmed. Students need instruction in using calendars for organizing their work, assistance in breaking down tasks, and support in working according to plans. They need direction and support in learning to organize their tasks and put them on a calendar time line. Counselors will further know that mastery of time management requires classroom work and follow-through. Students do not learn these skills in one sitting or merely through instruction. To help students master time management and connect it to classroom work, counselors will work with teachers to integrate time management and task analysis into teachers' course content and instruction. As further support, school counselors will organize academic support classes to provide follow-through instruction and support for making sure students master the time management and organizational steps they need to be successful.

Many educators hold the idea that intelligence and learning capability are innate. You either have it or you don't. You're either capable of academic success or you're not. Counselors in the new millennium will hold strongly to the position that learning capability can be increased and all children can learn. Because of this position, counselors will be knowledgeable about teaching strategies and techniques for increasing learning power. Critical areas for teaching and training include listening skills, cognitive mapping, note taking, reading, and textbook study strategies.

Listening Skills

Most instruction involves a teacher speaking to a classroom of students. The assumption is often made that when the teacher speaks, the students always listen. Or students can, at the very least, listen if they so choose. In the majority of schools, however, little attention is given to what students can do to become good listeners. This is surprising given that good listening can be taught. The student as listener can develop through instruction. School counselors in the new millennium will know how to conduct such instruction and train educators in how to teach it.

Active listening may come naturally to a small number of students, but most will need active instruction in this area to optimize their comprehension and retention of what they hear. Active listening involves visualizing the information that is presented. Some students do this naturally. If you read a passage or story to a group or class, you can ask students who among them created pictures in their minds while you were reading. You will likely find few students do this without instruction. Most need guidance. Students can increase their learning and memory through practice of visualizing while listening. Such practice can involve having students look at an individual object (e.g., an apple), removing the object from sight while they visualize it, and then checking how well their visualization matched the object. Students will need repeated practice at this skill to become adept and facile with it. Visualizing can then move to creating larger images of pictures, charts, maps, or other more complex objects. When visualizing more complex information, students should be guided to zoom in on details, to imagine the smaller parts, and then to put these together in more comprehensive visualizations. Again, this skill requires repeated practice for students to master. But master it they will, if given the opportunity to practice.

Following successful visualization of complex pictures, students should be guided in creating movies in the mind from spoken information. To facilitate this, school counselors and other educators can read a single sentence or paragraph and then ask questions that help students to visualize it. Examples from a social studies lesson might be

- What does the pharaoh look like?
- What is he wearing?
- Whom is he addressing?
- What do they look like?
- What does the setting look like?
- What is his tone of voice like?
- How are people responding?

Students may need to actually draw pictures of their visualizations before being able to answer comprehensive questions.

The detail given for active listening illustrates how basic skills for listening need to be taught. Only after students have mastered these basic skills can they be expected to learn more complex listening skills such as listening for topics, main ideas, and supporting details. Such complex listening skills will require further instruction, practice, feedback, and review.

One final listening skill involves teaching students to ask questions to clarify their understanding of information. Typically, students are not instructed in how to ask questions, so most don't ask them. However, asking questions is a good technique that aids learning. It also lets teachers know that a student is listening. Knowing how important this skill is to learning, school counselors can provide direction and support for asking questions, respond with appropriate rewards for asking questions, and expect all students to be able to demonstrate their ability to ask questions. Again, students need direct instruction in this skill, opportunity to practice the skill with guidance and support, and periodic review, practice, prompts, and evaluation of mastery to become competent learners. Subject matter here is not the focus. Listening skills can be taught in any subject area and need to be taught in all areas to be fully developed. Counselors in the new millennium will recognize this gap in teaching and learning and organize efforts to fill it.

Note-Taking Skills

Note taking is another one of those essential skills for learning that is seldom, if ever, taught. Students are expected to take notes from lectures, textbooks, information written on the chalkboard, research references, magazines and journals, encyclopedias, and perhaps even interviews and group meetings. Note taking is so basic that few educators would question it as a learning tool. Basic though note taking may be, it is generally not a focus of instruction and learning. As new millennium counselors become aware of this gap between expectation and practice, they will organize efforts to teach students to take notes.

Particularly important here is the organization of notes for later review and study. Cornell note taking has become the standard for taking notes from classroom lectures. This method organizes notes into a two-column format on regular-size lined paper. One larger column (two-thirds of the right side of the page) is used for writing notes on what is presented or read. Another smaller column on the left side of the paper, termed the recall column, is used for writing key words, phrases, and questions related to those notes. Once notes have been compiled, students organize their learning through the recall column. They challenge themselves in learning by being able to answer questions and define terms they write in the recall column related to the notes they have written. Folding the notepaper between columns to hide the answers aids in identifying what is known and what is not and needs to be learned.

Another aspect of note taking involves learning to write short notes rather than word for word notes. Writing key words and acronyms, and using shorthand notation and other methods for keeping brief notes, are important skills to learn. Students need to learn these skills when taking notes from written material such as library resources, textbooks, and even the Internet. To establish competence in note taking, students must be not only instructed, but also given opportunity to practice the skill both in and outside the classroom. They then need opportunities to receive feedback on their performance and practice the skill until they achieve mastery. All students can do this. Some, however, will take more time and practice than others. Counselors will recognize that learning mastery in note-taking skills is basic to success in school, and they will organize programs to ensure all students learn to do it well.

Test-Taking Skills

With the increasing emphasis on assessment and testing to demonstrate learning outcomes, students will benefit from guidance and instruction in how to prepare for and engage in a variety of tests. Many students—unfortunately many poor and minority students—have never learned how to study for and take tests. With the absence of encouragement and yet expectation for high performance, many students approach testing lackadaisically. They give what they get. Lacking knowledge about how to study for tests, how to approach questions, how to identify best answers, and how to organize a written response, students don't know how to do well on tests, and they form perceptions of themselves as inadequate and incapable of testing success. They learn to live down or up to the expectations they are given. Future counselors will understand this systemic relationship between expectations and student self-perception. They will also know that students can learn how to improve their performance on tests and demonstrate high levels of testing success.

Future school counselors will be prepared to teach and organize programs for developing test-taking skills. Test-taking skills will encompass the following: methods for studying and preparing for multiple-choice, short answer, and essay tests; understanding test instructions; strategies for identifying correct responses on multiple-choice exams; steps in writing essays; guided imagery for successful test performance; relaxation and anxiety-control strategies; positive self-talk; strategies for handling uncertainty and confusion; post-test actions; and analyzing test performance. Counselors will work with teachers and parents to support student test-taking skills. Knowing that success increases expectations and improves performance, future counselors will support teachers in developing student mastery of test taking.

Cognitive Mapping

One very useful tool for learning is cognitive mapping. Known by various names, such as brain mapping and web diagrams, cognitive mapping exercises the learner's visual, spatial, and kinesthetic modalities. The cognitive map is a spatial representation of a subject drawn with symbols, words, and colors. The map provides an overall picture of the subject and graphically shows the relationship of the parts to the whole. Cognitive maps give the learner an opportunity to conceptualize subject matter differently through the use of visual and spatial cues that invite imagination and creativity.

To create a cognitive map, a title or subject is written in the center of a piece of paper and enclosed in a circle, square, or preferably something related to the topic (e.g., outline of a leaf when studying plants). Each main heading or subtopic should be added as a branch emanating from the central topic or as symbols, pictures, or other geometric forms in the corners and along the sides of the paper. The branches, symbols, or pictures are labeled with the words of the subtopic or heading. Large or uppercase letters can be used to emphasize subtopics. Supporting details are then added to each main branch, symbol, or picture and labeled in lowercase or small letters. Small pictures and symbols can be added next to the words. Subtopics and detail can be drawn and labeled in different colors to enhance differentiation. The use of colors in cognitive maps is a terrific aid to learning and memory.

Each cognitive map the learner makes will be personal and unique, enhancing learning and memory. This type of spatial activity and the learning it generates can often be effective with students who struggle with the linear presentation of text and lectures. Also, for children who grow up with a primary language other than English, the use of cognitive maps can enable them to learn effectively in spite of language deficiencies. Cognitive maps actually increase the knowledge and use of language for those students who are learning second languages. The creativity and individuality that cognitive maps encourage enhance learning of the subject matter contained in the maps.

Cognitive mapping has several uses. A map can be made to provide a summary of information after taking class lecture notes. A map can also be made while previewing a textbook chapter to provide the reader with a framework or overview of the subject matter covered. During active reading of a chapter or article, a map can be used to record detailed information and ideas. A cognitive map can further provide an organized structure for written essays and reports. Students first draw a map of their ideas, then write about what is in their drawing.

Cognitive maps provide excellent study tools for exam preparation. Typically, students study by memorizing lists of information. This type of studying is inefficient and sometimes ineffective. Learning and memory are enhanced when students are assisted in understanding the relationship of detailed information to larger concepts. Cognitive mapping provides such relational learning tools.

Counselors can teach cognitive mapping to students as a part of their academic support program. Encouraging teachers to employ cognitive maps as part of their instruction can transfer this skill to many students while enhancing teaching effectiveness and improving learning gains. Students who are often the least successful in school, who have struggled with repeated low grades and failure, can achieve significant learning of subject matter by mastering the technique of drawing cognitive maps.

Learning Modalities

Recent research on learning modalities has illuminated understanding that learning occurs through various perceptual and experiential (physical) channels and can be strengthened by instruction that engages multiple channels. Instruction in learning modalities enables learners who have preference for or dominance in a particular learning modality to gain instruction in that mode, thereby maximizing their learning potential. The use of a multiplicity of learning approaches also increases learning for each individual student by helping him or her engage various learning modalities. The more ways in which information and ideas are communicated and reviewed, the greater the likelihood that they will be remembered and understood.

School counselors of the future will support student learning by teaching students about learning modalities and helping them identify their strong and weak learning channels. School counselors will also instruct students in strategies for engaging various learning modalities both within and outside the classroom. The goal here is to inform students so they can take responsibility for their learning. Equipped with the knowledge of how they best learn, students can increase their learning potential. With such knowledge, students will be more motivated to invest in the learning process and will accordingly raise their own expectations of success.

The main learning modalities are visual, auditory, and kinesthetic. Visual modalities include both pictures and words. Auditory channels include hearing the spoken word as well as reviewing learned information through words and sounds. The kinesthetic mode emphasizes physical movement. School counselors can help students learn by instructing and guiding them to use each learning modality. To gain mastery in the visual modality, students can create pictures, symbols, graphs, or outlines while they read or listen to lectures. The auditory channel can be employed through reading out loud, reciting information, and repeating the concepts and ideas one has learned. The kinesthetic modality can be engaged in such activities as role-playing, drama, running, touching, writing, and drawing.

It is an unfortunate fact that information about learning modalities and preferences is typically given to teachers, but not to students or their parents. Future school counselors will fill this gap by informing students and parents about learning modalities throughout their educational experience and by guiding students to engage all modalities in the classroom and in independent study. School counselors can also help students determine which modality is most effective for their learning and assist them in applying that modality to all subject areas.

Other Learning Support Programs

Teaching students how to learn will become a vital part of the academic support that school counselors will provide in the new millennium. School counselors will also design and implement other interventions and programs that directly affect student learning and achievement. Following are some academic support programs school counselors have initiated and should continue to initiate in the future.

Motivational Speakers

The familiarity school counselors have with the community surrounding the school enables them to bring successful community members into the school to talk about their careers and the importance of learning and education. Included in the list of resources school counselors can bring to students are politicians, civic leaders, successful business owners and managers, members of community-based organizations, college and university faculty and administration, law enforcement personnel, athletes, entrepreneurs, entertainers, medical service providers, and others.

Peer Helping Programs

Future school counselors will build student resources within the school to help students learn and achieve. Many students naturally like to help others. Organizing and training groups of students to be peer helpers has demonstrated positive outcomes for the peer helpers and those they serve. Peer helpers can be engaged as tutors for younger students and for students needing academic support. Peer helpers can also organize study groups before and after school. Some groups may organize in the school, others in the community.

Teacher Support Programs

Student learning, school success, and high academic achievement require high quality teaching. Recognizing this fact, future school counselors will work directly with teachers to support learning and improve teacher effectiveness in the classroom. The accelerating need for more quality teachers and the high percentage of relatively inexperienced teachers in classrooms will lead future counselors to develop this role. Supporting teacher improvement is a role many school counselors neglect. Some have little or no teaching experience and exclude themselves on this basis. What can they teach teachers if they haven't been there themselves? What teacher will listen to what a counselor has to say if that counselor has not already experienced and mastered the teaching job? Although teaching experience and expertise places the school counselor in a position to obtain credibility for working with teachers, such accomplishments are not necessary for working effectively with teachers to support and further their teaching effectiveness. Future counselors will have expertise they can bring to further excellence in teaching and learning—expertise that is not necessarily classroom based.

Counselors in the new millennium will employ their organization and team-building skills to organize small groups of teachers around the topic of improving teaching. Future school counselors will be adept at facilitating teachers talking to each other, sharing ideas and activities, and supporting creativity and teaching success. They won't avoid working with teachers, but rather will see their role as organizational and facilitative. They will pair veteran and novice teachers to provide support for new teachers. And they will work with expert teachers to organize in-service programs aimed at teaching excellence and mutual teacher support.

Weekend Schools

Future school counselors will organize after-school and weekend-school programs to support students who need additional academic support. Involving parents in weekend schools can be effective in teaching them how to help their children as well as provide a venue for parent education in a range of needed subjects (e.g., English as a second language, the use of computers, parenting skills, accessing community supports, career development and advisement, and so forth). School counselors will also organize medical and dental services to families through weekend schools.

After-School Homework and Tutoring Programs

School counselors with a new vision for school counseling will see their ability to organize homework support and tutoring programs as a major academic support activity. They will engage religious leaders and institutions, community-based organizations, school staff members, and others in helping students learn.

The Counselor as Advocate

School counselors in the new millennium will be advocates for all students to receive a challenging and high quality education. Educational equity will guide their efforts to organize the supports students need to be effective and successful learners. Their view of the school as a whole and knowledge of student progress over time, with different teachers and various courses, make them uniquely suited to see where the teaching and learning system may be weak or ineffectual and where change or additional supports are needed. This view is bolstered by counselors' knowledge of and involvement with the assessment and testing programs employed by schools to evaluate learning. Future school counselors will understand how to use data on individual students, classrooms, groups of students, and the school as a whole to highlight inequities and weaknesses and build teams of teachers and other school personnel to eliminate them.

Future school counselors will see that their role as advocates for student learning and achievement permeates all that they do. Students with a need for counseling and support regarding personal, emotional, and social issues will be provided services, with part of the accountability assessment for such services addressing learning and achievement gains. Career development interventions will also be examined with learning gains in mind. Guidance education and prevention programs will also contain an evaluative focus on learning and achievement. Future school counselors will further develop programs, such as teaching learning skills, that directly affect the success and achievement of students. The future of school counseling will lie in the ability of school counselors to have a strong, positive influence on the primary mission of schools—to help students learn.

About the Author

Charles Hanson completed graduate work in clinical and community psychology at UCLA in 1979. He is currently professor of counseling in the Department of Educational Psychology and Counseling at California State University, Northridge, in Los Angeles, California (CSUN). Dr. Hanson has been an elementary school teacher in the Los Angeles inner city. He is currently CSUN Project Director for the Initiative to Transform School Counseling. Supported by the Wallace/ Reader's Digest Fund, the initiative supports programs at six universities throughout the nation in working collaboratively with local school districts to reform the preparation of school counselors with the goal of closing the achievement gap between children of minority or low SES background and more affluent, non minority peers. Dr. Hanson is also active in community counseling as clinical supervisor and chairman of the board for the Valley Trauma Center, a rape crisis, sexual assault treatment and violence prevention program.

Section 5:

Preparing Student Support Professionals

Chapter Thirteen

Changing School Counselor Preparation: A Critical Need

Reese M. House, Patricia J. Martin & Colin C. Ward

In this chapter we propose a new approach to counselor education as a means of preparing school counselors to work in twenty-first-century schools. It is critical that school counselors move beyond their current roles as helper-responders in order to become proactive leaders and advocates for the success of all students in schools. When school counselors work in this fashion, they become an integral part of schools and educational reform. This vision places school counselors in the essential role of examining and questioning inequitable practices that do not serve the interests of all students.

We believe that school counselors must be taught to question the beliefs, assumptions, and values behind inequitable school policies, structures, or actions. This process of learning how to question needs to start in counselor preparation programs. This can be done in counselor preparation by emphasizing the value of experience, promoting active learning, engaging in reflective practice, and inviting dialogue among students and faculty. Such themes can guide program development, classroom exchanges, field experiences, interactions with colleagues, and collaboration with community members. Through these processes, school counselors are taught to take stands against injustices and join counselor educators and community stakeholders in thoughtfully constructing a blueprint for student success.

In this chapter we describe how counselor educators might prepare school counselors to become action-oriented critical thinkers. We also encourage the creation of learning communities among counselors-in-training and the schools, students, families, and communities that they ultimately will serve. We hope students who internalize and use the skills gained from this teaching will become professionals who embrace change, continually reflect on practice, and constantly seek to make schools better.

Rationale for Changes in School Counseling

Throughout the nation, communities are striving to improve their schools. To date, major American school reform efforts have focused on accountability for student performance by setting more rigorous academic standards, building new assessment strategies, and restructuring pre-service and in-service experiences for teachers and administrators (Mohrman & Lawler, 1996). In the United States, two primary events have fueled these efforts: (a) the unrelenting call for accountability for educating all students to higher academic standards, and (b) the economic demand for a more knowledgeable workforce. Concurrent with demands for accountability, reform is driven by awareness that the student population has become more diverse and now includes increased numbers of poor and minority children living in urban and rural communities. Data from states and local school districts show that poor students and students of color are systemically denied an education that would lead them to success in school and in the marketplace (Achievement in America, 2000). These data point out a significant achievement gap between poor and minority students and their more advantaged peers (Haycock, 1998).

The Achievement Gap

Educational equity in a democratic society requires that all children have equal access to quality education. Data collected on student achievement in America show that, except for a few schools, poor and minority students do not perform as well on any existing measures of academic proficiency as do middle- and upper-class White students (Achievement in America, 2000). Many poor and minority children do not obtain the skills and knowledge necessary to participate successfully in the twenty-first-century economy. This achievement gap has become the driving force for recent education reform efforts.

The achievement gap among students exists primarily because educators (a) expect less of minority and low-income children; (b) provide some students (usually White and middle class) with a rigorous, high quality curriculum and others with a watered-down, weak curriculum; and (c) provide fewer material resources to students who have the greatest need (Achievement in America, 2000). The need to raise academic achievement in our poorer schools is paramount, and is eloquently expressed by an African American high school senior:

> We are not only given the short end of the stick in terms of facilities and resources; but inner-city students aren't expected to excel. We are sometimes granted honors for completing only part of a task, while students in more affluent areas are expected to do more to get the same recognition. We are pitied by outsiders who sometimes try to "help" by giving us undeserved praise. Thus, we often don't expect much more of our own selves. We aren't pushed hard enough. We are babied by our teachers for too long. (Swasey, 1996–1997, p. 25)

School Counselors and Reform

The importance of educational reform is clear to us. Our global society is increasingly dependent on the development and better use of all our human resources. As Elam (1993) stated, High-level thinking, lifelong learning, and the capacity to make frequent career changes will be required in an increasingly competitive, high-tech, knowledge-driven, worldwide economy" (p. 276). Not addressing the need for educational change and continuing to foster low expectations and inadequate academic preparation for poor and minority students is paramount to benign neglect. Thus, school counselors support this neglect when they intentionally or inadvertently become part of the system that relegates large numbers of students to limited career options, virtually closing doors on their futures.

We believe that school counselors must be central players in reconstructing the system through leadership and advocacy. Yet, to date, education reformers have paid little or no attention to the key roles school counselors play in promoting the academic success of all students. School counselors, who have long been the keepers of records, have the opportunity to examine data about what is happening to students in schools; to engage in dialogue with teachers, administrators, parents, and community members to tackle these issues; and to develop strategies to change these debilitating patterns.

Current Forces Shaping School Counseling

Why don't most school counselors involve themselves in educational reform efforts and actively work to promote academic success for all students? The answer to this question is complex. Current school counselor behavior results from pre-service training, conflicting roles, strong administrative prescriptions, pliable and overly accommodating counselor behavior, limited professional development opportunities, and overt and covert pressures from school, community, and parental special interest groups (Walz, 1997).

Most importantly, when school counselors lack a strong personal and professional compass—their own well-conceived vision or mission, defined programs, and identified roles—they function at the direction of others. School administrators, parents with special interests, teachers, and others often insist that school counselors adopt their agendas (American School Counselor Association [ASCA], 1998).

Unfortunately, this means that school counselors often serve as maintainers of the status quo, advocating for the school system rather than for students and marginalized groups. They become "sorters and selectors," perpetuating the accepted placements and systemic barriers that cause an inequitable distribution between achievers and non-achievers based on race and socioeconomic status (Hart & Jacobi, 1992).

School Counselor Preparation Programs:
Current Status

Another major factor influencing school counseling is that, for the most part, traditional counselor education programs have not provided learning opportunities that prepare school counselors to be knowledgeable about education reform issues or how to be vital players in implementing reform strategies in schools. School counselors have not been taught about social and systems change, political climates, and power structures of schools and communities. Trainees have not been taught elements of leadership and collaboration that would enable them to instigate or facilitate effective systemic change. For the most part, counselor educators have not designed their curricula to teach advocacy, question the status quo, and challenge systems

(Capuzzi, 1998; The Education Trust, 1997).

Instead, school counselor preparation programs have moved more and more toward a mental health model, one that favors one-to-one counseling over educational, group, or institutional change practices (Collison et al., 1998). Large portions of counselor education curricula for pre-service school counselors focus on clinical practice. Yet clinical practice in schools frequently conflicts with the mission of schooling and the needs and priorities of teachers and administrators.

Clearly, some school-age students need mental health services. However, such a mental health model, based on a closed and confidential relationship between counselor and student rather than on a systemic approach to improving learning, creates a climate of mistrust between counselors and teachers. Teachers frequently comment: "What is the counselor doing behind closed doors with that student?" or "Jane is not doing any better in my class and you have been seeing her for six months. What is going on?" Such questions reflect the isolation promoted by a mental health model. Instead, school counselors need a model that emphasizes collaboration with teachers and administrators in order to minimize such mistrust and to be more effective on a larger population.

Schools have never been structured or staffed with low enough counselor-client ratios to allow school counselors to be effective mental health providers. Currently, the student-to-counselor ratio in the United States is 513 to 1 (American Counseling Association [ACA], 1999). With this ratio, school counselors find it impossible to provide effective mental health services concurrently with performing the many tasks vital to the operation of schools. Even when tasks performed by counselors are appropriate, and exclude the many clerical and administrative duties often assigned to school counselors, they are unable to serve effectively as mental health providers. Therefore, school counselors frequently experience dissonance between the mental health training they received and the work they actually do in schools (Walz, 1997).

Despite the revolutionary changes in K–12 education, counselor education seems to be maintaining the status quo. Bradley (1997) stated that "maintaining the status quo seems to be the mode of operation in higher education" (p. 30), and serves to neutralize both internal and external forces proposing change. Much time and energy is spent reacting to external pressures, such as state certification requirements and accreditation bodies, as well as currently publicized social issues such as violence, suicide, drugs, gangs, and so forth. To change, counselor educators need to move beyond this reactive approach and move to a proactive approach that addresses systems change.

Social-Critical Thinking and Systems Change

Education systems can either discourage or empower students to critically question systemic inconsistencies (Darder, 1991). Educational systems that discourage students perpetuate the creation of obedient, moldable, passive, and low-paid future workers incapable of changing systems. On the other hand, educational systems that empower students educate them to become critical, involved citizens (McLaren, 1989). In our proposal to change school counseling, we assume that school counselors can make a difference in promoting academic success if they first develop a broad social consciousness and a critical awareness of conditions in society and schools that impinge upon that success (Southers, 1991).

When counselor educators promote systemic change through critical inquiry, they empower counselors themselves to be leaders and change agents in society (Darling-Hammond, 1993). From this perspective, we as counseling professionals need to influence the social, cultural, and political dynamics that undergird academic success. Advocating for high achievement for all students is proposed here as a key role for counselors. It places them at the center of the mission of schooling and education reform.

The culture-centered training curriculum developed by Pedersen and Ivey (1993) provides a basis for focusing on these systemic issues. It emphasizes the incorporation of cultural worldviews in counseling training, utilizing the triad of counseling, consultation, and case-management strategies. This curriculum asks counselors-in-training to reflect on questions such as: (a) Is my present approach to helping efficient, effective, and relevant? (b) How do I determine the true meaning, scope, and effect on those I serve? (c) Do I see myself as a remedial expert, working one-to-one to provide direct service to selected individuals, or do I see myself as being systems-oriented? and (d) What effect am I having on the total school community? (Kurpius, 1992).

Motivating and Preparing for Action

What will prompt counselor educators to change? First, counselor educators must themselves believe that change is necessary. Second, they must be convinced that these changes will benefit the counselor education students, the students in K–12 schools, and the community at large. Then, the question becomes, "Is it possible to design such a system-challenging, visionary curriculum from within institutions that do not necessarily reward such change?" We recommend that counselor educators begin by critically questioning their own beliefs.

Examining Beliefs

Counselor educators may want to begin examining what they believe by asking themselves these fundamental questions:

- What do I believe about my own ability to be a leader and a change agent?
- What are the current gaps between preparation and practice in K–12 schools?
- What do I believe about changing systems?
- What do I believe school counselors need to know and be able to do?
- How do I currently change my teaching and my program to be responsive to the feedback I have received from counselors I have taught?
- What feedback is important enough to make a difference in how I prepare school counselors?
- How do I use data on schools and student achievement to make changes in my program?
- How do I teach others to think systemically about schools, learning, and achievement?
- As an instructor, how do I model leadership, advocacy, and systemic change?
- How do the graduates of my program demonstrate accountability for their work?
- What do I believe about the ability of all school-age students to reach high academic standards?
- How does my behavior as an instructor affect the students I teach?

Examining the Need for Change

Reflective inquiry about current program practices may help counselor educators decide the depth and breadth of changes that may be necessary. Reflecting on the following questions may stimulate necessary discussion:

- Are we currently preparing school counselors to work effectively in schools?
- What might cause us to be more proactive in our programs?
- How might we respond more actively in changing curricula to meet the current needs of school counseling students?
- What might we do differently in influencing the structure of our school counseling programs?
- What might prompt us to change our way of teaching?
- How can we create a cohesive school counseling curriculum that is closely aligned with the mission of schools and schooling?
- How would working actively in a learning community enhance my teaching?

Examining How Systems Change

After examining their personal beliefs and what steps might be necessary for change, counselor educators can look at the systems that need to change. Key elements in a system include the internal university environment (the department chair, the dean, the provost), the near external environment (the local area schools, community, business), and the more remote external environment (the state legislature, the board of education, the certification bodies). These entities all assist or deter change. Counselor educators may want to ask themselves the following:

- What are the beliefs, assumptions, and values behind a particular policy, structure, action, or orientation? Who shares these beliefs?
- What are the historical sources of these beliefs?
- Whose knowledge is considered legitimate?
- Who prospers if we act according to the identified beliefs?
- Who is empowered, disempowered, or disenfranchised by these beliefs?

The answers to these questions may offer insight into the feasibility of making changes in school counselor preparation.

Action Questions

Those ready to move toward implementation of a new approach to counselor preparation may want to ask the following questions to guide them in taking further steps:

- What is necessary to develop and nurture a community of learners in the classroom?
- How do we define ourselves as a learning community?
- How do we encourage dialogue that leads to generative solution-finding rather than presenting ourselves as having most of the answers?
- How do we decide what will be included or excluded from discussion or practice?
- How can we make a given situation more equitable, democratic, and accessible?
- What kind of pedagogy, experiences, and modeling best prepare critical, reflective practitioners?
- How do we encourage a diversity of views and alternatives?
- How do we call attention to social injustices and inequities?
- How have we exercised our voices for change?
- How have we helped students develop and exercise their voices?

Goals for School Counselor Preparation

After counselor education faculty have engaged in such reflective "soul searching," they then need to decide what changes to pursue. We suggest that counselor educators "begin with the end in mind" (Covey, 1992, p. 42) and look at the product of counselor education; that is, what school counselors themselves would do if they worked as leaders and advocates for change in the schools. We propose that in addition to being skilled counselors who work with students' personal concerns, school counselors need to do the following:

- Behave as if they expect all students to achieve at a high level.
- Actively work to remove barriers to learning.
- Teach students how to help themselves (e.g., organization, study, and test-taking skills).
- Teach students and their families how to manage successfully the bureaucracy of the school system; for example, teach parents how to (a) enroll their children in academic courses that will lead to college, (b) make formal requests to school officials on various matters, and (c) monitor the academic progress of their children.

- Teach students and their families how to access support systems that encourage academic success; for example, (a) inform students and parents about tutoring and academic enrichment opportunities, and (b) teach students and parents how to find resources on preparation for standardized tests.
- Use local, regional, and national data on disparities in resources and academic achievement to promote systemic change.
- Work collaboratively with all school personnel.
- Offer staff development training for school personnel that promotes high expectations and high standards for all students.
- Use data as a tool to challenge the deleterious effects of low-level and unchallenging courses.
- Highlight accurate information that negates myths about who can and cannot achieve success in rigorous courses.
- Organize community activities to promote supportive structures for high standards for all students (e.g., after-school tutoring programs at neighborhood religious settings).
- Help parents and the communities organize efforts to work with schools to institute and support high standards for all children.
- Work as resource brokers within the community to identify all available resources to help students succeed.

Widening the lens of what school counselors see as their job in these ways implies the formation of a new training model, one based on systems thinking about schools and schooling.

Necessary Programmatic Changes

We propose a mission-driven model for the program and the use of eight essential elements of change to revise school counselor preparation curricula. The eight essential elements are (a) criteria for selection and recruitment of candidates for counselor preparation programs; (b) curricular content, structure, and sequence of courses; (c) method of instruction, field experiences, and practice; (d) induction process into the profession; (e) working relationships with community partners; (f) professional development for counselor educators; (g) university–school district partnerships; and (h) university–state department of education partnerships. Counselor education faculty can use these elements as a framework for organizing thinking, planning, and implementing program changes.

Becoming a Mission-Driven Program

An overriding principle of any counselor education program and a prerequisite to using the eight essential elements as an organizational model is the development of a mission statement. A clear mission statement for school counselor preparation becomes the driving force of the program. A clear mission statement for school counselor preparation can determine the admissions criteria, the curricula of the program, and the type of pedagogy. In other words, the mission statement provides the guiding principles for (a) the program, (b) how we teach, (c) what is being taught, and (d) whom we teach. Thus, it shapes the curriculum as well as the practicing counselors graduating from the program.

We recommend an inclusive mission-creating process. When counselor educators include non-university community partners in developing a mission statement, the resulting mission takes on greater relevance to the needs of counselors, administrators, teachers, and students in schools. To develop a mission statement, school counselor educators can begin by looking at what they believe and value about (a) their teaching style, (b) their teaching methods, (c) school-age children, (d) educational attainment for all students, (e) future career options for students they serve, (f) what school counselors should know and be able to do when they complete the program, and (g) measurable outcomes for the work of school counselors.

1. Improving Criteria for Selection and Recruitment of Candidates for Counselor Preparation

Typically, counselor education programs have not actively recruited students to their programs, but instead have either accepted all applicants or used a screening process to select an identified number of students each year. Program faculty often state that graduate school requirements of certain scores on GRE qualifying examinations hamstring them.

Rather than following the "standard" procedures already in place, faculty can develop new criteria for selection based on the mission of the program. This will mean questioning the current systemic regulations that are preventing candidates from diverse backgrounds from enrolling in the program. Because of the increasing number of students of color in our schools, it is critical that school counselors represent diverse ethnic backgrounds. Questioning the rules and regulations provides a leadership and modeling opportunity for faculty. Seizing this opportunity to recruit more minorities to your campus might even bring critical acclaim when you are successful.

Instituting this "active admissions" process becomes a way for counselor educators to model leadership and advocacy. First steps include questioning all current procedures to see if they are serving the desired purposes and gaining the numbers of qualified students that you want in the program. After review of current procedures, implementation strategies might include such approaches as (a) working with local school districts to identify teachers that might be excellent counselors; (b) devising a nomination process so that community and school members could nominate prospective students; (c) creating an active recruiting committee consisting of faculty, practicing school counselors, students, community members, and school administrators; (d) making recruiting visits to historically Black and Hispanic institutions; and (e) working with the equity center on campus to recruit candidates.

In addition to these recruitment processes, it will be necessary to revisit the selection procedures. On what basis are students admitted to the program? What questions are asked of applicants? How are applicants screened? Are group or individual interviews conducted? Who is involved in the selection process? This may be an excellent opportunity to include school and community members in your program by inviting them to participate in the selection process. Thus, they become more invested in counselors working in schools.

After a review of the selection, recruitment, and admissions process, a new process is made public. The mission statement that includes the intent of the program should be included in the admissions materials. One by-product of this new process is that students will self-select from the program. If they are not seeking training to be advocates, leaders, and change agents, but rather want to be "helpers" and start a clinical practice, then this is not the program for them. On the other hand, word will spread about the kind of preparation the program entails, and the new admissions standards will attract more "qualified" candidates.

2. Altering the Content, Structure, and Delivery of the Curriculum

Once the mission has been clarified, it directs the content, structure, and sequencing of courses. The following questions may further stimulate discussions on needed changes:

- What course content, skills, and knowledge are essential to producing school counselors to meet the program mission statement?
- What is the rationale for the sequence of courses in the program?
- How does the program integrate its philosophy and mission into the teaching, curriculum, and course sequence?
- How does the mission influence pedagogy?
- How will we collaborate with other important stakeholders in the development of the new curricular content, structure, and sequence of courses?

Some innovations that might be considered are alternative methods of delivering coursework and developing a learning community.

Delivery of Coursework

Counselor educators need to consider alternative means of course delivery, such as (a) teaching at public schools or in the community; (b) inviting school counselors and administrators to co-teach some classes; (c) scheduling more courses on weekends; (d) offering more courses through distance education; or (e) teaming with faculty from educational administration to co-teach a course for both administrators and counselors. By diversifying the location or delivery of instruction, we move away from the concept of the university as the seat of knowledge. This broadens the universe from which knowledge is gained. The University of Wisconsin at Milwaukee designed one successful example of an alternative delivery method, in cooperation with the Milwaukee public schools. They admitted teachers from a large school district and worked collaboratively with school district personnel to co-teach these students in a cohort model. A majority of the classes were taught in the public schools at times convenient to teachers.

Developing a Learning Community

Strong learning communities can provide modeling, reflection opportunities, and group interaction for school counseling students (Ward & House, 1998). A learning community emphasizes inquiry and supports different social and cultural contexts. In the learning community, knowledge is challenged, redefined, and negotiated by all participants (Griffen, 1993). It is our premise that this approach allows future school counselors to gain insights into the social and cultural implications of different ways of knowing, different forms of knowledge, and different approaches to research.

One way to encourage the development of a learning community in the counselor education program is to utilize a cohort model of training, as defined by Paisley and Hayes (2000). These authors state that use of a cohort model creates the expectations among students that they ought to collaborate with others and provides a model usable later when students become school counselors. In a cohort model, a group of students enters and progresses through the program together. Also, instructors plan activities in courses, practica, and internships that require students regularly to work collaboratively. Osborne et al. (1998) elaborated on the use of a cohort model and emphasized the benefits of a cohort model coupled with a retreat experience designed to build cohesiveness.

In cohort models, individuals examine interpersonal dynamics and learn to value the unique worldview of each participant. Communication, negotiation, and conflict management become vehicles for enhanced learning. Cohort models use teaming, peer coaching, generative problem-solving, and collaboration, methods that are critical to school counselors becoming leaders and advocates in their schools and communities.

3. Methods of Instruction, Field Experiences, and Practice
Developing Constructivist Methods of Delivering Instruction and Field Experiences

In this new approach to teaching school counselors, the methods of instruction, field experiences, and practica would be transformed to include (a) early experiential learning in the schools, (b) early and continuous integration of theory and practice, and (c) frequent opportunities for counselors to know and understand schools and schooling. The program faculty would focus on (a) learning rather than teaching; (b) induction-oriented, interactive teaching rather than lecture; (c) sharing belief systems; (d) modeling advocacy, leadership, and community involvement; (e) collaborating and teaming with school and community stakeholders; (f) modeling the use of data to make informed decisions for systemic change; and (g) placing students in the school system early and frequently.

Courses could be designed and taught in a collaborative yet focused fashion that implements the program's mission. For example, the research course could help students to (a) examine current use of data and explore biases in data collection strategies; (b) analyze data samples disaggregated by race, ethnic group, and gender; (c) identify educational inequities reflected in such data; (d) generate hypotheses for action research; (e) develop an action plan to garner support for such disaggregated data collection; and (f) work collaboratively with the instructor and representatives from the school district and community to build strategies for such change in schools and districts. Teaching strategies for such a course might include

- understanding social and cultural issues that affect all members of society (e.g., racism, sexism, socioeconomic status, and ageism), utilizing guest speakers, videos, and class member experiences;
- introducing methods and strategies of advocacy to instigate social change;
- providing examples of advocacy projects initiated by the faculty member teaching the class;
- requiring a group project on an issue that the students identify as needing change;
- teaching the students how to collect and utilize data to determine the need for change; and
- collaborating with students in developing and carrying out a plan of action based on needs and data, and evaluating the plan.

Direct Experience in the Schools

Counselor educators' ongoing experience in the schools models for students an investment in collaborative work. The vast differences between how counselors are often taught and how they actually work in the schools may be reduced by building such collaborative relationships with school district administrators, supervisors, teachers, and counselors, and by early, frequent, and direct experience in the schools. Students and faculty are thus exposed to the daily lives of students, families, teachers, counselors, administrators, schools, and the community. In this process they learn counseling models, child and family counseling approaches, social service case-management approaches, community resources, and systemic paradigms of change. In addition, they become familiar with education reform issues, gain knowledge of the achievement gap, learn how to collect and use data, and gain an understanding of standards-based assessment, testing, and interpretation; special education; and school policy.

<u>Teaching Reflectivity</u>

Reflectivity, as it applies to schooling, is a conscious effort by school counselors to identify contradictions and hidden or distorted understandings extant in the schools (Lather, 1986). Learning to practice reflectivity helps future counselors to "think outside the box" and question the status quo.

Such a reflective inquiry method can highlight the social and political patterns preventing access and equity to a quality education for all students in public schools. In this reflective mode, students are asked to contemplate fundamental questions such as (a) What do I do? (b) How do I do it? and (c) What does this mean both for myself as a professional and for those whom I serve? Reflective practice includes recognizing professional dilemmas and inconsistencies, using them to construct meaning, and from such meaning developing guides for action (Mezirow, 1994; Colton & Sparks-Langer, 1993). Strategies that counselor educators could employ in their classes to teach reflectivity include

- **Reflective journaling:** writing out confusions, frustrations, questions, intentions, hypotheses, and assumptions pertaining to students or classroom events.
- **Retrospection:** drawing together materials (case notes, reflective pad, or literature) that link practice to the articulation of those values, beliefs, and concepts.
- **Reflective supervision:** reviewing during supervision the purpose, beliefs, and assumptions of school counseling to aid in clarifying patterns and themes necessary for learning and professional growth.
- **Reflective dialogue:** reviewing journal entries and other reflections with peers, focusing on what happened, what is being learned, and the meaning of the events.
- **Extension:** extending this reflective dialogue beyond peers to school and community members to widen and enrich the learning.
- **Action research:** reviewing the literature, applying the relevant findings to counseling in schools, conducting

an action research study, and reflecting on this research process.

It is important to note that in this process of teaching students to be reflective, they will begin to challenge, question, and push the envelope on a variety of issues with the instructors. This becomes an opportunity to dialogue with students about advocacy, leadership, and change. This is not a passive exercise, but an active, involved, and engaged process in which open dialogue and exchange of ideas are encouraged and supported. The classroom becomes a place for safe practice of introducing new ideas and new ways of looking at systems change, and the process prepares students for such exchanges in schools. This is a very different way of teaching than a lecture style or planned discussion on selected topics.

4. Improving the Process of Induction into the Profession

Preparation to be a school counselor does not stop with completion of the program. Often the most difficult part of becoming a school counselor is putting into practice in the schools the skills and knowledge learned in the program. Developing and maintaining professional relationships and making a difference in the profession become critical functions for the new school counselor. For school counselors to work as questioners of the status quo and initiators of action, they need continuing support, constant reflectivity and feedback, and a period of mentoring by a practicing counselor who understands and engages in a social-critical approach to counseling. Questions for counselor educators to consider during the new-counselor induction phase include

- What critical experiences and professional involvement are needed during the preparation program?
- What kind of follow-up support does the faculty provide for new school counselors?
- Who are designated as mentors and how can faculty secure mentors for new professionals?
- How does the program emphasize the importance of continuing professional development?
- Have we included adequate information about entering the profession during the preparation program?
- How does the faculty contribute to continuing professional development activities for school counselors that support the program philosophy, mission, and goals?

- How does the faculty encourage and support new school counselors to take risks for youth, including those that challenge the system?
- How does the program assist new school counselors to obtain allies who might support them in their work?

5. Developing Working Relationships with Community Partners
One of the tenets of the education reform movement is the belief that schools cannot function successfully without supportive community partnerships (Gerstner, Semerad, Doyle, & Johnston, 1994; Schorr, 1997). The creation of successful school counselor training programs also depends on strong and viable community partnerships. The essential nature of this endeavor is based on the concept that change agents receive ultimate direction from the community (Homan, 1999). As Homan explains, "You are working with a community rather than having a community working with you. The change agent must listen to the community as well as offer direction. It is the community who must act, not just the change agent, and the final decisions will always reside with the community. After all, whose change is it anyway?" (1999, p. 10).

As counselor educators consider working with community partners to gain insight and information, they might consider the following questions.
- What is the relationship among the community, local schools, and the counselor preparation program?
- How do we engage critical stakeholders in meaningful dialogue about training school counselors?
- What collaborative efforts exist to support closing the achievement gap among students of different socioeconomic classes and races?
- How have we used data to engage the community in efforts to improve student achievement?
- Who are the unofficial community leaders who can galvanize the community to action on behalf of marginalized students and their families?

6. Increasing Professional Development Relevant to School Counseling
Counselor educators need to choose professional development activities that increase their knowledge of schools. They may need to consider such questions as (a) What professional development activities will help me to prepare

school counselors in a new model? and (b) How am I engaged in focused, reflective discussion on the current changes in philosophy, program, and role of school counselors? For example, many counselor educators teaching in school counselor preparation programs have either not worked in schools or not worked in schools in a long time. Counselor educators can begin their professional development by becoming directly involved in the schools (Hayes, Dagley, & Horne, 1996). Such involvement helps educators to better understand current education reform issues faced by educators as well as current mandated accountability measures.

7. University–School District Partnerships

Close and continuous collaboration with school districts is an essential ingredient in this new process of preparing school counselors. Best practices happen both at the university and in K–12 schools. Neither higher education nor school districts can independently design and implement necessary changes needed for school counselors. While school counselors and administrators are anchored in the reality of schools, students, and learning, counselor educators are steeped in research and theory. Together, a cohesive, reality-based, research-guided curriculum can be designed and implemented. Working as collaborative stakeholders to create this new curriculum ultimately ends in greater acceptance of the new directions.

8. University–State Education Department Partnerships

Influencing policy at the state level becomes an integral part of success in this new model. State department entities determine policy and thus program directions. However, there is not often a clear working relationship and open lines of communication among state departments and universities and school districts. It is important to become a part of the process and influence changes made at the state level, determining such policies as testing, certification, accreditation, and licensing.

Groups that have a wide base of community, school, and university representation most often influence state departments. Therefore, a first action step is to use one's collaborative stakeholder group to determine what policies at the state level might be changed to enhance both the university and school district. This collaborative group must develop a united and focused approach based on the interest of serving all children. A thoughtful and planned approach, utilizing data and including key stakeholders, will often make the difference in policy changes.

Conclusion

As leaders and advocates, counselor educators and school counselors need to reexamine recurrent professional role patterns and think in a more systemic fashion. They must be willing to reach and influence people beyond their jurisdiction, have political skills to cope with conflicting requirements of multiple constituencies, and question the status quo. When working from this framework, counseling professionals will be active creators and definers of systems change, rather than passive respondents to or victims of environmental circumstance. Preparation that produces school counselors who can practice as leaders and advocates to influence the attainment of high achievement for all students aligns school counselors with educational reform, and places them in the middle of the changes needed to support all students.

In this chapter we purposely look beyond the usual boundaries and faculty roles of the university as we propose changes in school counselor preparation. We suggest anchoring learning in the experience of the schools and communities by forming collaborative working relationships with key stakeholders in school districts and communities.

We propose that counselor educators teach school counselors to be advocates, leaders, helpers, collaborators, risk takers, and data users. To do this, counselor educators need to both teach and model these roles themselves. We hope the questions presented in this chapter can guide counselor educators to (a) reflect on their practice, (b) participate in a planned dialogue with colleagues and others, (c) infuse new principles in their teaching of school counselors, and (d) be social activists in their roles as counselor educators. By doing this, they will influence a new generation of school counselors to become leaders and advocates in the schools.

References

Achievement in America: 2000 [Computer diskette]. (2000). Washington DC: The Education Trust.

American Counseling Association. (1999). *U.S. student-to-counselor ratios*. Alexandria, VA: Author.

American School Counselor Association. (1998). *The national standards for school counseling programs*. Alexandria, VA: Author.

Bradley, F. O. (1997). Status of school counseling: Structure, governance, and levers for change. Washington, DC: The Education Trust.

Capuzzi, D. (1998). Addressing the needs of at-risk youth: Early prevention and systemic intervention. In C. C. Lee & G. R. Walz (Eds.), *Social action: A mandate for counselors* (pp. 99–116). Alexandria, VA: American Counseling Association.

Collison, B. B., Osborne, J. L., Gray, L. A., House, R. M., Firth, J., & Lou, M. (1998). Preparing counselors for social action. In C. C. Lee & G. R. Walz (Eds.), *Social action: A mandate for counselors* (pp. 263–277). Alexandria, VA: American Counseling Association.

Colton, A. B., & Sparks-Langer, G. M. (1993). A conceptual framework to guide the development of teacher reflection and decision-making. *Journal of Teacher Education, 44*, 45–54.

Covey, S. R. (1992). *Principle-centered leadership*. New York: Fireside.

Darder, A. (1991). *Culture and power in the classroom: A critical foundation for bicultural education*. New York: Bergin & Gravey Press.

Darling-Hammond, L. (1993). Reframing the school reform agenda. *Phi Delta Kappan, 74*(10), 752–761.

The Education Trust (1997, February). *The national guidance and counseling reform program*. Washington, DC: Author.

Elam, S. (Ed.). (1993). *The state of the nation's public schools*. Bloomington, IN: Phi Delta Kappa.

Gerstner, L.V., Semerad, R. D., Doyle, D. P., & Johnston, W. B. (1994). *Reinventing education: Entrepreneurship in America's public schools*. New York: Penguin Books.

Griffen, B. (1993). ACES: Promoting professionalism, collaboration, and advocacy. *Counselor Education and Supervision, 33,* 2–9.

Hanson, C., & Geary, P. (2000, March). *Mission Driven Programs: New Directions for School Counselors.* Paper presented at the meeting of the American Counseling Association, Washington, DC.

Hart, P. J., & Jacobi, M. (1992). *From gatekeeper to advocate: Transforming the role of the school counselor.* New York: College Entrance Examination Board.

Haycock, K. (1998). Good teaching matters: How well-qualified teachers can close the gap. *Thinking K–16, 3*(2), 1–2.

Hayes, R. L., Dagley, J. C., & Horne, A. M. (1996). Restructuring school counselor education: Work in progress. *Journal of Counseling & Development, 74,* 378–384.

Homan, M. S. (1999). *Rules of the game: Lessons from the field of community change.* Pacific Grove, CA: Brooks/Cole.

Kurpius, D. J. (1992). Outreach, advocacy, and consultation: A framework for prevention and intervention. *Elementary School Guidance and Counseling, 26,* 176–189.

Lather, P. (1986). Research as praxis. *Harvard Educational Review, 56*(3), 257–277.

McLaren, P. (1989). *Life in schools: An introduction to critical pedagogy in the foundations of education.* New York: Longman.

Mezirow, J. (1994). Understanding transformation theory. *Adult Education Quarterly, 44*(4), 222–244.

Mohrman, S. A., & Lawler, E. E. (1996). Motivation for school reform. In S. H. Fuhrman & J. A. O'Day (Eds.), *Rewards and reform: Creating educational incentives that work* (pp. 115–143). San Francisco: Jossey-Bass.

Osborne, J. L., Collison, B. B., House, R. M., Gray, L. A., Firth, J., & Lou, M. (1998). Developing a social advocacy model for counselor education. *Counselor Education & Supervision, 37,* 190–202.

Paisley, P. O., & Hayes, R. L. (2000). Counselor under construction: Implications for program design. In G. McAuliffe & K. Eriksen (Eds.), *Preparing counselors and therapists: Creating constructivist and developmental programs.* Alexandria, VA: ACES and Donning Publishers.

Pedersen, P. B., & Ivey, A. (1993). *Culture-centered counseling and interviewing skills: A practical guide.* Westport, CT: Praeger Publishers.

Schorr, L. B. (1997). *Common purpose: Strengthening families and neighborhoods to rebuild America.* New York: Anchor Books.

Southers, C. L. (1991). Home economics teacher education reform: Prime time for a phoenix agenda. *Journal of Vocational Home Economics Education, 9*(2), 56–69.

Swasey, M. (1996–1997, Winter). Student voices: School system shock. *Rethinking Schools, 11*(2), 25.

Walz, G. R. (1997). *Knowledge generalizations regarding the status of guidance and counseling.* Washington, DC: The Education Trust.

Ward, C. C., & House, R. M. (1998). Counseling supervision: A reflective model. *Counselor Education and Supervision, 38,* 23–33.

About the Authors

Reese M. House is a nationally recognized counselor educator. He is professor emeritus at Oregon State University where he focused on preparing school counselors to be proactive change agents and advocates for social, economic, and political justice. He has experience as a school counselor, community activist and HIV/AIDS educator. He currently works at the Education Trust in Washington, DC, on the Transforming School Counseling Initiative.

Patricia J. Martin, senior program manager at the Education Trust, is on leave from Prince George's County Public Schools, where she has worked as a school counselor, a supervisor of school counselors, and an assistant superintendent of schools.

Colin C. Ward is an assistant professor in the Counselor Education Department at Winona State University, Winona, Minnesota.

Chapter Fourteen

Counseling in the Future

Joseph D. Dear

Schools and *everyone* associated with schools have a personal and moral obligation to be committed to carrying out the primary mission of the school and school district. The basic structure of existing school districts is not likely to change in the next 20 years. When students are assigned to attend school in a certain district, it is incumbent upon the district to accept that youngster unconditionally, for the most part, and to do everything within that team's power to educate the young person. Naturally, there are some exceptions in extreme cases, but generally speaking, school districts must accept the challenge they receive. A great variety of kids come to any school district. Some kids possess the most desirable characteristics of the ideal young person, whereas others come to the district with many shortcomings. The district is equally obligated to educate kids from both extremes of the desirability spectrum.

School is often the place where children have their closest contact with people from diverse backgrounds. Schools must be at the forefront of developing a multicultural attitude in children, especially in states such as California, Texas, Florida, and New York. Just as schools have special activities during American holidays, they can acknowledge and have special activities during holidays of people from different cultures. Changing demographics require different procedures in all aspects of the educational system. The student of the year 2021 should leave the K–12 system as an academically, socially, and psychologically balanced, civic-minded person ready to enter society and become a responsible, productive individual with basic skills in reading, writing, mathematics and thinking critically, as well as competence in the use of computers and other emerging technologies.

To improve the chances of the school system producing such a student, the future pupil service provider will need to learn to bring about a better relationship, agreement, and level of commitment among the *learners, teachers,* and the *end users* of the person being taught.

The learners will need to bring to the table all the resources they have available, such as their natural skills and competencies; their experiences and other relevant personal attributes; the collective experiences and knowledge of their family, friends, peers, and mentors; their knowledge of other resources, such as those in the community; and an attitude of wanting to learn, to the extent possible.

The teachers will need to bring to the table all the resources they have available, such as their natural skills and competencies; their experiences and other relevant personal attributes; and resources from their department, school, district, and colleagues, including knowledge of other resources.

The end user will need to bring to the table all the resources that entity has available, such as its existing strengths, flexibility, sensitivity, access, and willingness to include, involve, accept and provide.

This concept can apply to the higher education system: For example, the learner as credential counselor candidate must bring to the table a positive attitude and commitment to carry out, to the best of his or her ability, the required schedule of competencies. The teacher as counselor educator must bring to the table a positive attitude and commitment to make use of all resources available through his or her personal experiences, colleagues, department, university, and the system as a whole. The end user, such as the school that employs the student support counselor, must provide an induction experience for that recently hired counselor to be welcomed and sufficiently oriented, mentored, coached, and gradually integrated into the school, beginning with a reasonable workload, assessment, and support for two to three years, enabling the counselor to intensely and continuously upgrade his or her skills throughout employment.

The same scenario would work for the K–12 student as learner, the K–12 teacher as teacher, and the potential employer as end user. For example, students would bring to the table the resources of family, friends, and peers, as well as knowledge of other resources. Teachers would bring the resources of their department, school, district, colleagues, and others of which they are aware. End users (colleges or universities, employers, volunteer or quasi-volunteer organizations) would work at being flexible, sensitive, and willing to include and provide for that employee so that the individual can realize his or her full potential and be as productive and as "fulfilled" as possible.

The Role of Pupil Service Providers

The pupil service provider (PPS) would need the following skills, which are not currently (or sufficiently) required in most counselor education programs:
- computer skills and other skills in the use of technology
- cultural, linguistic, and academic development skills
- increased knowledge about and skills in handling integrated services and the concomitant knowledge of formulating joint agreements, relationships, and partnerships based on shared resources
- sufficient understanding of relationships, communication, conflicts, violence, self-esteem, and issues of equity
- practice of learned competencies *throughout* education and career
- sufficient skills in learning to bring about change in any existing system

Most educators who have been in the profession for a number of years know that where academic performance is high, relationships among students and staff are generally okay. Generally speaking, in schools where the vast majority of people genuinely care about one another and are committed to working together as a team toward a common educational goal, the educational quality is higher.

If this is an accurate and acceptable premise, then a major goal of schools might be to increase the number of participants who genuinely care about one another and are committed to working together as a team toward their school's stated educational mission. School districts throughout the United States are finding success through the effective utilization of the human resources available to them.

School counselors are primarily pupil advocates and partners with other educators, parents, and the community at large. Ultimately, their goal is to foster optimum teaching and learning conditions and to prevent school failure. They are the professionals in the school who are between the school administrators and the teachers. They are the "climate control" of the school and the liaison with the community.

In addition to the academic challenges students must face at school, they encounter personal and social situations that impede their learning. Pupil service providers are (or should be) trained to serve as schools' experts in the two extremes of the human behavioral continuum. On the one end are such behaviors as motivation, self-esteem, personal growth, nurturing, positive reinforcement, and support; on the other end, crisis prevention and intervention, conflict management and mediation, problem solving and decision making, and the development of refusal skills.

With the agreement and support of colleagues, including other support staff, teachers, and administrators, support personnel could take a number of positive steps in schools:

- They could take the lead in initiating student forums, which involves an ongoing search for student leadership from all segments of the student body to do, among other things, such activities as promote student responsibility and initiate the establishment of campus chapters of strong academic, social, and civic groups, clubs, and organizations.
- They could initiate a mechanism that gives students training in communication skills.
- They could solicit assistance from other support staff and teachers to help students learn about the nature and extent of such things as good citizenship, relationships, communication, and so forth. For example, staff could implement a series of "what if" exercises, using video and role-playing techniques to examine common situations, such as a student making a joke about a serious subject.
- They could encourage interaction among different ethnic groups (supervised initially, if deemed necessary) through the various scheduled school forums and other student gatherings. This interaction could allow students a way to talk about what's going on at school without identifying themselves.
- They could initiate regular meetings of small staff teams to discuss positive ways of improving the school climate and relationships, encouraging potential positive or success-oriented situations, and addressing problem situations.
- They could initiate a system for identifying problem

students and staff and develop strategies to neutralize the impact of these students and staff on the smooth functioning of the school. Pupil service providers could work on ways to make these students and staff more productive and positive elements in the school environment.

- They could model appropriate and consistent responses to student behavior: Good behavior is encouraged and elicits positive consequences; bad behavior is discouraged and elicits negative consequences. This behavior policy oftentimes requires training and continuous communication with students and staff to make certain everyone knows the difference. Behavior that falls in the middle is continuously clarified.
- They could explore and document student expectations for use in the educational process. Likewise, they could explore and document teacher and other educator expectations of students in order to improve the educational process at every opportunity.
- They could continuously seek ways to engage students in work and other activities of interest to them. Undoubtedly, this requires getting to know something about the students and their interests.

Student Leadership

Some pupil services staffs have found ways to carry out their school's mission primarily by effectively using student resources. This is one source for suggested practices that is virtually untapped, yet it is an unlimited resource on every school campus—potentially the entire student body. Let's review a few facts:

Fact. Students listen to other students.

Fact. Young people join gangs and get involved with the wrong crowd because these gangs and other crowds fill needs: "loving" relationships, security, social outlet and acceptance, and on and on and on.

Fact. Peer pressure works.

Students need more good student role models. They need to see more people who look and speak like them doing things that matter. Students could take the leadership in matters of school harmony and safety. They are able to ask questions straight up and get straight up answers.

213

There are a number of students who are enthusiastic about learning and getting involved in school. Many already know that learning is a process, sometimes short, but sometimes long. We all probably know one or two students who don't give up at the first sight of defeat or failure but who keep on believing and trying. Well, with some support, they could teach others the same relatively simple concepts.

With the assistance of school staff, students could design and plan a strategy to "get to work" in their own schools. They could then work on identifying other student leaders and analyzing where the new recruit fits in the leadership training process—at the beginning, in the middle, or toward the end.

Students have not fully developed and accepted all the learned stereotypes, biases, and misconceptions of adulthood. They are still somewhat innocent and impressionable and therefore in a better position than are most adults to find problems in school systems and to develop solutions. Students need to start working on solutions for today's problems in preparation for the bigger and more challenging problems of tomorrow.

Creating Student Leaders

Students need to be recruited to help make schools functional. The heroes of the school should be the good and smart kids; the student body should look up to the good kids instead of the bad kids. Schools should plan strategies to make that the case.

Students should be identified first in every district, then in each and every school, to serve as "leaders with a purpose." They should be recruited, carefully, and trained to accomplish the following:

1. Develop a "picture" of the school, including all the significant elements that make up a school, such as attendance, grades, troublemakers, good and bad things going on, the school climate, who is respected and why, who is not respected and why, the movers and shakers of the school and why they have that influence, and so forth.
2. Recruit other potential leaders.
3. Identify other students' weaknesses and strengths.
4. Teach other students to solve problems and mediate differences; develop their own self-esteem and assist others with developing self-esteem.

5. Develop their own, and assist others with developing, personal and social responsibility.

Students at the elementary, middle, and high school levels should be identified to serve in this capacity—with an eye to continuously expand the number of leaders at every grade level. Students at each level would learn specific leadership skills:

Elementary: become aware of and learn to observe other students and the school environment; learn terminology and basic elementary ideas and concepts related to leadership, responsibility, and respect.

Middle/junior high school: become "shadows" of experienced leaders; learn more advanced ideas and concepts related to leadership, responsibility, and respect; participate in low-level training and experiences that lead to more advanced participation in the school and in leadership.

High school: beginning in freshman year, learn and experience the above ideas and concepts and begin training others to be leaders.

Pupil Service Providers: Leading the Leaders

Ultimately, counselors and other support staff of 2021 should not only work hard to acquire certain skills and competencies, but they should also work toward assisting students to acquire the same competencies. Among those coveted qualities are leadership, mentorship, organization, and advocacy:

Leadership: Demonstrate leadership and show others how to be a leader and how to follow a leader.

Mentorship: Demonstrate being a mentor to someone; demonstrate receiving support from a mentor; show others how to do both.

Organization: Demonstrate personal organization and show others how to be better organized.

Advocacy: Become a model advocate for students, staff, and the community; show others how to be an advocate to others.

Even though educators and American corporate executives have known the key to successful operations and projects for years, it took the Japanese automobile industry to drive the point home several years ago. A company works best when everyone associated with it has become personally committed to carrying out the company's primary mission. That same concept works for schools, too. Teachers, students, bus drivers, administrators, counselors, parents, psychologists, custodians, secretaries, social workers, librarians, cafeteria workers, and everyone else at a school must work together as a team for the betterment of their school. I don't think this is a new concept in education.

About the Author

Joseph D. Dear, Ed.D. has served as state coordinator of all 64 pupil personnel services training programs in California for the state's Credentialing Commission since 1989. He facilitated the 25-member advisory panel that wrote California's new counselor standards, which are being implemented between 2001 and 2003. He has been a counselor educator, newspaper editor, TV program host and producer, Upward Bound director and private consultant. He has published major reports and articles on the topics of school violence, counseling and substance abuse in the Black community. Dr. Dear completed his B.A. in psychology, M.S. in community mental health and Ed.D. in counselor education, all at Northern Illinois University, DeKalb, Illinois.

Chapter Fifteen

Support Programs for Students with Disabilities in the Public Schools

Leo M. Orange & Martin G. Brodwin

> Together, we've begun to shift disability policy in America away from exclusion, towards inclusion; away from dependence, towards independence; away from paternalism, towards empowerment.
> —President Bill Clinton
> Statement to the National Council on Disability, April 16, 1993

This chapter has been written as if it were 20 years from today. We are looking into the future (as much as one can) and attempting to outline changes we hope will have occurred in public schools, specifically in the area of the provision of support programs for students who have disabilities. Our approach is most optimistic; this optimism is based, in part, on the successful passage of both the Americans with Disabilities Act of 1990 and the Individuals with Disabilities Education Act of 1990. The Americans with Disabilities Act was developed to end discrimination against people with disabilities in employment, public transportation, public accommodations, and telecommunications. The Individuals with Disabilities Education Act is an amendment and retitling of the Education for All Handicapped Children Act of 1975, which was originally stimulated by congressional concern for and dissatisfaction with the complete exclusion of millions of children with disabilities from the public school system and the inappropriateness of educational programs that were available for these students (Price-Ellington & Berry, 1999–2000; Rubin & Roessler, 2001).

One major emphasis of these education acts was the idea that school-age children must be placed in the least restrictive school environment possible. This resulted in a greater degree of mainstreaming and inclusion of children with disabilities into regular classrooms and schools to be educated with their nondisabled peers.

Our vision for all students who have disabilities in 2021 is based on four premises: (a) that every public school will have support services for students with disabilities; (b) that rehabilitation counselors will be available for these students in every school; (c) that architectural barriers that impede access for people with disabilities to move freely about their environment will no longer exist; and (d) that U.S. society will adopt a philosophy of total inclusion of people with disabilities in all aspects of life and living, including public education. This chapter, admittedly optimistic, foresees positive change for students and all people who have disabilities in American society.

The Future

We predict that the public school of the future will provide full accommodation, allowing students with disabilities a free, appropriate, and equal opportunity for education to the greatest extent possible. To facilitate this, educational administrators and public school teachers will work closely with rehabilitation counselors in developing curricula and assessing what kinds of accommodations can be made within the school. A rehabilitation counselor will be available for all students who have disabilities; each school will have a center for students with disabilities where students go to arrange reasonable accommodations when needed. The public school system will become an ideal setting for the education of children and youth who have disabilities. The goals of the 1975 Education for All Handicapped Children Act will be finally realized by the year 2021.

We are hopeful that the accommodations described later in this chapter will be established at the beginning of the twenty-first century, enabling inclusion of most students with disabilities to occur within every public school. Rehabilitation counselors will assist both students and schools in providing accommodations and permitting a free and appropriate education in the least restrictive environment possible. Examples of accommodations are provided in the next section.

Inclusion and Integration

Inclusion is the activity of making individuals with disabilities members of a larger group (Rubin & Roessler, 2001. When full integration occurs, individuals with disabilities join other members of society in all aspects of education, employment, and leisure-time activities. Federal law mandates inclusion. The Individuals with Disabilities Education Act states that all individuals with disabilities have the right to a free and appropriate education in the least restrictive environment possible.

Federal law mandates integration. The Rehabilitation Act of 1973, the Rehabilitation Act Amendments of 1992, and the Americans with Disabilities Act of 1990 discuss the integration of individuals with disabilities into society. The purpose of each of these federal laws is to make the social environment accessible to individuals with disabilities. Once physical barriers are removed and accommodations made (ramps rather than steps, assistive technology for computers and telephones, interpreters, etc.), people with disabilities will be able to interact with other individuals within society.

Students with and without disabilities need each other in the educational environment (Hanley-Maxwell, Szymanski, & Owens-Johnson, 1998; Price-Ellington & Berry, 1999–2000). Studies show that when two different groups interact in a positive or beneficial way, attitudes of the people in the groups become more positive. Ideally, integration results in the development of ongoing personal interactions, which may range from casual acquaintances to intimate relationships. In our public schools of the future, we visualize inclusion of students with disabilities resulting in greater acceptance by nondisabled students of people who are different, leading to further inclusion of people with disabilities in all aspects of society. Along with this trend, we see a gradual diminishment of societal discrimination toward people with disabilities, leading to greater opportunities in education, work, and social activities.

Accommodation within the Public School

We now want to change focus to the theme of this chapter: a view of what public schools will look like in 2021 in terms of providing accommodations for students who have disabilities or chronic medical conditions. The public school of the future will accommodate verbal communication limitations; visual communication limitations; stamina limitations; limited use of the upper and lower extremities; and cognitive limitations. Let us jump ahead to where the future is the present, to see what changes are in effect in public schools in 2021.

Verbal Communication Limitations

In 2021, computer technology is of great value for students with disabilities who either have limited verbal skills or are completely nonverbal. This includes students who have limitations of hearing, total deafness, or difficulty interpreting verbal information. Students in the latter category include those with learning disabilities, traumatic brain injury, cerebral vascular accident, mental retardation, and some types of neurological deficits. Through the increased use of written material and computer-based communication, the rehabilitation counselor and teacher, working together, have been able to mainstream into regular classes many children and youth with verbal communication limitations. This occurred early in the twenty-first century.

In the year 2015, basic sign language became part of the curriculum for all students. This functional language is presented to students in innovative and creative ways to stimulate an interest in learning; most students enjoy learning sign language because of the way it is presented to them. In developing this newly required language in the public schools, rehabilitation counselors stressed its importance not only to youth, but to all people as they become elderly. Hearing loss occurs to everyone as they age; by the time this occurs to most people, it is usually too late to learn alternative means of communication. For hearing-impaired and deaf students, each public school now has amplified telephones, telecommunication devices, audio loops, flashing lights and alarms, well-lighted areas, and, for individual students, vibrating pocket pagers. Since 2002, all public schools have had TDDs (telephone devices for the deaf). When needed by students for particular projects or activities, qualified interpreters are available (Brodwin, Parker, & DeLaGarza, 1996).

Visual Communication Limitations
Students with limitations of sight or total blindness have benefited from legislation and its application by rehabilitation counselors and by specialists in orientation and mobility. For

children and youth with residual vision, accommodations have included greater use of the other senses. Specialists in visual disabilities have assisted school administrators to use improved lighting and greater illumination in certain areas, and color and contrast in room design, space and arrangement, and size and distance. Closed-circuit television enlarges print electronically; personal computers and peripherals with large print magnification, speed output, and optical scanning are available at the office for students with disabilities, an office existing within all public schools.

Textbooks in Braille are ordered from the U.S. Library of Congress months ahead of when they are needed, so they arrive before the beginning of classes to give students sufficient preparation time. The combination of a scanner, speech synthesizer, Braille printer, and regular-print printer give students who are blind access to most of the information used in the classroom environment, and permit the student to produce a work product in a format accessible to everyone (Espinola & Croft, 1992).

Before school opens in fall for the academic year and on the first days of school, an orientation and mobility specialist helps any visually impaired students who are new to the school to navigate on campus. Other students participate in these activities to help them become familiar and comfortable with disability and to enable them to provide assistance as the academic year progresses. Administrators, teachers, and an orientation and mobility specialist work together to remove or minimize the impact of architectural barriers. Equipment and furniture is not moved about during the school year without blind students being fully informed and oriented to any changes.

Stamina Limitations

Many disabling conditions and chronic illnesses, such as paralysis, multiple sclerosis, respiratory conditions, neurological diseases, and muscular dystrophy, can cause constant or intermittent problems with physical stamina, fatigue, and mobility. A significant problem encountered by people with severe disabilities concerns energy expenditures. The development of home-based education through use of the Internet and closed-circuit television, allowing the individual to be "part of" the classroom, has helped students with stamina limitations.

The home-based program is designed to allow students with

these and similar problems to take work home and maintain full class participation through closed-circuit interactive television, computer modems, and the Internet. The system allows for seeing, hearing, and interaction as if the individual were actually in the classroom. In fact, when the younger students are initially introduced to this, some feel that the student at home is actually in a room adjacent to the classroom instead of at home. Several of the younger students go as far as looking around the area adjacent to the classroom to find the student who, in reality, is at home.

Limited Use of the Upper Extremities

This limitation of function may be caused by paralysis, paresis (partial paralysis), severe incoordination, an absence of one or both upper extremities, congenital deformities, and certain neurological conditions (e.g., cerebral palsy). Because of the wide range of possible limitations, there are many potential accommodations. Custom-designed prosthetic and orthotic devices help maximize a student's ability to grip, pinch, and hold objects, and extend the joints through a normal range of motion (Brodwin et al., 1996). The devices selected allow for easy functioning by the individual, and take into consideration his or her highest level of capability. Almost any part of the body that has voluntary control can operate some type of computer interface. Sensors can detect the slightest movement if the person lacks the strength to operate a switch on a computer. Many people with disabilities can effectively and efficiently use a standard computer keyboard with a single finger, mouth stick, or head pointer.

Limited Use of the Lower Extremities

Some disabling conditions, such as spinal cord injury, amputation, other permanent injuries of the lower extremities, polio, cerebral palsy, and multiple sclerosis, can cause difficulty in ambulation and mobility. Full accessibility for wheelchairs on campus has occurred within the first two decades of the twenty-first century. Rehabilitation counselors and school administrators prompt attendance at classes. Power wheelchairs and small motorized vehicles allow for easy ambulation on campus. Parking spaces close to buildings are available for students who drive to school. Rehabilitation counselors work with school staff to minimize walking distances and ambulation for students with limited use of their lower extremities or those who are easily fatigued (Crewe & Krause, 1987; Temkin, 1996).

Cognitive Limitations
Intellectual functioning limitations and learning deficiencies may cause deficits in many areas or in one specific area, such as language or mathematics, depending on the individual (Brodwin et al., 1996). Through advances in medicine and medical treatment, many of these limitations have been minimized or resolved. Advances in computer technology have allowed professionals to become adept at developing individualized programs to maximize the potential of individuals who have some form of cognitive impairment. Caring, involvement, and understanding among all school staff have decreased the emotional impact of these conditions, both on the person with a disability and on others. Mainstreaming—full integration whenever possible—and acceptance by nondisabled students have created an atmosphere "near normal" for all individuals within the school. School staff is made aware that there can be occasional emotional volatility, and each person is sensitized to this possibility and informed on how to react if such problems occur. Assistive technology has helped students with limitations of cognitive-intellectual functioning. Computer software technology has enhanced written language skills, and the advances in artificial intelligence have minimized limitations of many students. Word processing, spelling- and grammar-check programs, and the development of "thinking" computers have become valuable assists to students with limitations in cognition. Supercomputers help with learning, making associations and inferences, and decision making. Availability of information has been greatly enhanced since the turn of the twenty-first century.

Attitudes: Acceptance, Inclusion, Independence, and Empowerment

Disability has broad sociocultural implications that go beyond physical, mental, and emotional limitations. Public school personnel now realize that sociocultural considerations include discrimination in education and employment. Although schools in the twenty-first century are fully inclusive, some employers still discriminate against people who have disabilities, regardless of the individual's knowledge and abilities to perform the particular job. In the past, and still in the present, social and psychological reactions of employers and the sociopolitical structure of society have created a "disabling environment" that has resulted in significantly diminished job and career potential. People with disabilities often have found themselves unemployed or underemployed, earning salaries significantly less than nondisabled workers. Although society has been changing, residuals of discriminatory behavior have remained, especially in the area of employment. Students with disabilities are taught to advocate for themselves, especially when apparent discriminatory practices exist, and nondisabled students are encouraged to advocate for their disabled peers when they see discrimination occurring (Brodwin et al., 1996; Maki & Riggar, 1997; Orange, 1995).

A great advance in the arena of attitude is that schools have been teaching students to view disability-related functional limitations as located within the environment, not within the person with a disability (Hahn, 1982, 1988; Orange, Brodwin, & Johnson, 1993). In this model, the architectural barriers of the past and the negative attitudes and behaviors of society, rather than the disabilities themselves, are seen as the cause of any limitations persons with disabilities have. When the barriers in society no longer exist, disabilities will be minimized.

Within the early twenty-first century, we have seen the removal of many architectural barriers, allowing people with disabilities greater access to education and employment, as well as social and leisure-time functions and activities. This, along with the changing attitudes of society, has helped people with disabilities become more included in daily life. No longer perceived as being outside the minority group model, the 43 million people with disabilities in the United States are now afforded all the rights and privileges of other minority groups. The civil rights movement and consumerism movement for persons with disabilities were given strength by the Americans with Disabilities Act of 1990. Unemployment for people with disabilities has decreased and underemployment has diminished. Although opportunities and salaries for people with disabilities are not yet equal to their nondisabled peers, the gap has narrowed, and opportunities continue to grow.

Assistive Technology

We are in an age of rapid technological change. No sooner is a personal computer introduced than an even more technologically advanced model replaces it. Legislation of the

1970s mandated strong support for people who have severe disabilities and chronic illnesses, and with it developed a national focus on meeting these individuals' independent living needs, including their educational achievement. The successful inclusion of students with disabilities requires that public school curricula become fully accessible to all students—regardless of the severity of the student's physical, emotional, or intellectual limitations—whenever possible. Technology can be a valuable and practical assist for inclusion of students with disabilities into the mainstream of education. The use of the microcomputer in education is a vital assist to students with disabilities in their educational achievement, as well as in other areas of daily living and independence. Use of technology to its full potential requires public school administrators, teachers (including those in special education), and rehabilitation counselors to become even more aware of and adaptable to the uses of technology in the school setting by individuals with disabilities.

In 2021, with the increased and evolving presence of technology in the classroom and at home, and the infusion of technology into the curriculum, accessibility is immediately enhanced, and solutions are only a keystroke, mouse click, or Internet "surf" away. All too often, technology has been viewed as a stand-alone classroom component, a place where students go when they have completed all of their required assignments, or where they can prepare their practice activities and homework. Technology is a powerful vehicle for instruction, curricula access, and accommodation if that technology is used within the curricula and not viewed as an adjunct to teaching and learning activities. Computer technology in 2021 is seen as a tool, much like paper and pencil, and students are encouraged to learn and use advanced technology across all learning activities, both within and outside the classroom.

In an inclusive setting, the use of technology has become a device for learning and providing access to the curriculum. Infusing educational curricula with technology occurs at the lesson- or unit-planning phase of curriculum development. Thereby, it becomes an integral and integrated part of the educational process. Once the curriculum is developed, methods are explored to provide accommodation for students with disabilities, thereby allowing them to achieve their maximum potential in the least restrictive environment possible.

In becoming productive, independent, and able to assimilate into and achieve within society, people with disabilities must overcome numerous obstacles. To maximize vocational potential, the individual needs a quality and comprehensive education. Technology of 2021 allows students access to an equal education, whether it is within a regular school environment or, for those with the most severe limitations, at home or in an institution.

Assistive technology has helped provide persons with disabilities greater independence in the areas of social, educational, vocational, and leisure-time pursuits. Two major drawbacks of assistive technology are its expense and the rapid obsolescence of equipment. In working with students, rehabilitation counselors attempt to locate funding sources that have the means to purchase the needed assistive technology for the student.

The microcomputer as assistive technology has had tremendous impact on the lives of people with disabilities. These computers have become readily portable and fully accessible; a laptop version is used in the classroom. The student can use the computer both as a conversational and as a classroom aid. The various interfaces (standard keyboard, mouse, touch-key switches, and sensors) allow students with disabilities to operate computers effectively and efficiently. Since the beginning of the twenty-first century, with government support and incentives, electronics companies have been designing computers and peripheral equipment with the needs of people with disabilities in mind. With the use of modern assistive technology, individuals who have disabilities are on an equivalent playing field in this information age.

Career Counseling and Employment

Legislation that passed in the 1990s ensured that students with disabilities would be provided equal opportunities to participate in the decision-making process; this included career planning and employment. As has always been the case for students who do not have disabilities, the thought of going to work in the future is instilled beginning in kindergarten. In the past, poorly developed self-concepts, ambivalence about obtaining meaningful employment, and limited information about occupations have been obstacles to employment for people with disabilities; in 2021, these problems have been replaced with strengthened self-esteem, the concept of working as a reality, and the provision by counselors of sufficient occupational information to make informed choices. Disempowerment has been replaced by mainstreaming in education, inclusion in all aspects of society, and self-empowerment.

The American with Disabilities Act of 1990 went far in helping diminish discriminatory practices in the workplace. Today's employers concentrate more on an individual's abilities, rather than his or her limitations. With the more progressive philosophy of career development for students with disabilities, teachers and counselors look at careers and career paths for these students, instead of looking at low-paying jobs with little probability of advancement. Employers are more knowledgeable and cooperative than they once were in offering advancement and career path positions. The words of Kosciulek (1998, p. 114), "The goal of empowering people with disabilities to live independently, enjoy self-determination, make choices, contribute to society, and pursue meaningful careers should be a common one for all professionals serving individuals with disabilities," have now become a reality and a part of everyday practice.

The empowerment philosophy emphasized by Emener (1991) has been adopted by our public school systems. Paraphrased, the four tenets of this philosophy are the following:
1. Each individual is of great worth and dignity.
2. All people have equal opportunities to maximize their potential and are deserving of help from society, whenever necessary, to achieve this potential.
3. People strive to grow and change in positive ways.
4. Individuals are free to make their own decisions about managing their lives and futures.

Career counseling is no longer done *to* the student; the student is an active participant in all phases of the process. Professionals have learned through experience that active involvement of the person with a disability is one of the essential elements to successful career counseling interventions. Computers have enhanced the career counseling process for all students. Students with disabilities have benefited from the latest in computer technology and access, and can be instructed to guide much of this process independently. Processing of information has become simpler; students can now access information on careers from their homes and spend as much time on it as they feel they need.

Conclusion

The future for inclusion of people with disabilities in all aspects of American society is an outcome that would have a most positive impact on this country and its citizens. Through mainstreaming and inclusion, students in our schools will have greater opportunities to become productive members of our society. Legislation occurring just before the turn of the century paved the way for these changes. The Individuals with Disabilities Education Act and the Americans with Disabilities Act produced change in two most important areas: education and employment. These legislative acts and others, with the current removal of architectural barriers and the positive change in attitudes that has been occurring, prompted us to take an optimistic approach when looking toward the future.

We believe that all public schools of the future will have (a) ready access to a rehabilitation counselor, and (b) a wide range of support services for their students who have disabilities. Although persons with disabilities currently show higher rates of unemployment and underemployment, the gap is narrowing, due in part to the Americans with Disabilities Act and also to a gradual change in employer attitudes toward workers who have disabilities. We believe that future changes within the educational system will provide for greater inclusion of students with disabilities in the public schools. With more positive societal attitudes, full accessibility in a barrier-free environment, and uses of computer technology, much that we have written within this chapter will come to fruition by the year 2021. The words of President Clinton at the beginning of this chapter provide a most positive vision of the future for persons with disabilities: "Together, we've begun to shift disability policy in America away from exclusion, towards inclusion; away from dependence, towards independence; away from paternalism, towards empowerment."

References

Americans with Disabilities Act of 1990, 42 U.S.C. § 12101 *et seq.*

Brodwin, M. G., Parker, R. M., & DeLaGarza, D. (1996). Disability and accommodation. In E. M. Szymanski & R. M. Parker (Eds.), *Work and disability: Issues and strategies in career development and job placement* (pp. 165–207). Austin, TX: Pro-Ed.

Crewe, N., & Krause, J. S. (1987). Spinal cord injury: Psychological aspects. In B. Caplan (Ed.), *Rehabilitation psychology desk reference* (pp. 3–35). Rockville, MD: Aspen.

Education for All Handicapped Children Act of 1975, 20 U.S.C. § 1400 *et seq.*

Emener, W. (1991). Empowerment in rehabilitation: An empowerment philosophy for rehabilitation in the twentieth century. *Journal of Rehabilitation, 57,* 7–12.

Espinola, O., & Croft, D. (1992). *Solutions: Access technologies for people who are blind.* Boston: National Braille Press.

Hahn, H. (1982). Disability and rehabilitation policy: Is paternalistic neglect really benign? *Public Administration Review, 43,* 385–389.

Hahn, H. (1988). The politics of physical differences: Disability and discrimination. *Journal of Social Issues, 44,* 39–47.

Hanley-Maxwell, C., Szymanski, E. M., & Owens-Johnson, L. (1998). School-to-adult life transition and supported employment. In E. M. Szymanski & R. M. Parker (Eds.), *Rehabilitation counseling: Basics and beyond* (3rd ed.) (pp. 143–179). Austin, TX: Pro-Ed.

Individuals with Disabilities Education Act of 1990, 20 U.S.C. § 1400 *et seq.*

Kosciulek, J. (1998). Empowering the life choices of people with disabilities through career counseling. In N. C. Gysbers, M. J. Heppner, & J. A. Johnston, *Career counseling: Process, issues, and techniques* (pp. 109–122). Boston: Allyn & Bacon.

Maki, D. R., & Riggar, T. F. (Eds.). (1997). *Rehabilitation counseling: Profession and practice.* New York: Springer Verlag.

Orange, L. M. (1995). Skills development for multicultural rehabilitation counseling: A quality of life perspective. In S. Walker, K. A. Turner, M. Haile-Michael, A. Vincent, & M. D. Miles (Eds.), *Disability and diversity: New leadership for a new era* (pp. 59–65), Washington, DC: President's Committee on Employment of People with Disabilities.

Orange, L. M., Brodwin, M. G., & Johnson, S. (1993). Early intervention to facilitate employment of persons with spinal cord injury. *California Association for Counseling and Development Journal, 13,* 9–15.

Price-Ellington, D., & Berry, H. G. (1999–2000). Postsecondary education, vocational rehabilitation, and students with disabilities: Gaining access to promising futures. *American Rehabilitation, 25*(3), 2–10.

Rehabilitation Act of 1973, 29 U.S.C. § 701 *et seq.*

Rehabilitation Act Amendments of 1992, Public Law No. 102-569, 106 Stat. 4344.

Rubin, S. E., & Roessler, R. T. (2001). *Foundations of the vocational rehabilitation process* (5th ed.). Austin, TX: Pro-Ed.

Temkin, A. (1996). Employment and spinal cord injury: Reflections on the impact of managed care. *Spinal Cord Injury Rehabilitation, 2,* 71–77.

About the Authors

Leo M. Orange, M.S., is the coordinator of disabled student services at Oxnard College in Oxnard California, and a part-time assistant professor at California State University, Los Angeles, in the rehabilitation-counseling program. Mr. Orange has many publications in the professional literature of rehabilitation and counseling on subjects of attitudes, reasonable accommodation, multicultural counseling, and medical and psychosocial aspects of disability. He has presented papers and workshops at local, state, regional, and national conferences and conventions on various topics of disability studies.

Martin G. Brodwin, Ph.D., C.R.C. is a professor of education and coordinator of the Rehabilitation Counselor Education Program, Charter College of Education, California State University, Los Angeles. Since 1980, he has testified as a vocational expert for the Office of Hearings and Appeals, Social Security Administration, on issues of disability. Dr. Brodwin has written more than 50 article and book chapters on topics including multicultural counseling, medical aspects of disabilities, private-sector rehabilitation, attitudes, and sexuality and disability. In 1997, he was honored with the Outstanding Professor Award by California State University, Los Angeles.

Chapter Sixteen

Pinching the Future of Higher Education Counseling

Edmond C. Hallberg

It is a rare privilege to have the luxury to envision almost 20 years ahead to the year 2021. In this day and age, most of our time is taken by day-by-day crisis management, which all but precludes speculations about the future. Therefore, it is with pleasure that I look to the future of our field—college counseling.

Speculations in this chapter lead briefly through key and scary future university trends and values; then we will be able to look at four areas that will shape college and university counseling. Each trend offers a unique brand of excitement and a challenge to be faced, although the reader will note a certain amount of agitated nostalgia on my part as well.

Trends in Higher Education

Five major trends seem to be important as background when looking at college counseling in the year 2021. These college trends do not clearly represent directions—visible only is an erupting kaleidoscope of change and choice. However, these five trends seem to be important:

1. computer dominance
2. the university without a place
3. the university as a major source of societal power (and, therefore, money)
4. the narcissism of individuality
5. the faculty as entrepreneurs

Computer Dominance
The good news about the computer, as we well know, is its speed, storage, and memory, which cannot be disputed.

However, little is known about the downside. Patterns indicate bothersome "click-throughs": Office mates e-mail each other instead of having eye-to-eye contact. Personal contact is getting lost in the tiny flag that stands on the AOL mailbox. Personalities seem detached and demeaned to a small icon on the 'net. Although communication continues, the computer allows ¡the community of scholars to remain anonymous—faceless. Increasing computerization, along with faculty overspecialization and the death of a small town campus, have all but "done in" the community of scholars.

Computer dominance has eroded even the classroom, which allows the "unlearned" to select their own teachers and subjects on the Internet. Wisdom, compassion, authority, and trust, past principles of the learning process, seem unimportant, passé. Information is thought to be an education, being informed equates with being literate. Each of these developments twists alma mater beyond recognition.

The University without a Place
Second, it appears that the "place" of the university has all but disappeared. Today colleges are a place for the occasional comings and goings of faculty and students—Penn Station instead of Penn State. In the future, faculties will spend less time on campus. Students will be part-time, dropping in and out for a year or two, and then returning to take a course here and there. Students will be given a "ticket to ride," coming and going and transferring to the trains of their own impressions. College will be a place to manufacture, classify, and retain information, a factory of sorts, not dusty and noisy like those in the past, but a factory nonetheless. The college and university of the future will be without concrete or ivy or walls—or a community of scholars. Satellite U and virtually U will be all we need.

The University as a Major Source of Societal Power
The third trend has to do with the campus as the Fort Knox of the year 2021. Within the new specialized campus trappings mentioned, economic events will be fueled by dollars and cents generated at universities.

If we follow Toffler's (1991) logic in *Power Shift,* we find we are readily shifting from an agricultural, through a post-industrial, to an information-based world economy. Within each wave, economic values (dollars, that is) were in land, then natural resources, and then information, respectively. If information is today's "serious bucks," and the university is a place where information is developed, stored, and accessed, then the college and university will be the richest institution in the land. Possibly, tomorrow's stock market will record daily fluctuations in the stock of Harvard, Yale, Cal State, and ABC Community College.

If these speculations seem far-fetched, remember we are talking about the year 2021. Keep in mind that after World War II, American colleges and universities tied themselves closely to the federal government. At one point, the University of California at Berkeley was receiving 27% of its funding from the federal government. During the cold war, some portions of Stanford's Physical Science Department received 80% of their monies from outside sources. These universities provided research monies remunerated to faculty by the federal government or other outside sources. Professors invented the transistor, started Silicon Valley—yes, they even invented Viagra—and continually advanced their own economic positions, *as well as* knowledge for its own sake.

Today, Merck's research professors receive millions of dollars to run college and university labs. A professor at UC San Diego explores DNA with a beginning class at the university in the morning, and then in the afternoon, to augment his salary, runs next door to the Salk Institute to do research. Toshiba proposes building a microbiology building at UC Irvine to house the UC faculty members, raising questions as to who has ownership of products.

The Narcissism of Individuality

Fourth, we find a trend that is fueled by computer dominance: the narcissism of individualization. This is a mouthful, but "narcissism" runs deeper year by year in our society. Deep concern for self, so characterized by characters on *Ally McBeal, Seinfeld,* and *Friends,* may close the learner to all but his or her own introspection. Is "me" sufficient to learn, or do we need a more humble learner able to explore and risk beyond self?

Many colleges today propose that students should be consumers. This obviously fuels the narcissism of individuality. Will the future B.A. be as valuable as its predecessors? The last century focused on the development of knowledge of the faculty. Will we make the mistake of being preoccupied with focusing on the learner in this century? A balanced collaboration between faculty and students seems necessary for the superior transmission of knowledge.

Today, student narcissism dominates even the classroom in many places. Ask any professor who tries to keep the class together for 16 weeks—students miss class without remorse, postpone midterms to take a holiday, and discount key subjects as "not for me." "Vocamania" (the pursuit of preparation for lucrative employment) has all but buried the liberal arts in many colleges. Courses about history, philosophy, and the arts are for the "fringe people." An applied-knowledge future seems to be the curriculum.

The Faculty as Entrepreneurs

The fifth and last trend is that faculty will become entrepreneurial. In the future, faculty will work for an institution of higher learning and become a partner in a biotech company at the same time. Colleges will contract their faculty to work in industry or government. Faculty will be responsible for the disciplines they will develop and research. They will apply their discipline to industry or government, and teach students who will participate with them in industrial applications. Students will have assignments within a discipline, as well as those in other industrial applications.

Faculty tenure will be eliminated due to the pace of change occurring within the universities and colleges as well as in the industrial marketplace. Tenure will have no place in this profitable stew of competitive academe. Professional journals and articles, the bulwark of faculty promotion and its "billboard" (the number of peer reviewed publications), will disappear as the customary counting device for promotion. Instead, the constant ratios for results-based projects within the community and those related to students' success ratios will become the measure of faculty.

Many faculty will live on the campus two or three nights a week, or in industrial "faculty clubs," and then go home. Their teaching will be provided through distance learning, as well as at a "company," or campus. Faculty training and retraining will be a big part of each discipline.

Librarian faculty will be the highest paid professionals in the organization. By the year 2021, "data guides" and "mappers" will see one through the maze of research, Internet, and hologram topics. An overwhelming amount of material and information that is stored and classified will need to be accessed, which will demand that librarians act as information guides for the faculty member or the project team leader.

If information is wealth, "academic thieves" will be everywhere, gathering information for their purposes. The ownership of intellectual property will be one of the major preoccupations of the day.

Inasmuch as the universities and colleges are the center of information and enterprise, people will be able to "buy a byte" and go into the database of the colleges and universities for a fee. There will also be "knowledge brokerage fees," similar to what Dean Witter and Charles Schwab have today.

Not only is the faculty going to have to change, but the process of higher education as we know it will also change. Faculty will become resource mentors, as mentioned earlier. Students will learn at different rates, with different goals and learning styles. The lecture as the sole teaching method will die in approximately 2010 due to changes in classroom authority, diversity, culture, age, and multipurpose self-education.

Faculty will preside over student assessment in mentoring teams, which will monitor student progress until graduation. Public funds will be allocated accordingly. Many counselors, as well as other faculty, will teach student development courses, which will be set within the corporate setting, as well as in classrooms of English and mathematics.

Moreover, good teaching and research will be tied inextricably to individual student progress. Today's legislators, parents, and students alike are asking penetrating questions for the first time. Two such questions are "How come I can't find any faculty on campus?" and "Why is it that you as faculty lose two-thirds of your students who wish to graduate?" We will be held accountable for the answers to these questions in the next decade.

The students in the year 2021 will be somewhat indentured. They will have long-term educational plans for learning that may last 20 or 30 years. Things will move so fast, students and faculty will constantly need updating. Student tuition could be in excess of $300,000. Many students will have to take out a "knowledge mortgage," similar to a home mortgage, to pay for this increasing cost of education. The average age of students will be 40 years old. Commencement will cease to exist.

Trends in Higher Education Counseling

Given these five speculations regarding trends in the

university and college, we are now able to look more closely at the changes in college counseling in the year 2021. We will look at college counseling in the following ways:

1. going with the force
2. discarding post-industrial counseling organization
3. counselers as teachers
4. student development as a discipline

Going with the Force

Although those of us in counseling long for a connected, simpler life unencumbered by lifelong tuition and profitability, we have no choice. If we continue to resist and we do not join in with the changes in the university, we will be squashed like a bug crossing the super highway. I know you wish to return to the tweed jackets, pipe smoking, and 13 hours of counseling you had with your favorite client. Of course, you hope to slough off accountability so you can continue to ruminate about the good old days, but this will be impossible. The first trend in counseling in the year 2021 will see counselors changing their attitudes, moving through their own resistances to excitement. Counselors will go with the force, or be forced into permanent sabbatical.

Discarding Post-industrial Counseling Organization

The second trend relates to new organizations. What will the organization of college counseling look like in the year 2021? It will be much like the new organization suggested in the trends stated above: entrepreneurial and computer driven. But, more specifically, the new organization of counseling will have several different elements. First, we will get rid of the words "student services." Are we educators or not? Although everybody needs technical support, counselors with master's degrees will be hired to provide education and to change behavior, not merely to support it. The erroneous assumption that all we have to do is "deliver the student to the classroom in optimal condition for learning" will reach its final resting place. Besides, "student services" sounds like an international oil company! I know of no college or university where they have departments of English services or mathematics services. The question we need to answer is, "What is it we do to educate students directly?"

We must recognize that medical, real estate, and banking services should be provided by the outside community. College financial aid services belong to the local bank. College housing services belong to the local real estate broker, and all but emergency medical services generally belong to the city hospital. This does not mean that we do not have a calling. Fortunately, our calling in a results-based society goes to the center of the direct education of students.

In the next century, college financial aid offices will offer topics such as budgeting college money, financial planning through the life cycle, and preparing financially for a family. These courses, or seminars, will be fundamentally much more educational and important than vying with the local bank to provide loans and other financial services. Housing education in conjunction with other disciplines will include important areas of student leadership and personal relationships. Housing departments will initiate an entire curriculum of living together, sexual orientation, and relationship conflict. Health services will educate college students concerning AIDS, abuse, stress, and immunity management. Teaching these programs is important.

If our narrowed purpose in the future is to educate students directly, two camps, instruction and student affairs, are unnecessary. I know how some of you feel, because I spent five years of my life as a dean of students fighting with the vice president of instruction. While results indicated that we were both bloodied after the five years, we also deviated from purpose, and yet we were fighting for the same territory, the same concern—to directly educate students. The waste of power between instruction and student affairs will be seen as an unnecessary expenditure in the year 2021, or possibly before then. Naturally, somebody has to be in charge of the direct education of students, but the battle to determine and keep the territory rights is over.

Counselors as Teachers

For those of us in counseling, the new century will demand new skills in three areas. First, we will need new skills related to changing behavior, not merely presenting information. Second, we will need to move from therapy to direct teaching of content; and third, we will need to move from being artists to being scientists. Each carries with it enough challenges and excitement to erase the nostalgia for the past decades.

The need to add to or change student behavior demands a much more prescriptive process than allowed in the traditional counseling approaches. Counselors will need to understand how to change behavior, how to set goals, and how to move a student from point A to point B. Traditionally, we have placed the onus on the client to change. The student as a consumer, picking and choosing unilaterally, attempting to educate him- or herself through the client-centered therapeutic method, is of the twentieth century. In the future, directions need to be *prescribed* by faculty in concert with students. This does not mean that students forfeit their internal locus of control to the faculty direction. Within instructional guidelines, maintaining an internal locus of control and taking responsibility for one's learning are paramount. Despite past counselor training, counselors have had the luxury of not being accountable for student progress. This will not be the case in a results-based student success curriculum. This will be difficult for counselors to learn because of previous training or passivity toward the learning process.

Moreover, for the first time counselors will be responsible for college success—a content or "master student" approach, a discipline of affective development foundational to the learning of other subjects. The student development curriculum will provide content and goals, methods of presentation, sequencing of experiences, qualified instructors, and methods of evaluation. The formation of this discipline is underway but will take a good portion of the new, beginning century to complete.

Last, the art of counseling, which we have worked on so diligently over the years, will be supplanted by the steel gray, postmodern industrial science of measured, planned student success. This is not all good, but the banner of results will be based on metric assessments and "success engineering," the new accountability for counselors in the future. It will also be the basis for increased funding and job security within higher education.

Student Development as a Discipline
The student success curriculum will have several elements of counselor responsibility. These are assessment, identification of foundational characteristics, and prescribed interventions.

Assessment of goals, outcomes, and accountability, while thought to be discrete by some, are all part of the same process. One should not exist without the others. Let's look at assessment. First, before the year 2021, we will begin to realize that assessment of prior achievement is insufficient for those students who need to improve in basic subjects. The next century will give us a set of measured causes of lack of achievement, and offer measured interventions for improvement.

An analogy may clarify here. In 1960, if you went to your

cardiologist, he or she would test your blood pressure. If high, you would be given some digitalis and be sent home. Measurement indicated a problem with hypertension, but solutions to the problem were unknown. Today, college counseling personnel are still measuring achievement by a lack of it! Measurement tells students they are doing poorly in a subject and probably will do poorly in the future, but so what? We must tell the student why he or she is doing poorly and what to do about it.

Today in medicine things are different. Thirty years of extensive research have provided six indices of heart disease: stress, high and low density cholesterol, lack of exercise, diet, obesity, and heredity. Through extensive research findings, indices allow for a direct intervention to improve the quality of life and possibly to extend it. In student development, we must uncover and measure the causes of lack of success. Each specific cause will elicit interventions, which will increase the probabilities of college success.

Along this line, I am working on identifying eight factors of success. These are in the *College Success Factors Index* (Hallberg, Sauer, & Hallberg, 1992). These factors exist as foundational to achievement, and have been found to be valid in the literature as well as empirically.

Control/responsibility. If we do not have control over the responsibilities we assume at college, less success is possible.

Competition. The need to compete is part of our culture, and thus is an aspect of college and career success. For successful students, competition becomes internalized—they compete with themselves.

Task precision. A strong goal or task orientation, and a desire to complete the task in a near perfect manner, are very important in college success.

Expectations. Successful students have goals that are related to assignments, areas of study, and future careers.

Wellness. How healthy one is relates to college success. Stress, anger, sleeplessness, alcohol or drug use, and inadequate diets are deterrents to college success.

Time management. How people maximize the time they have, and schedule activities to affect productivity, will directly affect success.

College involvement: Being involved in the college environment, and knowing how to use school resources, are important factors in persistence and retention.

Family or significant other involvement. Family encouragement and participation are important motivating factors in a student's success.

These factors are measured in the *College Success Factors Index* and lead to specific interventions designed into a curriculum entitled *Making the Dean's List* (Hallberg & Achieris, 1998). In terms of the factors stated here, control and responsibility interventions include assertiveness training or self-esteem education. Conflict resolution and communication skills are included for competition, and it utilizes time management theory and exercises.

In the future, then, the formation of a college success curriculum must answer five questions.

1. Have we committed ourselves to the purpose of college, which is to increase student success?
2. What are the factors that affect student success in college?
3. Are we able to measure these variables that lead to success?
4. Once we have measured factors of success, can we identify causes and communicate these factors to the students and the college community?
5. Is there a student success curriculum related to these factors that we can teach to students and measure their progress to increase their chances of success?

The formation of the college success curriculum will develop in the next 10 years, and it is my belief that student development professionals should be at the center with their success partners from other disciplines, as well as students.

Although I have outlined the path to the year 2021 in a broad manner, nevertheless, I hope the reader will add a few skips of his or her own flat rock across the lake. I only wish my tenure were just starting. When I began, counselors were considered "suspect at best," but the future will find counselors indispensable to the success of learners in higher education. Let's take the challenge.

References

Astin, A. W. (1975). *Preventing students from dropping out.* San Francisco: Jossey-Bass.

Hallberg, E. C. (1971). *The affective curriculum.* Unpublished manuscript.

Hallberg, E. C., & Achieris, R. (1998). *Making the dean's list.* Sacramento, CA: Ombudsman Press.

Hallberg, E. C., Sauer, L., & Hallberg, K. (1992). *College success factors index.* Sierra Madre, CA: Ombudsman Press.

Hallberg, E. C., & Thomas, W. (1973). *When I was your age.* New York: Macmillan.

Pascarrelia, E. T., & Terenzini, P. T. (1991). *How college affects students.* San Francisco: Jossey-Bass.

Tinto, V. (1975). Dropouts from higher education: A theoretical synthesis of recent research. *Review of Educational Research, 45,* 89–125.

Toffler, A. (1991). *Power shift.* New York: Bantam Books.

About the Author

Edmond C. Hallberg is co-author of *The College Success Factors Index* and *The School Success Factors Index.* His background includes being a professor of higher education counseling at California State University. He has also served as dean of admissions and registration, coordinator of academic advising, and dean of students. Hallberg has his doctorate from Stanford University. He has been a consultant or speaker at more than 40 community colleges and four-year colleges. A past president of the California College Personnel Association, Hallberg has been featured in *People* and *Money* magazines, and has appeared as a popular speaker at conferences and on numerous radio and televisions programs. In addition to having researched college success issues for more than 20 years, he has equally broad experience as a management development trainer. He has had extensive experience as a seminar leader and conference speaker.

Section 6:
Riding Political and Technological Currents

Preparing Students for the Globalized Society of the Twenty-First Century: A Comparative Perspective on the Ideological Roots of Guidance

Lonnie L. Rowell

The future of school counseling is bound to political processes interwoven with the contemporary education reform movement and with the social and economic conditions of the emerging global economy. More specifically, 20 years from now school counseling and guidance will reflect the dynamics at work within three distinct yet overlapping domains: the contemporary school reform movement, the professionalization of school counseling, and the relationship between counseling and the critical social and economic issues of the twenty-first century. The context within which school counselors work today has been increasingly shaped by a sustained effort to bring about a particular set of changes in the form and content of American education. In the short term, the politics of school reform influence all aspects of what counselors do and do not do in schools, how the profession is viewed within education circles and within the larger society, and how many counselors will be working in schools over the next 20 years. In the longer run, how school counseling positions itself in relationship to the professionalization of helping, the changing demographics of American society, and the increasingly unequal distribution of wealth will be defining elements in whether school counseling continues its development as a minor actor in the unfolding drama of global corporate domination or realigns itself with the heritage of progressive reform that marked its beginnings in the early twentieth century.

Ultimately, all aspects of counseling practice are tied to political processes. Politics are present both in the large domain of the special interest we represent as professional counselors and the smaller domains of how we wield the power of our expertise in counseling sessions and the everyday decisions we make, or that are made for us, about the allocation of time in the performance of our work and the living of our lives. In addition, all the counseling research imaginable—on guidance and counseling outcomes, on the efficacy of comprehensive counseling programs, and on the specific methods that most enhance effective counseling—passes through the crucible of politics. By politics I am referring simply to individual and organized actions affecting the distribution of power within various social systems. From a practice as well as research perspective, all the new models, new standards, new programs and new techniques in school counseling are either privileged into practice or shrugged off to institutional backburners or academic dustbins by the political decisions of legislatures, governors, credentialing commissions, licensing boards, counselor education programs, accrediting bodies, school boards, superintendents, principals, and others. In short, although we often would prefer to deny it, there is simply no escaping the press of politics in our lives.

Thus, it should come as no surprise that to understand fully where school counseling is headed as we begin the new millennium, some kind of political analysis is needed. How is it that time after time reform efforts steer clear of addressing the links between home and neighborhood conditions and school experience? Why do the powers that be in education most often marginalize the significance of prevention-oriented counseling and guidance and yet point with pride to the crisis-response teams of counselors, social workers, and psychologists rolled out when the latest schoolyard, hallway, or classroom tragedy bites the national psyche? In its broadest terms, a political analysis of school counseling entails a concern with how counselors in schools "reinforce the values, institutions, and human behaviors on which our present social order rests or . . . challenge those values, institutions, and behaviors" (Galpers, 1975, ix).

In an effort to address these and other issues, I offer a brief analysis of the future of school counseling through the dual lens of institutional theory (DiMaggio, 1988; Knoke & Prensky, 1984;

Laumann & Knoke, 1987; Ogawa & Bossert, 1995; Salganik, 1985; Scott, 1987) and progressive social commentary (Galpers, 1975; McKnight, 1995). The analysis explores how school counseling, represented by its organizational actors, or "institutional entrepreneurs" (DiMaggio, 1988), and by its formal and informal networks of influence (Laumann & Knoke, 1987), has sought to find its voice among the calls for changes in the institutional structures of American education and to define its place in the professionalization of American life in general. The crucible of politics I examine is tied to an understanding of the educational reform agenda of the 1980s and 1990s, to an understanding of how school counseling reform is positioned within this larger reform, and to the limitations of the dominant reform agenda in relationship to some pressing issues facing us at the turn of the new century. My findings point to the need for a more carefully developed political awareness as well as a more pronounced political involvement by school counselors and all those who support guidance and counseling.

The visible contours of the political processes at work in school reform are relatively easy to spot. For example, we look one direction and see new laws and policies being enacted by legislatures and school boards to increase student achievement and hold teachers more accountable; we look another and see national commissions, task forces, and committees hard at work on recommended changes in virtually every aspect of education; we look again and see the corresponding counseling task force, commission, or committee redefining counseling and guidance, setting new standards for the profession, or advocating for its inclusion in the newly emerging institutional configurations of education. The subterranean contours of these politics, however, are harder to see. Here, I believe, a political analysis is needed that confronts the relationship between school reform, globalization, and a corporate domination of society that, among other things, "establishes the market as the patron of educational reform" (McLaren & Farahmandpur, 2000, p. 25). Such an analysis also must address the overlapping of demographic factors and the normative elements reflected in cultural values and beliefs with the interests of various political actors (Lipman, 1998; Oakes, 1992). These less visible political processes are no less significant to the future of school counseling, and we can better understand what is occurring beneath the surface of school reform and school counseling reform by bringing these deeper elements to light.

I am well aware that some readers may be turned off by a

partisan call for political awareness and activism. Many counselors have made it clear that they are not "into that political stuff." Some feel that they must preserve their energy for "the kids." For others, politics seems too tiresome or too interwoven with shrewdness, expediency, or contrived interactions to be considered a priority. All I can ask in the face of these objections is that you temporarily suspend your disbelief and consider an alternative view. In this view, given that politics are unavoidable, it is essential for us to learn to do our politics wisely—with care, skill, and humility—on behalf of, first and foremost, children and youth. Helping skills are indeed an honorable set of tools for use in all aspects of human relations. But such skills do not exist in a vacuum, and the people who employ, and are employed by virtue of, those skills have a responsibility to conduct their practice in ways that reflect democratic and humane values, that is, in ways that empower people. Furthermore, I assert that we must develop our capacity to put those values to work among and between counselors, learning to work politically in ways that challenge and nurture us individually and strengthen our collective capacity for collaborative action. In my view, this task also must be made a high priority for all who wish to be advocates for social justice and who believe that our democracy must be revitalized and transformed into an authentic participatory system based on the genuine practice of citizen-power. In this context, I suggest that counselors have a direct stake in articulating and creating linkages between counseling practice and progressive social movements.

School Reform, School Counseling Reform, and the National Standards

The first domain to examine in this political analysis is the contemporary school reform agenda. This examination includes consideration of the reform of school counseling and the place of school counseling within the larger reform movement. Readers are no doubt familiar with the call for greater accountability and standards in education and are well aware that this particular education reform alarm was sounded in the 1980s with the publication of a series of papers, books, and pamphlets decrying the poor state of American education and proclaiming the need for urgent action to better prepare America's students for the soon-to-arrive twenty-first century (Pulliam & Van Patten, 1995). Following publication of A Nation at Risk in 1983, more than 30 other major reports and examinations of public education in America were released over a 10-year span (Pulliam & Van Patten, 1995, pp. 196–198). Throughout the 1980s and into the 1990s, education was a top national priority.

The recently adopted National Standards for School Counseling Programs (Campbell & Dahir, 1997) provide the clearest link between the contemporary school reform movement and school counseling, and it seems clear that sustained advocacy for the standards will constitute the centerpiece of the formal political future for school counseling. As Campbell and Dahir describe it, the call for reform and revitalization in school counseling, evident since the late 1980s, is the counseling profession's response to larger school reform initiatives "enacted in the name of achieving excellence in education"(p. 2). Campbell and Dahir explicitly tie the standards to "the current educational reform agenda that focuses on raising expectations for teaching and learning" (p. 1).

The standards imply a dual political strategy for school counseling in relation to the larger school reform efforts. On the one hand, the standards take their cue from the increased emphasis on higher achievement and accountability in education: they thus are dependent on, and contribute to, the momentum of the larger reform agenda. On the other hand, the standards acknowledge the struggles of many students against the numerous barriers to learning that so often block school success: in this context, the standards give at least some voice to the fairness, equity, and social justice issues often marginalized by the current reform agenda. Politically, from another perspective, advocacy for the standards most likely will bring gains for school counseling as a recent professionalized addition within the institutional framework of American education. Although, as will become evident, these gains make perfect sense in terms of larger trends for professionalization and specialization in helping, they need to be weighed against the need for, and potential of, a far more concerted populist effort in relation to crucial social and economic issues currently brushed aside in favor of the corporate interests that underlie the current school reform agenda. In my view, the tension between these two positions captures some of the deeper issues school counseling will face in the coming years.

Although many students are motivationally prepared to meet the challenge of higher academic standards, a very high percentage are not, and the barriers to learning that these students face put them seriously at risk of failure and of unproductive and troubled futures in the larger society. Yet with programs and services that address these barriers and promote healthy development for all students continuing to be seen both as "supplementary" and as items that interfere with activities directly related to instruction in reformed schools (Center for Mental Health in Schools, 1999), the dominant reform agenda appears oddly out of sync with the lives of the estimated 40 to 50% of American students who manifest some form of significant learning, behavior, and emotional problems (Center for Mental Health in Schools, 2000, p. 1).

On the other hand, the national standards define the counseling and guidance program as the cornerstone of student success and present a case for ending the "support services" view of school counseling in favor of a more comprehensive approach. Without this change, some argue, the emotional, physical, economic, and interpersonal barriers to learning found among so many students will continue to be addressed in a piecemeal manner, thus insuring that not all students will be able to meet the more rigorous expectations of higher academic standards (Center for Mental Health in Schools, 1999). In addition, the lack of a comprehensive approach to guidance and counseling creates unbearable pressures on classroom teachers to incorporate into their already excessively burdened classrooms ever-new and expanding curriculum related to such things as character education and development, conflict resolution, and violence reduction. From this standpoint, the challenge is to incorporate an updated understanding of learning and the development of the whole child within the drive for higher educational standards and to expand current school reform models "to fully integrate 'educational support activity'" (Center for Mental Health in Schools, 1999, p. 1). In short, the case for comprehensive school counseling and guidance is built around the idea that we cannot "win" the battle to maintain America's place in a changing world market if we simply leave behind those who are "at risk" and if we ignore the need to integrate academic achievement with the development of the whole child. Thus, although the standards reflect some of the priorities of the dominant school reform agenda, they have potential as a focal point for discussion of reform directions that promote not only the value of greater productivity but also the humane recognition that for today's youth, growing up in a "cold new world," to borrow part of the title of William Finnegan's recent book, extraordinary efforts are needed from caring adults to bridge the growing divide between generations and to end the isolation of the American adolescent "tribe apart" (Hersch, 1998, p. 1).

Another locus of activity linking school counseling and school reform has been the work of the College Entrance Examination Board. The College Board recognized in the 1980s that school reform efforts were overlooking counseling and guidance and appointed a Commission on Precollege Guidance and Counseling to examine the issue (College Board, 1986). The commission found, among other things, that "those initiating programs of educational reform must recognize that in the interest of justice and equity for all students, higher standards of performance can be achieved only by mutually supportive systems of instruction and guidance" (College Board, 1986, p. 31). Following a two-year investigation and completion of a major report, the board initiated three projects to field-test recommendations contained in the report (Nailor, 1999). The projects demonstrated that school counselors have a crucial role to play in school reform and that when counselors are active in the planning and implementation of such reforms, the whole school benefits. The Board's total effort provided evidence that the piecemeal approach to school counseling is an ineffective and inefficient use of educational resources, and that, conversely, carefully planned and systematically implemented high quality school counseling and guidance programs are crucial elements in student achievement as well as in successful school reform efforts (College Board, 1986, 1994, 1996).

In many respects, the alignment of school counseling reform with the broader school reform agenda constitutes a reasonable foundation both for building a better future for school counseling and for advocating for success for all students. If carefully planned and systematically implemented, high quality school counseling and guidance programs are crucial elements in student achievement, and if standards now exist that clearly identify what those programs ought to consist of, then, from an institutional politics standpoint, the future is clear: The formal and informal networks of professional counseling should simply continue advocating for the implementation of what they know works. With leadership from the American School Counseling Association (ASCA) and the College Board, among others, the key political work is to advocate for the careful planning of, and to secure the systematic implementation of, high quality counseling programs in which the role of school counseling is clearly defined according to the new national standards.

Such efforts are presently underway across the country. Teams of national standards trainers are at work in virtually every state. County offices of education and state departments of education are forming committees and task forces and sponsoring workshops and academies to disseminate the national standards or to develop localized versions of the standards. (I have just completed seven months' work on just such a county task force). An impressive mobilization on behalf of reforming school counseling programs is now underway, and it is unlikely that this mobilization will slow in the next several years. There is easily two decades worth of hard work and agonizing political mountains to climb on behalf of the changes described above.

The Politics of Professionalization and the Reform of School Counseling

Nevertheless, the reform mobilization described in the above positive narrative primarily positions school counseling advocates as a cautionary chorus behind the divas singing the praises of higher academic standards for students and greater accountability for teachers and administrators. While specific reforms for improving instruction and reorganizing school management have become the centerpieces in school districts' efforts to implement higher academic standards, counseling and mental health advocates have had limited success in gaining recognition that higher student achievement requires more than good instruction and well-managed schools. Although advocacy for comprehensive approaches has met with some success (e.g., in the Memphis City schools and the Central O'ahu District in Hawaii, according to the Center for Mental Health in Schools, 1999), these institutional and infrastructural solutions are few and far between and often mask an ongoing inability of our dominant educational structures to respond in meaningful ways to the needs of the children and youth. In addition, by not aligning with efforts to create a modernized progressive agenda that could perhaps more convincingly articulate the limits of "assembly-line, multiservice 'care'" (McKnight, 1995, p. 19) in a variety of helping settings, and more genuinely define a compelling vision for change, school counseling reform advocates inadvertently raise false hopes about what they can deliver and ultimately contribute to the deepening of public cynicism about service providers.

To fully understand this point and its implications for the future of school counseling requires further clarification, including a quick glance at the history of guidance and counseling in schools. Concern for those marginalized by the dominant agenda of contemporary school reform calls us back to the emergence of school guidance and counseling and the broader reforms of the progressive movement at the beginning of the twentieth century. As Gladding (1988) describes, counseling "developed out of a humanitarian concern to improve the lives of those adversely affected by the Industrial Revolution of the mid to late 1800s" (p. 5). Similarly, "most of the pioneers in the early guidance movement, which evolved into the profession of counseling, were social reformers" (p. 9). Gerald Stone (1986) discusses the era's "reform ideology" (p. 13) whose basic sentiment was humanitarian and arose in part from the individualism expressed in religion, the ideas of the Enlightenment, the pioneer spirit of the frontier, and the ideals of democracy. Whatever its sources, this humanitarian concern, stressing the improvability of humankind through the application of reason and scientific procedures, was expressed in diverse forms and in many localities across the country.

The reform ideology of this period was broad in scope, with reformers active in education, children's rights, treatment of the mentally ill, women's rights, workplace safety and workers' rights, food inspection, electoral reform, and challenges to the growth of monopoly capital (Zinn, 1980). Stone (1986) cites John Dewey and Frank Parsons as two of the most influential reformers in relationship to guidance and counseling. Dewey's ideas concerning the importance of schooling as preparation for vocation, citizenship, and responsible adulthood provided "fertile ground" (Stone, 1986, p. 14) for the growth of guidance, and Frank Parsons's founding of the Boston Vocational Bureau in 1908 was a critical first step in institutionalizing vocational guidance (Gladding, 1988). Dewey, in particular, has been acknowledged as a leading figure in the progressive education movement (Pulliam & Van Patten, 1995).

Most often, writers in counseling and counseling psychology focus on the humanitarian intentions of reformers. Authors such as Gladding (1988) and Stone (1986) stress the link between the emergence of guidance and a concern with improving the lives of children and youth through the application of rational and scientific procedures that would enable young people to learn more about themselves and to make rational choices about vocations. Little is usually said, however, concerning the relationship among the emergence of guidance, the broader progressive education movement, and the broader yet progressive movements. In my view, this omission limits our capacity to develop cogent political analysis and contributes to the tendency of counseling, like its famous relative psychology, to be ahistorical. I suggest that this tendency needs to be challenged, and that such a challenge is critical to the future of counseling.

A more historically based understanding would take into account the political dynamics that both opened up possibilities for reform of institutions and limited the scope of such reforms. For example, Zinn (1980) asserts that the reforms of the earlier progressive era were principally aimed at siphoning off popular sentiments for more fundamental changes in the society. It was, in Zinn's (1980) words, a period of "reluctant reform" (p. 341) in which business interests took the lead politically to initiate changes to "stabilize the capitalist system in a time of uncertainty and trouble" (p. 342). As Richard Hofstadter (1955) discusses in a classic work, the urban crowding, poverty, crime, corruption, and immigration chaos summed up as "the social question" (p. 235) in the late nineteenth- early twentieth-century reform era was answered by policies and programs intended to "minimize the most outrageous and indefensible exploitation of the working population" (p. 235). Yet, with their primarily conservative impulses, the reformers feared the poverty and restlessness of the growing urban masses. Reforms of this period helped perpetuate the economic domination of big money and big business rather than initiate creation of social systems more conducive to human well-being.

Such an analysis is not intended to generate guilt regarding the reform heritage out of which modern professional counseling emerged. A fuller historical understanding can help illuminate some conflicting interests found within the contemporary school reform movement and can open up possibilities for alternative perspectives that can free us from constricting and self-defeating strategies. At present, for example, a clear conflict exists between the interests of a new corporate elite which is expanding and consolidating, without constraints, all over the world and the interests of children and youth expected to achieve higher standards, yet not given the necessary assistance that would enable them to do so. It is perhaps not as gruesome a scenario as Zinn's (1980) description of the treatment of indigenous people on the island of Haiti by Columbus, but it has its parallels. In one Haitian province the Spanish conquerors were convinced that vast amounts of gold could be found and everyone fourteen or older was ordered "to collect a certain quantity of gold every three months. When they brought it, they were given copper tokens to hang around their necks. Indians found without a copper token had their hands cut off and bled to death" (p. 4).

I suggest that too close of an alignment with the dominant agenda of contemporary school reform threatens to identify counselors with an emerging managed-care, semiprivatized education system that, when it comes to the poor and disadvantaged in particular, will metaphorically cut off their hands. Without strong and broader advocacy for those increasingly marginalized by the rush to higher standards, the risk is that the national standards, like other aspects of the reform agenda, will primarily benefit those already in privileged positions within the educational system. Those who do not bring in the gold, so to speak, will be left to bleed to death (often quite literally) on the mean streets of urban decay and gang warfare.

A recent California lawsuit provides an example of this dynamic. In May 2000, the American Civil Liberties Union filed suit in California on behalf of students in a number of urban school districts contending that a "two class system" exists in which poor and non-White students attend schools with "terrible slum conditions, unqualified teachers, and few up-to-date textbooks" (Associated Press, 2000, May 22). The same conditions are not found, the suit contends, for White middle- and upper-class children. According to the Associated Press article, similar "adequacy funding" suits have been filed in 20 other states, with about half being successful to date. These lawsuits raise important issues regarding setting higher standards and providing adequate resources to ensure that all students have the opportunity to achieve them. In this context, the effort to pair good instruction and well-managed schools with comprehensive approaches to addressing barriers to learning and developmental issues is only part of the problem: The differential distribution of educational resources tends to systematically marginalize some students and privilege others, and unless this disparity is also addressed some students will be consigned to a much higher risk of failure regardless of program standards. Ironically perhaps, from the standpoint of the juvenile justice system, the unequal distribution of resources works in the opposite direction. A recent major study indicates that Black youths are 48 times more likely to be given juvenile prison sentences than Whites, and that White youths "convicted of violent offenses are imprisoned for an average of 193 days" (Glasser, 2000, p. 28) while Black youths are imprisoned for an average of 254 days. These disparities, and more, contribute to results such as the recent Los Angeles Times poll in which 58% of Latino parents and 94% of Black parents rated local schools as fair to poor (Sahagun, 2000).

However, as in the prior reform era, the current culture of school reform reflects an inherently conservative agenda, with a reworking of the status quo emerging from a "reform mill" (Oakes, Hunter Quartz, Ryan, & Lipton, 2000, p. 265) environment dominating education. As an alternative, Oakes and her associates assert the importance of reinfusing a sense of "civic virtue" into school reform. In their view, the process of transforming American schools "must itself be educative, socially just, caring, and participatory" (p. 262). Here, it would seem, we catch our first glimpse of the potential for linkages between comprehensive school reform, a revitalized progressive movement, and the reform of school counseling. In my view, the more progressive reform heritage of counseling needs to be reclaimed as the yardstick by which the political work of school counseling is undertaken. Ultimately, we need to ask how counselors can contribute politically to heading off the antihumanitarian tendencies reflected in the dominant late twentieth and early twenty-first century school reform agenda. Here, a relevant question for the future of counseling is, are school counselors the political actors in education best situated to take leadership in a reform process that is socially just as well as caring and that combines the legitimate expertise of helpers with genuine participatory practice in relationship to parents and students?

Unfortunately, thoughtful reform processes seem a luxury today, and school reforms have come at a sometimes dizzying pace in state after state. Teachers, principals, administrators in California, for example, are said to be "shell-shocked" (Brydolf, 1999, p. 24) by the proliferation of reforms, and the state's superintendents and school boards have sent a message to the governor to "back off and give the districts a break" (p. 24). Similarly, researchers at the University of California recently reported that the state needs "breathing space" after the "reform frenzy" of recent years (Associated Press, 2000, May 27). The Policy Analysis for California Education (PACE) report describes school reforms in California as "pieces of a jigsaw puzzle just dumped from the box" (Associated Press, 2000, May 27). The hundreds of new education laws and programs coming out of legislatures and governors' offices around the country may create quite a whirlwind of activity in school district offices, but these reforms appear to have done little to generate genuine participation in building school community or to address issues of civic virtue in any substantive way.

Of course, in a larger sense it is not simply the reform process that is problematic. In a close examination of the outcomes of previous school reform efforts, Tyack and Tobin (1993) address why the current institutionalized forms of schooling in the United States have been so hard to change for the past nine decades. They coined the phrase "the grammar of schooling" to refer to "the regular structures and rules that organize the work of instruction" (p. 454). These structures and rules, as evidenced in particular in the graded school and the Carnegie unit of high school credit, have remained stable despite significant and determined efforts to change them. Although considerable evidence points to the archaic nature of existing structures and rules in education, it is the reform efforts that, time and time again, have faded. Perhaps this helps explain why so many veteran teachers and school counselors appear cynical in relationship to reform: They simply no longer believe that it is possible to work in education from a stance based on "norms, policies, and practices that promote the public good through a citizenry educated to come together across differences and solve common problems in a democratic public sphere" (Oakes et al., 2000, p. 5). Reforms, like fashions, come and go. Yet little substantive change occurs, and when substantive change does occur it often lasts only as long as the determined efforts of the most vocal reformers.

In this context, we might say that if school counseling reform is to be more than complimentary rhetoric following the basic rules of the grammar of schooling, then school counselor leaders not only need to align more closely with those proposing fundamental changes in the rules but they also need to take care to sustain the reform process. As a preliminary step I suggest that reclaiming the progressive heritage of school counseling requires a more honest assessment of the role of school counseling in ideological and structural relationship to a whole set of institutional actors and forces in education. In particular, I suggest, professionalization as a force in counseling needs to be critically reexamined and new directions for the future of counseling need to be charted, directions that build community rather than undermine it and that enhance the individual and social capacities of youth and adults rather than pathologize the challenges people face.

Perhaps, for example, the national standards need to be recognized as an action taken by organized actors working to institutionalize structural elements within education that advance the interests of professionalized helping. There is no mystery in this, as actors within institutional settings take action to put in place structural elements favorable to the actors' interests (DiMaggio,1988). These actions also fit well with larger trends of modernization. According to Scott (1987), the nation state and the professions are the two primary agents that shape modern institutions. As Scott describes it, the structures of our dominant public and private institutions are created through political contests between these two agents. Thus, the politics of the national standards and related efforts reflect actors concerned with the marginalization of school counseling as a nonessential support service (a subordinate institutional form from the standpoint of professional school counseling) locked in a political contest as the nation state works to advance its interests (at least those interests identified with corporate and global capitalism) through new structural elements in education that promote higher expectations for teaching and learning.

Clearly, ASCA and the College Board have taken actions consistent with the interests of those they represent. In this sense, they are using their organizational power quite appropriately. As Laumann and Knoke (1987) indicate, organizational actors, rather than individual actors, possess the resources needed to reshape institutions, so it is entirely fitting that the ASCA, the College Board, and others have taken prominent positions in the political contests defining the institutional forms of education for the twenty-first century. Yet, if in this scenario you begin to have some difficulty hearing the genuine voices of children, youth, and parents, then you are on the trail of the problem too often masked by the preeminence of political contests between the organizational gladiators of modern society. As we shall see, the involvement of all these experts in institutional reform, particularly reforms of human service (and, I would argue, educational) institutions, often creates a social and political environment in which the negative consequences of reform contradict the potential positive effects (McKnight, 1995). A chief contradiction to be faced, whether or not counselors and counselor advocates like the idea of facing it, is the effect of increasing specialization in human services of all types on the community-building capacity of ordinary citizens. McKnight's (1995) critique puts the problem this way:

> The community, a social space where citizens turn to solve problems, may be displaced by the intervention of human service professionals acting as an alternative method of problem-solving. Human service professionals with special expertise, techniques, and technology push out the problem-solving knowledge and action of friend, neighbor, citizen, and association. As the power of profession and service system ascends, the legitimacy, authority, and capacity of citizens and community descend. (pp. 105–106)

Over the past 40 years, many authors have examined the emergence of experts and managers of all types, and the institutional and organizational forms that reflect their interests, as a defining characteristic of modern American history (e.g., Bellah, Madsen, Sullivan, Swidler, & Tipton, 1985; Marcuse, 1964; McKnight, 1995; Roszak, 1969). As Roszak (1969) described it, "in the technocracy everything aspires to become purely technical, the subject of professional attention. The technocracy is . . . the regime of experts "or of those who can employ the experts" (p. 7). Szasz (1961) contributed significantly to the critique of psychotherapy as a particular domain of technocratic rationalization. He concluded that the popularity of psychotherapy, in all its forms, can be attributed to a "pervasive wish to deny, alter, or avoid facing up to well-defined conflicts of human interests, whether these be interpersonal, social, economic, or ethical" (p. 220). Ultimately, in Szasz's view, the problems that we all face, but that are particularly problematic for some, are the problems of human social interaction: They are problems of freedom, responsibility, and power.

As Bellah et al. (1985) saw it, the professions have been granted prominence in society because of the problem of "invisible complexity" (p. 207). In this view, people experience great difficulty making sense of both what is happening in society at large and how they relate to it. Special professions have been created to interpret the often overwhelming and paralyzing complexity and to run the society. Hence, "the therapist is a specialist in mobilizing resources for effective action" (p. 47), and counselors and therapists of all types have proliferated as experts on the "management" of personal life.

In relationship to school counseling, the proliferation of narrowly defined experts may have been a critical factor in the effort to shift the emphasis from guidance to counseling in schools. According to Forster (1997), guidance became associated with the authoritarianism and paternalism of a bygone era, and leaders in the counseling profession saw a separation of guidance from counseling as a way to align with newly emerging paradigms of service. From another viewpoint, however, because guidance could be effectively done by virtually any educator, it may have lost favor with those advocating for the professionalization of counseling.

Whatever the case, by the late 1950s a new cultural sensitivity was emerging that called for a different approach to guiding the nation's youth. The emphasis on client-centered approaches that began to develop in counselor education programs across the country seemed to fit with the emerging cultural milieu emphasizing communication, listening, and a kind of "articulate energy" (Bellah et al., 1985, p. 123) that better enables us to handle "diverse, rapidly changing, and often demanding interaction with others" (p. 123). These are the interactions that predominate in the more impersonal and individualized social environments of the corporate culture we now inhabit. Schools play their part, of course, and large impersonal schools help prepare children and youth for a future in the community-less social landscapes of adult life. The functional differentiation of counseling from guidance, and the new emphasis on the development of a particular set of communication skills based on psychological knowledge and clinical skill rather than moral values (Bellah et al., 1985, p. 122), also fit with the emergence in popular discourse of the "expressive individualism" (p. 47) that has come to be the dominant social force defining the modern American character. Again, whereas guidance for good character is a function performed by all educators, counseling has come to be defined as a specialized activity centered on fostering a more expressive self. This activity can only be legitimately performed by, of course, professionals.

As McKnight (1995) sees it, the "professional problem" (p. 16) has three causes. First is the "inefficiency argument" (p. 18); that is, the contradiction in which more and more funding goes into professionalized services of all types while the public perception grows that the problems defined as the jurisdiction of professionals "have consistently grown worse" (p. 19). The second cause is the arrogance and elitism of professions. As McKnight sees it, consumer revolts provide evidence of a simmering dissatisfaction with "modernized systems of assembly-line, multiservice 'care' that institutionalize the individual professional" (p. 19) but provide little genuine care. Third, in McKnight's view, is the iatrogenic nature of modern professions; that is, the tendency of "technological, specialized professionalism" (p. 20) to generate harmful negative side effects that amount to "professionally administered injury" (p. 20). One example of this is the excessive pathology labels applied to children and youth in the name of helping them.

As a specialization within counseling, school counseling has benefited from and contributed to "the united effort called professionalization" (Sweeney, 1995, p. 117). Although most effort and interest within the specialty is now focused on strengthening its position within education, McKnight's critique suggests a quite different emphasis needs consideration. In his scenario, to the degree that they promote an agenda based on excessive professionalization of roles and functions, school counselors are part of the problem and more often than not, however unintentionally, will contribute to the further weakening of communities and will generate parent and student revolt against the systems of care put in place by counselors.

Alternatives to this scenario were widely discussed in the 1960s but have been largely invisible within counseling circles in the 1980s and 1990s. For example, Vocations for Social Change (VSC) served as a "decentralized clearinghouse" for those "struggling with one basic question: How can people earn a living in America in 1969 and ensure that their social impact is going to effect basic humanistic change in our social, political, and economic institutions?" (Goodman, 1970, p. 729). In relationship to counseling and therapy, Jaffe (1973) explored the differences between "alternate services" and "established services" as experienced both by consumers and by service providers. For clients, as he saw it, "choosing an alternate service is thus based on a rejection of established services and a search for a process which is more connected with their often unarticulated values" (p. 37). The emphasis for both those providing services as well as those receiving services was on choices related to a more engaged sense of community and of opposition. The helper and the client were engaged as equals in an effort to create a new society.

An interesting recent example of the tension between genuine caring and the professionalization of helping is provided by the newsletter of the Center for School Mental Health Assistance (On the Move With School-Based Mental Health, 2000). In a recent issue, a teen health center in Brooklyn is described as a "model for youth involvement" (Silverman & Barra, 2000, p. 3). The authors describe the center as a "strength-based approach to mental health services that focuses not on 'fixing the client' but on co-creating a program with the adolescents they serve" (p. 3). The distinction between "fixing" and "co-creating" is emphasized as a key element of the center's effectiveness. Yet when the developer of the primary method used at the center declares that his "Performance Social Therapy (PST)" is really an "anti-therapy" (p. 3), one begins to wonder. Isn't pathology implicit when youth attendance at center activities is still called "mental health visits" (p. 3) and when the primary method used in working with the youth is labeled a therapy? Nevertheless, as described in the article, this center deserves considerable credit for focusing on the strengths of youth and on inclusiveness and collective responsibility. As Silverman and Barra explain, "group members build their community and create an environment in which each of them is supported in their efforts to grow emotionally" (p. 3). At least here the professional helpers are encouraged to question the dominant paradigm in which, as the experts, they apply a pathologizing label on attitudes and behavior that only they can then fix. This kind of work offers a solid alternative to the scenario described by McKnight and others.

What position should school counselors take on these difficult issues in the coming years? Should the primacy of the professions as one of two shapers of modern institutions, and counseling's part in that primacy, be questioned? What alternatives to the present scenario might exist? The overlapping political domains of school reform and the professionalization of school counseling are complex. Critics of the present school reform agenda have noted that although the shortcomings of the American educational system turn up on virtually everyone's list of social concerns (Unger & West, 1998; Brydolf, 1999), the agenda for school reform has predominantly been shaped by those preoccupied with preparing the workforce for an emerging global economy. As an adjunctive element in the dominant reform agenda, comprehensive guidance and counseling is required to make its case in terms of adding value to the mission of higher academic standards, and the role of school counselors becomes to provide specialized professional services tied to "student competencies" in three domains–academic development, career development, and personal-social development. Yet the comprehensive, developmentally based school guidance and counseling program that so many earnest reformers are working tirelessly to create runs the risk of becoming yet another, in McKnight's words, modernized system of "assembly-line, multiservice 'care' "(p. 19) that institutionalizes professionals, in this case, school counselors. I suggest that in this context the rush toward the professionalization of counseling represents a rightward drift from counseling's roots in the progressive reform movement.

In my view, counseling runs the risk of becoming a postliberal co-celebrant in seeking to align the education system with the entire sociopolitical-economic infrastructure being invoked for the convenience of an emerging global market economy (McLaren & Farahmandpur, 2000). As McLaren and Farahmandpur describe it, postliberalism is defined by the corporate domination of society, the oppression of nonmarket forces and antimarket policies, the gutting of free public services, the elimination of social subsidies, limitless concessions to transnational corporations, the market as the patron of educational reform, and private interests controlling most of social life in the pursuit of profits for the few (p. 25).

Is it even possible at this historical moment to question the assumptions, values, and guiding principles that have dominated the past three decades? Can school counselors begin to work with students in ways that authentically engage them both in co-creating programs and building community in schools? Can school counselors help reinvoke civic virtue through the creation of a new moral discourse that supersedes the incessant "me-ness" of expressive individualism?

It is not that there is anything wrong with working to strengthen the practice of school counseling; to demand recognition by the mainstream educational establishment that professional counselors in schools enhance academic achievement, career development, and personal-social development of students; to improve the quality of the training entering professional counselors receive; or to contribute new knowledge concerning how best to help children and youth grow and develop into mature, caring, socially responsible, economically productive, happy, and lovable adult citizens. These are worthwhile activities, and if they collectively constitute a foundation for the practice of professional counseling, then clearly professionalism does not have to be at odds with building community. The challenge is to take the best of what it means to be a professional—that is, the advanced study of some field— and put it to work in service of something. The challenge is also to balance any technical expertise one has acquired through a profession with the humble recognition that, as the Russian proverb declares, "the poor will never forgive us our help." The arrogance of much that passes for professionalism may seem like a nice escape from the "real world," but it disempowers people and promotes a cult of expertism in which only, for example, the counselors know how to fix people's problems, talk with kids, understand someone's emotions, develop plans for a future of promise, or help someone move on a little from a bad situation to a better one. What would serve us so well at this time, it seems to me, is honest conversation among counselors, counselors and teachers and administrators, and between counselors and students, counselors and parents, and counselors and counselor educators. While it cannot be foretold what would come out of such a conversation, holding it would represent something hopeful. From that conversation might emerge new directions for the professional practice of school counseling and new strategies for advancing a revised agenda for school reform.

Toward a Progressive Agenda for School Counseling Reform: Grounded Reflections on Critical Social and Economic Issues

The third domain in this analysis is the relationship between counseling and critical demographic, social, and economic issues. These issues take us outside the confines of school reform and school counseling and turn our attention to the neighborhoods, apartments, malls, parks, streets, and homes where America's children hang out and live and interact with the significant adults in their lives. As Joyce Carol Oates (1998) describes in a review of William Finnegan's (1998) Cold New World: Growing Up in a Harder Country, alarmingly high numbers of young Americans "live in poverty of varying kinds: economic, social, intellectual, spiritual" (Oates, 1998, p. 12). Her description of the modern "shadow world . . . populated by near-invisible, politically powerless (or indifferent) Americans who have no share in our national economy" (p.13) is bound to disturb many a caring person. Yet this description needs to stand as the backdrop for our brief examination of three considerations that stand out regarding the future of school counseling: the demographics of the coming decades, issues of family and community in the twenty-first century, and wealth distribution and social fragmentation.

Demographics and Dollars

Overall, trends show a dramatically changing U.S. population. According to Melnick, (1993), demographic projections for the United States include

- The aging population phenomenon: Average life span is increasing and will continue to do so.
- A more diverse population: By 2000, 1/3 of Americans will be minorities: U.S. population growth for Asians since 1980 has reached 108%; for Hispanics, 53%; for African Americans, 13%; for Whites, 6%.
- The concentration of the population in large metropolitan areas: By 1993, 50% of Americans were living in the 39 largest metropolitan areas.

How might these projections relate to the future of school counseling? I will begin my analysis with the third trend: As the population in large metropolitan areas grows, even slightly, the effect is sprawl, or continuous development linking city and suburb into a mass of fragmented landscapes, concentrated poverty, regional malls, gridlocked freeway networks, and costly demands for expanding infrastructural elements such as police and fire services and schools (Florian, 1999). According to a recent Newsweek study (Pedersen, Smith, & Adler, 1999), "over the lifetime of a child born today, the developed area of the nation will more than double" (p. 24). By 2021, then, or roughly a quarter of the way through the average lifetime of millennium babies, the large metropolitan areas will have grown considerably, and those graduating from high school will have grown up with, and had their lives largely defined by, a social, cultural, and economic environment of sprawling development and loss of undeveloped land.

We cannot know with any certainty how sprawl will affect schools, parents, children and youth, teachers, and counselors. From the earlier age of reform, we know that the tremendous growth in cities, overcrowding and poverty, poor sanitation and public health, and rampant crime and corruption of the late nineteenth- and early twentieth-century period fueled reforms in education, government, and business and industry, among others. Perhaps sprawling development will lead to another intense period of reform. From a psycho-social perspective, one wonders how Americans will respond emotionally and psychologically to the projected loss of undeveloped land? Our "wide open spaces" are as much a part of the American psyche as apple pie and baseball. How at peace will we be as a people when we are jammed further together in a tangle of fragmented landscapes, concentrated poverty, community-less malls, gridlocked freeway networks, and confusing infrastructures?

Regarding the aging of America's population, some hard political realities await school counseling. Lacking real political power, children and youth are easily overlooked, and with an aging population of adult voters, it seems likely that attention will be increasingly focused on the needs of the older segments of the population. The altruism and abiding love of grandparents and the flurry of current school reform initiatives notwithstanding, the needs of children and youth and policy questions concerning K–12 education may be quietly pushed further into the background in the years to come. Melnick (1993), for example, cites projections indicating that as the population ages, the political agenda of the nation increasingly will focus on adult health and safety issues. As a Newsweek (1990) special edition on the twenty-first century family asserted, "by 2030, the entire baby boom generation will be senior citizens. No other change in the twenty-first century will have a more profound effect on the way American society looks, feels, thinks, and behaves" (p. 3). How does increased funding for education and school counseling stand up against baby boomer senior citizens asserting their needs for adequate care and services? I suggest this will be another crucial political question throughout the first half of the twenty-first century.

The aging population and continued sprawl, coupled with a slow-changing political climate, likely will create ongoing difficulties for school funding and, within that, the funding of counseling in schools. More development will mean a continued emphasis on building new schools. This often translates into making sure there is a "seat" for each child and pushes into the background the critical questions of just what will go on within the walls of these sparkling new sites. Given the "grammar of schooling" (Tyack & Tobin, 1993), once the bricks and mortar are set, what gets put in the building is more often than not more of the same curriculum, staffing patterns, pedagogical approaches, and views of home-school relations. For school counseling this most likely means laboring under the support service umbrella, and this means, furthermore, that when school funding falters, counselors will be at the front of the line for reductions and elimination.

The issue of diversity will be a critical one for the coming decades. Counselors must be able to interact with a broad array of diverse populations. In addition to ethnic diversity, populations inhabiting social domains such as sexual orientation, the homeless, children and youth being raised by grandparents, the religious right and faith communities in general, single parent homes (dads or moms going it alone), and a huge variety of blends of everything above, and then some, also need to be heard, interacted with respectfully, and looked to for solutions to the problems associated with the complex variety of lifestyle and situational domains that now constitute the American experience.

The changing nature of the majority-minority designation and the higher dropout rates for Hispanic and African American students will remain two of the most critical diversity issues. Regarding the minority designation, for example, by the year 2030 in Texas, nearly half the population will be Hispanic (R. Vazquez, personal communication, October, 1999). In California, by 1994 54% of the state's K–12 students were members of ethnic minority groups with Hispanic/Latino students constituting 33% of the school population (State of California Association of Teacher Educators, 1994). Given that "the students most likely to drop out of high school in the United States are Hispanic" (DiCierbo, 2000, p.1), reforms that raise standards but do not meaningfully address the issues and concerns of Hispanic/Latino youth are bound to fail. And the increasing percentages of ethnic minority students in the nation's schools indicates that reform proposals lacking in even the most basic cultural sensitivity will carry increasingly higher stakes when they fail.

Family and Community in the Twenty-First Century
Changes in the family structure have been the focus of much concern for the past 20-plus years now. We are, by now, all familiar with the basic statistical litany: an increasing percentage of single parent families; declining percentage of traditional nuclear families; and increasing variety of family forms (e.g.,

single parent, step-parent, living alone, cohabitation, surviving a spouse, etc.) (Melnick, 1993). With less than 5% of year 2000 American families likely to be constituted as the traditional nuclear family and a projected 50% increase in single parent families over the twenty year period 1980 to 2000, the numbers provide convincing evidence of fairly dramatic change.

The status of the American family has been lamented by critics from both the left and the right, and the lamentations often invoke a deep nostalgia for an allegedly lost paradise of family life (Futrelle, 1992). Yet, as Arlene Skolnick (1992) describes it, this nostalgia arises out of a misleading moralizing about the decay of the family. Skolnick asserts that the large-scale demographic and social changes impacting the family have been in motion for the past 100-plus years and reflect, not a decay, but reasonable responses by Americans to changes brought about as a result of industrialization and middle-class affluence. What American families face on a daily basis are not the simple moral truths proclaimed by "family values" advocates, but an at times dizzying array of decisions about such things as the amount of TV time and the selection of programs appropriate for children, the division of labor for the domestic work of running a household, transportation schedules for after-school activities, the homework schedule, and so forth. For economically marginalized, impoverished, or single parent families, the choices are far more constrained, and the demands of keeping the household functioning are more pressing. The political rhetoric of family values aside, there is simply no longer much shock about the alleged collapse of the family. The 1990 Newsweek special edition on the twenty-first century family reported that "as many as one third of children born in the 1980s may live with a stepparent by the age of 18" (Kantrowitz & Wingert, 1990, p. 30). Whatever the parenting configuration, on a day-to-day basis what stands out in America's neighborhoods is not the lack of values. Rather, one senses that everyone is doing the best he or she can to cope with the complexities of reconfigured families and the intensification of the invasion of market forces into family life (Bellah, Madsen, Sullivan, Swidler, & Tipton, 1991).

Yet, alongside all this determined effort, a weariness can be detected. The tangible social supports that families need so they can function in a healthy way have eroded, and in their absence the difficulties and challenges of family life seem to have worn many of us down. With the lack of adequate child care, the increasing number of hours per week adults are spending at work, and the lack of adequate treatment programs for adults wishing to kick drug and alcohol habits (often so that they can become better parents or can retain custody of their children), among other issues, the structural elements of daily living often stack up against a healthy family life. Here, what is at issue is governmental indifference and not the weakness of, or absence of, family values. As Hewlett and West (1998) describe it, "American policy has never been more anti-family" (p.33). Their examples include the failure to address television programming issues, the lack of a remedy to marriage penalties in the tax code, and the lack of improvement in day care quality and availability for working parents. In this context, perhaps talk about family values is attractive to politicians because it is so nebulous: One does not really need to do anything other than proclaim the importance of those values. The phrase, in other words, is useful as an ideological construct and as a mask that obscures real injustices, inequalities, and contradictions in contemporary family life. As Futrelle (1992) points out, the family values debate ensnares us in a moral discourse oddly blind to important issues of race, class, gender, and sexuality (p. 531).

Against this backdrop, what do the next few decades hold in store for families, and how might school counseling be positioned in this scenario? On the surface, the challenges families face would seem to provide a huge boost to the case for school counseling. The fragmentation of lives that is so often cited as a consequence of the "weakened" family is an invitation to guidance and counseling provided by professionalized helpers of all sorts, including school counselors. If the busyness of adult lives makes it extra difficult for parents to cover all the bases in helping our children develop good character and learn to uphold standards of personal responsibility, then isn't it a real plus to have other caring adults involved in our children's lives? If, for whatever reasons, guidance from home has broken down or is under severe strain, then how thankful we ought to be that caring, well-trained professional counselors are there to fill the void. But as any aware reader recognizes, the scenarios just described are far too often more wishful thinking than reality as accurate descriptions of the relations between parents and counseling.

During the family values debates, school counseling, like other elements in education, has been a victim of the climate of opposition between home and school. Some have even challenged the work of counselors as maliciously usurping the authority of parents to guide (American Counseling Association

[ACA], 1996). Ultimately, the family values debate that emerged in the 1980s seemed to be more about generating guilt and assigning blame than about acknowledging the large-scale changes that impact American families and promoting democratic dialogue about how best to address changing economic and social conditions. Instead of increasing parents' capacities to responsibly handle the new conditions and providing practical means for solidarity between home and school in the task of educating children and youth, school reform policies have led to increased pressure on educators to do more in relationship to academic achievement. Many parents, in particular single parents and poorly educated working-class parents, have felt that they are being blamed for not providing family environments conducive to learning. In response, as parents were pressured to take more responsibility for the success of their children, they in turn expected more from the schools. From a public policy and fiscal standpoint, neither side was provided with the resources adequate to the tasks they were being assigned.

This scenario often resulted in a hardening of tensions between home and school. This tension has been reflected in political battles such as that over the proposed 1996 Parental Rights legislation. In this instance, counselors were set up as a target for all the frustrations parents were feeling toward the educational system. Indeed, because the legislation supported parents suing counselors if they offered guidance "in any way contrary to the parents' views and preferences" (American Counseling Association, 1996, p. 3), the ACA Advocacy Kit pointed out that one simple solution for districts fearful of litigation from parents "would be to end all guidance and counseling services for students" (p. 3).

Clearly, an alternative to this litigious milieu would be cordial and respectful home-school relations. Yet, when an emphasis on home-school collaboration can be found, it often seems glib and without real substance. In California, for example, although legislation was passed to better prepare educators, including counselors, to establish "effective, collaborative partnerships between educators and families" (Dear, 1998, p. 1) and the rhetoric of "family-school partnerships" abounds in the state's official "education news" (California Department of Education, 1997, p. 2), the practical elements for addressing the issues that lead to tensions between schools and families often cannot be found. Rather, the "concept of family-school partnerships [as] a comprehensive approach to connecting families and schools to support student learning" (p. 2) amounts to a kind of ideological exhortation for everyone to work harder to enjoy the "benefits" of greater collaboration. Despite the "overwhelming evidence that family involvement in the education of children is critical to effective schooling" (California Commission on Teacher Credentialing, 1997, p. 7), the structures and public policies for facilitating authentic involvement seem to elude school officials, governors, and legislators over and over again. In part this is undoubtedly because the conditions of family life work against having this partnership take on anything other than a symbolic, ideological meaning. Given all the other pressures on them, most parents simply do not have time to partake of the "potential benefits" (California Department of Education, 1997, p. 2) of the partnership.

School counselors, in the coming decades, have an opportunity to work collaboratively with parent and community groups to define new directions for home-school collaboration. This collaboration, I suggest, will involve advocacy for major state and federal policy changes concerning the relationship between schools and communities as well as specific program reforms at the local level that foster more authentic interaction between homes and schools. Current policy initiatives at the state level are often worse than Band-Aid approaches: they provide the paper cover for the Band-Aid, but when you tear open the cover, there is frequently nothing inside. From a political standpoint, Hewlett and West's (1998) call for a national parent movement whose objective would be to "retake some of the ground lost to the influence of popular entertainment, poverty, governmental indifference, and public hostility" (Johnson, 1998, p. 20) is a concrete and realistic alternative. As currently defined by the educational technocrats, home-school collaboration still smacks of condescension, and school counselors could work to change this.

Wealth Distribution
Perhaps in no area is the importance of connecting the future of school counseling with an activist stance more evident than in the domain of wealth distribution in the United States. The growing urgency of concern about the living wage as a family issue is one result of the growing gap between the haves and have nots in American society. (Living 125 miles south of Los Angeles, the city with "the widest gap between rich and poor of

any major American city" [Candaele & Dreir, 1999, p. B9], is a powerful reminder of this issue.) By 1999 the average family income in the top 5% of the earnings distribution stood at more that 19 times that in the bottom 20% (Lardner, 2000). This gap was up from 10 to 1 in 1979 to 16 to 1 in 1989. The 1999 figure was the largest gap since the U.S. Census Bureau began compiling this statistic and stands as the highest income gap of the world's advanced industrial nations (Lardner, 2000). In terms of the concentration of wealth, 1% of the U.S. population holds approximately 40% of the nation's household wealth (Lardner, 2000).The bottom 20%, it should be noted, contain more than five million children (Kozol, 1990).

The gap in income and wealth is increasingly recognized as a social problem (Lardner, 2000). As Jonathan Kozol (1990) put it in the 1990 Newsweek special edition on the twenty-first century family, "The willingness of the nation to relegate so many of [the] poorly housed and poorly fed and poorly educated children to the role of outcasts in a rich society is going to come back to haunt us" (p. 48). Even from a middle-class perspective, as a Newsweek article puts it, in the midst of "one of the greatest economic booms in U.S. history . . . many of us are feeling a little grumpy" (Bryant, 1999, p. 37). Yet adult angst is only secondarily our concern. In education, the financing of schools reflects the disparities in wealth, and as the trend of economic segregation continues (Lardner, 2000), we can anticipate an intensification of the disparities between schools serving the affluent and those serving the poor. In the words of a seventh grader attending a run-down California urban school: "I feel like I'm someone bad to go to a bad school like this" (Associated Press, 2000, May 22).

What are the overall implications of these projections and trends in demographics, family and community life, and wealth distribution for school counseling? First of all, cross-cultural skills and competencies for counselors and second-language capability will continue to be crucial considerations. The demographic projections are convincing evidence that our schools will be ever more diverse settings. The adults in these settings must have a whole set of skills, awareness, and knowledge regarding this diversity. Yet there are deeper aspects of this issue that cannot be adequately responded to simply in terms of counselor skill development, and counselors need awareness and knowledge that goes far beyond the focus of current training. McLaren (1999) has suggested, for example, that all educators learn from the work of the late Brazilian educator Paulo Freire. Recognized as a controversial thinker and radical activist who had a deep understanding of the interrelatedness of education and social and economic transformation, Freire asserted throughout his career that "educational change must be accompanied by significant changes in the social and political structures in which education takes place" (McLaren, 1999, p. 49). I suggest that study of Freire's work and the closely related work of many others in the area of critical pedagogy is an important direction for school counselors and counselor educators to take in the coming years.

The themes of parents, students, and educators working together to achieve the goals of education and authentically valuing the family are intertwined. As Hewlett and West (1998) point out, if we really want to value the family, we need public policy that provides a living wage, adequate health and child care, and adequate parental leave. Without the specific policies, all the additional training of educators and all the exhortations to parents to collaborate will not make a difference. I suggest that these issues will continue to dominate public discourse about education and families, and they will be at the core of the relationship between school counseling and the family as well. To strengthen the relationship with families, counselors need to become strong advocates for the kinds of movements called for by West and Hewlett. As they indicate, the "economic facts of family life preclude a return to traditional structures" (p.122), and school counselors should work together to avoid positions that reinforce nostalgic notions of family or inadvertently reinforce the redomestication of women.

Indeed, demographics impact policy indirectly, after they have been filtered through the values, beliefs, and interests of various political actors (Welner & Mickelson, 2000; Lipman, 1998). As part of developing an increased political awareness, counselors can begin by more explicitly aligning their values, beliefs, and interests with programs and policies that benefit those marginalized by the current agenda of school reform. This also will necessitate participating in the articulation of an alternative future, one tied to real lives in real communities rather than to a Disneyesque global culture of shopping malls, superficial media, and theme park lifestyles. Putting counseling skills at the service of genuine dialogue with children, youth, parents, and other educators simply seems more personally and socially worthwhile than continuing to push the obsessive professionalization and rampant pathologizing that lie just beneath the surface of most school counseling today.

Opening up a more authentic dialogue about values, beliefs, and interests may take us in unexpected directions, but this step seems a precondition to reconnecting with a progressive heritage. For example, I recall the words spoken by a respected legislator here in California (a strong supporter of education) in a conversation with two university counselor educators advocating for a bill mandating school counseling in California. (I was one of those advocates, and the senator's words have stuck in my mind.) The legislator listened calmly and then asked two simple questions: "How much will it cost?" and "Where will the money come from?" Upon hearing the answer—"$350 million a year, and it will be new money"— the legislator replied, "That, my friends, will be a hard sell."

Why was this "sell" so hard? Why was it harder than, say, selling the $3.6 billion annual budget of the California Department of Corrections (CDC)? In fact, while California sleepwalked through a 20-year decline in support for school counseling, the prison budget trebled in the 10 years from 1987 to 1997 (Parkes, 1997). This despite research showing that so-called "intermediate sanctions" (such as house arrest and electronic monitoring), appropriate for as many as a quarter of California's new prisoners, could save as much as $14,000 of the $22,000 annual cost of incarcerating one person in the state (Parkes, 1997). The CDC has been confident enough of its future funding to request 17 more California prisons. Clearly, the difficulty of the "sell" had to do with more than simply the value-for-dollar of prevention versus incarceration. Perhaps California as the "Golden State of Jails" (Parkes, 1997, p. 1) is a preview of the coming safety issues agenda of an aging population? Whatever the case with this particular example, whatever the sudden temporary enthusiasm for counseling in the wake of tragic events at schools (e.g., "More Counselors Needed," 1999), and whatever the current temporary good fortune for school counseling based on sudden economic upturns, given the trends discussed, I suggest that the "sell" for school counseling will not become significantly easier in the coming 20 years without a fundamental reconceptualization of education (e.g., Oakes et al., 2000; Glasser, 1992) and of school counseling's role within this reconceptualization.

Summary and Conclusion

School reform is a quintessentially American enterprise: We love to tinker toward opportunity for all and success for all who work hard (Unger & West, 1998). Yet when one looks beneath the surface of our contemporary tinkering, as we have seen, the view can be troubling.

The trends and projections I have examined inform us about the momentum of daily living: They help us understand in a larger sense what is happening around us. They also can assist with planning ahead by informing us about what can only be dimly perceived on the horizon and providing a basis for calculating the resources needed to respond to emerging challenges. Although the numbers alone will not tell us just what will happen in the next 20 or so years, they may indicate the parameters within which public policy debates take place, the likelihood of one particular type of institutional change taking precedence over other types, and they may illuminate the political choices faced by those interested in a progressive agenda for school counseling. As Scott (1987) reports, the nation state and the professions likely will remain the primary shapers of modern institutions. Yet institutional actors working within the structures of professionalized helping can help or hinder the emergence of new consciousness among those being helped, and to do this these actors must have a keen sense of the values and beliefs that inform their efforts.

In the post-Columbine environment of late twentieth-century American education, it was easy to find headlines stressing "more counselors needed in schools" ("More Counselors Needed," 1999, p. 5). This was quite a change from the anxious moments of the late 80s through the mid-90s, when some asked "is it possible for counselors to remain an integral part of the educational system, or are they, like the rain forest, disappearing forever?" (Anderson & Reiter, 1995, p. 268). Was it merely the tragic shootings at campuses around the country that has brought the change about? I suggest that although this dramatic new expression of profound anger, opposition, and alienation has a lot to do with the newfound appreciation of the counselor, far more has been at work. Among the formal and informal networks of influence in education, the political processes of school reform have posed a threat to, as well as opened up opportunities for, the professionalized helping provided through school support services. As "institutional entrepreneurs" (DiMaggio, 1988), school counselors have acted reasonably in asserting a position on school reform that advances the professional interests of school counseling and seeks to move it out of a subordinate institutional position and into a central, if not dominant, position. Yet, perhaps because of the primacy of concerns over institutional jockeying for position, present school counseling advocacy efforts do not adequately challenge the limits of the current school reform agenda. Something larger is needed, and I suggest that school counseling reestablish its intellectual, theoretical, and spiritual ties to the progressive reform heritage out of which it emerged nearly a century ago. Without this effort, school counseling will most likely serve as a handmaiden for a reform agenda that marginalizes the issues faced by our most disadvantaged children and youth and that blindly follows a global corporate agenda that intensifies income inequality and removes all constraints from a corporate elite that is expanding and consolidating its hold all over the world.

I have offered a brief political analysis of the future that stands humbly in the face of a veritable firestorm of bad news for children and youth preceded, and followed, by a sad litany of societal indifference and by evidence of limited vision and contradictions on the part of those guiding current reform efforts in education. Yet my view is not an antistandards position: I simply question the extent to which we want to camp out on that doorstep. As a recent guidance leadership document puts it, "every aspect of education has to be accountable in terms of student outcomes" (National Consortium of State Career Guidance Supervisors, 1999, p. 2), and in a sense this is the wave of the future. For school counseling and guidance, the new national standards provide a yardstick by which states, school districts, and schools can measure the extent to which their utilization of school counseling and guidance is in keeping with the practices identified through research as most likely to yield positive outcomes for students, teachers, parents, and all other stakeholders in education. In addition, for districts not currently utilizing school counselors, the standards provide a time-and-effort-saving framework and organizational tool for broadening and deepening reform efforts underway in those districts. In particular, higher standards can realistically lead to increased achievement when district reform efforts are broadened to include, in addition to the two components of improved instruction and better managed schools, a third component, equally as fundamental, that addresses comprehensively enabling learning by lowering barriers that interfere with development, learning, and teaching (Center for Mental Health in Schools, 1999) and that increases the number of students finishing school with the "academic preparation, career awareness, and the personal/social growth essential to choose from a wide range of substantial post-secondary options, including college" (Campbell & Dahir, 1997, p.1).

Moments of sweeping historical change do occur, and there is much evidence to suggest that we may be approaching one of those historical crossroads in which the prevailing order of things is fundamentally altered. The challenge is to avoid the momentary fun of wishful thinking based on the notion that because we are entering a new century, things will somehow be magically different. Rather, we have the responsibility to engage in careful reflection on what changes are occurring and on the implications of these changes for, in this instance, school counseling. My hunch is that the immediate period beyond the millennium promises to be one in which the tensions among the "enduring institutional forms" (Tyack & Tobin, 1993 p. 453) of modern American education; the "shadow world" (Oates, 1998) of nearly invisible and politically powerless Americans with its crush of economic, social, intellectual, and spiritual poverty; the intensification of problems arising from the barriers to learning faced by increasing numbers of students; and the jarring transformations associated with economic, political, and environmental global change will continue to rise. I believe it will take more than two decades before the full scope of global change impacts America's schools, and hence, school counseling. Thus there is time for rethinking our direction and for taking steps that go beyond strengthening the position of school counselors as organizational actors in the broad political contests that are redefining the institutional forms that education will take in the twenty-first century. In addition to engaging on existing infrastructural battlegrounds (probably an inevitable occurrence given the overall position of professionalization within American society), I suggest that school counselors also need to reach out in bold new ways to students, parents, and communities, not merely in times of tragedy and grief but through the quiet daily work of raising consciousness and forging a new sense of common purpose as Americans.

The questions we face are both personal and political. How do we get through, in the words of singer-songwriter Leonard Cohen, this historically "shabby moment" (Iyer, 1998, p. 68) in which people are simply "holding on in their individual way to an orange crate, to a piece of wood, and we're passing each other in this swollen river that has pretty well taken down all the landmarks, and pretty well overturned everything we've got" (p. 68).

Robert Heilbronner's (1980) *An Inquiry into the Human Prospect* was an early, and somber, look ahead. His "updated for the 1980s" edition began with "an oppressive anticipation of the future" (p. 12). Heilbronner was concerned not only with the nature of the external challenges to the human prospect but also, and perhaps more important, with our individual and collective capacities for response to the threats. The "civilizational malaise" (p. 19) Heilbronner wrote of had as much to do with the human spirit as it did with such elements as economic crises, world demographics, the prospect of nuclear terrorism, global warming, and other confidence-shaking events. The hope he saw, limited as it appeared to be in the 1980s, could be found in the exercise of individual responsibility. Now, some two decades later, it remains increasingly too easy, in the face of mounting economic, environmental, and global political problems, to answer "who cares" to the question of "what's to be done?"

In my view, reestablishing a progressive agenda for the future of counseling, and for school counseling in particular, means fostering a sense of critical consciousness among counselors and among those they serve. In Freire's views concerning educators and liberation, literacy was the crucial vehicle for the development of a "critical consciousness" among the poor, and it was from this consciousness that new personal meanings as well as common purpose among the oppressed could be created (McLaren, 1999). In this context, perhaps it is in the domain of a kind of emotional literacy that counselors will be able to help children, youth, and parents better articulate their views of what's needed to improve schools and better address the contradictions that have left our educational institutions tied in knots or chasing their tails.

References

American Counseling Association. (1996, October). *Advocacy pit: "Parental rights" legislation.* Alexandria, VA.: Office of Government Relations, American Counseling Association.

Anderson, R. S., & Reiter, D. (1995). The indispensable counselor. *The School Counselor,42*, 268–276.

Associated Press. (2000, May 22). ACLU sues state for school funding. *Las Vegas Review Journal*, p. 3B.

Associated Press. (2000, May 27). Study: School reform efforts for California not pieced together. *Las Vegas Review Journal*, p. 9B.

Bellah, R. N., Madsen, R., Sullivan, W. M., Swidler, A., & Tipton, S. M. (1985). *Habits of the heart*. Berkeley: University of California Press.

Bellah, R. N., Madsen, R., Sullivan, W. M., Swidler, A., & Tipton, S. M. (1991). *The good society*. New York: Vintage Press.

Bryant, A. (1999, July 5). They're rich and you're not. *Newsweek, 134*(1), 37–43.

Brydolf, C. (1999). Reforms rock—around the clock. *California Schools: Quarterly Magazine of the California School Boards Association, 58*(1), 24–32.

California Commission on Teacher Credentialing. (1997, June). *Preparing educators for partnerships with families*. Report of the Advisory Task Force on Educator Preparation for Parent Involvement. Sacramento, CA: Author.

California Department of Education. (1997, Fall). *Education news: A newsletter of the California Department of Education, 1*(2).

Campbell, C. A., & Dahir, C. A, (1997). *The national standards for school counseling programs*. Alexandria, VA: American School Counseling Association.

Candaele, K., & Dreir, P. (1999, October 8). Labor makes a stand in Los Angeles. *Los Angeles Times*, p. B9.

Center for Mental Health in Schools. (1999, Spring). Expanding school reform. Addressing Barriers to Learning, 4(2), 1–9.

Center for Mental Health in Schools. (2000, Winter). *Addressing Barriers to Learning, 4*(2), 1–9.

College Board (1986). *Keeping the options open: Recommendations.* Final report of the Commission on Precollege Guidance and Counseling. New York: College Entrance Examination Board.

College Board (1994). *Strengthening educational guidance and counseling in schools.* New York: College Entrance Examination Board and National Association of College Admissions Counselors.

College Board (1996). *Keeping the options open: Continued, 1992–94.* New York: College Entrance Examination Board.

Dear, J. (1998, February). *A focus on the family.* Presentation at the annual conference of the California Association for Counseling and Development, Los Angeles, CA.

DiCierbo, P. (2000, Spring). Risking a future: How do we keep Hispanic youth in school? *On the Move With School-Based Mental Health, 5*(1), 1, 6.

DiMaggio, P. J. (1988). Interest and agency in institutional theory. In L. G. Zucker (Ed.), *Institutional patterns in organizations: Culture and environments* (pp. 3–21). Cambridge, MA: Ballinger.

Finnegan, W. (1998). Cold new world: Growing up in a harder country. New York: Random House.

Florian, E. (1999, July 19). Oh no, it's spreading. *Newsweek, 134*(3), 25.

Forster, J. R. (1997). Reframing guidance and counseling in the schools with a constructivist perspective. In T. L. Sexton & B. L. Griffin (Eds.) *Constructivist thinking in counseling practice, research, and training* (pp. 141–154). New York: Teachers College Press.

Futrelle, D. (1992, April 20). The family thing. *The Nation,* 529–531.

Galpers, J. H. (1975). The politics of social services. Englewood Cliffs, NJ: Prentice Hall.

Gladding, S. T. (1988). *Counseling: A comprehensive profession.* Columbus, OH: Merrill.

Glasser, J. (2000, May 8). And justice for some. *U.S. News & World Report, 128*(18), 28

Glasser, W. (1992). *The quality school* (2nd ed.). New York: HarperCollins.

Goodman, M. (1970). *The movement toward a new America.* New York: Alfred A. Knopf.

Heilbronner, R. L. (1980). *An inquiry into the human prospect: Updated and reconsidered for the 1980s.* New York: W.W. Norton.

Hersch, P. (1998). *A tribe apart: A journey into the heart of American adolescence.* New York: Fawcett.

Hewlett, S. A., & West, C. (1998). *The war against parents: What we can do for America's beleaguered moms and dads.* New York: Houghton Mifflin.

Hofstadter, R. (1955). *The age of reform.* New York: Random House.

Iyer, P. (1998, November/December). Leonard Koan: What's the sound of one world-weary, enigmatic rock 'n' roll idol searching for his soul? *Utne Reader, 90,* 65–68.

Jaffe, D. T. (1973). A counseling institution in an oppressive environment. Journal of Humanistic Psychology, 13(4), 25–46.

Johnson, D. (1998, July 16). My blue heaven. *New York Review of Books, 45*(12), 15–20.

Kantrowitz, B., & Wingert, P. (1990, Winter/Spring). Step by step. *Newsweek 114* (27), 24–34.

Knoke, D., & Prensky, D. (1984). What relevance do organization theories have for voluntary associations? *Social Science Quarterly, 65*(1), 1314–1339.

Kozol, J. (1990, Winter/Spring). The new untouchables. *Newsweek, 114*(27), 48–53.

Lardner, J. (2000, February 21). The rich get richer. *U.S. News & World Report, 128*(7), 39–43.

Laumann, E. O., & Knoke, D2. (1987). *The organizational state: Social choice in national policy domains.* Madison, WI: University of Wisconsin Press.

Lipman, P. (1998). *Race, class, and power in school restructuring.* New York: SUNY Press.

Marcuse, H. (1964). *One dimensional man.* Boston: Beacon Press.

McKnight, J. (1995). *The careless society: Community and its counterfeits.* New York: Basic Books.

McLaren, P. (1999). A pedagogy of possibility: Reflecting upon Paulo Freire's politics of education. *Educational Researcher, 28*(2), 49–54.

McLaren, P., & Farahmandpur, R. (2000). Reconsidering Marx in post-Marxist times: A requiem for postmodernism? *Educational Researcher, 29*(3), 25–33.

Melnick, R. (1993). *Approaching the year 2000: Some significant trends and projections affecting higher education.* Presentation at the Western States Universities Government Relations Conference, Tempe, AZ.

More counselors needed in schools. (1999, May 11). *School Board News, 19*(8), 5.

Nailor, P. C. (1999). *Developing school counselors as change agents for schools of tomorrow.* Unpublished doctoral dissertation. Johnson & Wales University, Providence, RI.

National Consortium of State Career Guidance Supervisors. (1999, May). *National Guidance Leadership Academy proposal.* Unpublished paper, Center on Education and Training for Employment, Columbus, OH.

Newsweek (1990, December). *The twenty-first-century family.* [Special edition]

Oakes, J. (1992). Can tracking research inform practice? Technical, normative, and political considerations. *Educational Researcher, 21*(4), 12–22.

Oakes, J., Hunter Quartz, K., Ryan, S., & Lipton, M. (2000). *Becoming good American schools: The struggle for civic virtue in school reform*. San Francisco: Jossey-Bass.

Oates, J. C. (1998, July 16). A lost generation. *The New York Review of Books, 45*(12), 12–14.

Ogawa, R. T., & Bossert, S. T. (1995). Leadership as an organizational quality. *Educational Administration Quarterly, 31*(2): 224–243.

On the Move With School-Based Mental Health [On-line serial], 5(1). Available: http://csmha.umaryland.edu/csmha2001/onthemove-spring2000.php3

Parkes, C. (1997, March 8–9). Golden state of jails. *Financial Times*. London, 1.

Pedersen, D., Smith, V. E., & Adler, J. (1999, July 19). Sprawling, sprawling. . . . *Newsweek, 134*(3), 22–27.

Pulliam, J. D., & Van Patten, J. (1995). *History of education in America* (6th ed.). Englewood Cliffs, NJ: Merrill.

Roszak, T. (1969). *The making of a counterculture*. Garden City, NY: Doubleday and Co.

Sahagun, L. (2000, April 11). L.A. Unified gets dismal ratings from public. *Los Angeles Times*, pp. A1, A22.

Salganik, L. H. (1985, April). *Schools under pressure: The external environment and recent organizational reforms*. Paper presented at the annual meeting of the American Educational Research Association, Chicago, IL.

Scott, R. W. (1987). The adolescence of institutional theory. *Administrative Science Quarterly, 32*(4), 493–511.

Silverman, B., & Barra, K. (2000, Spring). *Let's talk about it: A model for youth involvement* [7 paragraphs]. On the Move With School-Based Mental Health [On-line serial], 5(1). Available: http://csmha.umaryland.edu/csmha2001/onthemove-spring2000.php3

Skolnick, A. (1992). *Embattled paradise: The American family in an age of uncertainty*. New York: Basic Books.

State of California Association of Teacher Educators. (1994). The future of teacher education in California [Special issue]. *Issues in Teacher Education, 3*(2).

Stone, G. L. (1986). *Counseling psychology: Perspectives and functions*. Monterey, CA: Brooks Cole.

Sweeney, T. J. (1995). Accreditation, credentialing, professionalization: The role of specialties. *Journal of Counseling and Development, 74,* 117–25.

Szasz, T. S. (1961). *The myth of mental illness*. New York: Dell.

Tyack, D., & Tobin, W. (1993, Fall). The "grammar" of schooling: Why has it been so hard to change? *American Educational Research Journal, 31*(3), 453–479.

Unger, R., & West, C. (1998, November 23). Progressive politics and what lies ahead. *The Nation,* 11–15.

Welner, K. G., & Mickelson, R. A. (2000, May). School reform, politics, and tracking: Should we pursue virtue? *Educational Researcher, 29*(4), 22–26.

Zinn, H. (1980). *A people's history of the United States*. New York: Harper & Row.

About the Author

Lonnie L. Rowell, Ph.D., is an assistant professor in the Counseling Program at the University of San Diego. In his 30 years of experience in K-12 and higher education, Rowell has served as a teacher, administrator, counselor, program developer, and counselor educator. He received his doctorate from the University of Southern California and his Master of Science from San Diego State University. Rowell has been involved extensively in the state professional association, including serving as chairman of the state legislative task force, past president of the California School Counselors Association, co-director of the Summer Counseling Institute, and past president of the California Association for Counselor Educators.

Chapter Eighteen

The Impact on Future Guidance Programs of Current Developments in Computer Science, Telecommunications, and Biotechnology

Lynda K. Mitchell & Philippe L. Hardy

We are living in an era of incredible technological change. The purpose of this chapter is to envision how this technological revolution will affect the guidance, counseling, and student support programs of the future, specifically those of 20 years hence, around 2021. We have chosen to concentrate on a period of 20 years because those who specialize in envisioning the future, often called futurists, usually advise that 20 years or so is about the limit for which reasonable extrapolations can be made based upon the present.

The best way to begin to grasp the extent of change that might occur in the next 20 years is to think about the changes that have occurred in the last 20 years. What was life like in 1981? At that time, although some of the incipient technology existed, few of the products, services, and biotechnology advances that have become such a ubiquitous part of our daily lives had been created. Just as a few examples, in 1981 there were essentially no personal computers, no CD players, no CD-ROMS, no wide-screen or flat TVs, no VCRs, and no video cameras. There was no voice mail, no Internet, no global positioning system, and no virtual reality. There was no cloning and no gene mapping. The developments of the past 20 years, and the fact that change is accelerating more or less exponentially, suggest that we should expect even more dramatic developments in the next 20 years. As an aside, we should note that much of this exponentially accelerating change has occurred because during the past 50 years, computer capacity has doubled (and halved in price) every 18 months, a phenomenon known as Moore's law (Kahu, 1998). Given that it would have been very difficult for most of us to envision in 1981 what the world of 2001 looks like, in reality our minds probably cannot grasp what changes the next 20 years will bring about. Nevertheless there are numerous people who make their life's work trying to anticipate such changes, and in this article we attempt to pull together their predictions into three categories: computer science, telecommunications, and biotechnology. We will then discuss the potential impacts of these developments on the guidance programs of approximately 20 years hence. It's worth noting that developments in these three categories are inevitably converging because of increased computing capacity. For example, as Kahu (1998) points out, the number of genes that can be sequenced in the human genome project doubles every two years because the computers that drive the process are becoming ever more efficient.

Computer Science

The major immediate development in computer technology will probably be speech-directed computers. Microsoft Corporation, for example, has directed a considerable portion of its research and development budget in that direction (Gates, Myhrvold, & Rinearson, 1998). Several models of speech-directed computers already exist, but the technology requires the computers to be "trained" to your voice, and the computers still make many errors of comprehension. As Isaacson (1998, p. 34) notes, "ask a computer to 'recognize speech' and it is likely to think you want it to 'wreck a nice beach.'" As the technology becomes even more widely available, however, it should provoke a huge upsurge in computer use by technophobes who currently avoid dealing with windows, computer mice, and so forth. Imagine the ease of being able to verbally instruct your computer to power up, go online, print a document, or pay your monthly bills. Or imagine having a computer in your car that you can chat with as you are driving. Isaacson (1998, p. 35) believes that "in a decade or so . . . we'll be able to chat with our . . . telephone consoles, browsers, thermostats, VCRs, microwaves, and any other devices we want to boss around." Another recent development still being perfected is "digital ink" that turns paper into a computer screen.

Similar developments are expected with regard to how

computers output information. There is no particular reason why we should have to get all of our information from a computer by staring at a screen. In the future, computers will probably communicate with us through a variety of sensory input. For example, a stockbroker may have a computer that communicates the number of shares traded via a sound, such as a waterfall. As the volume of shares increases, the sound gets louder and louder (Gross, 1997). From speech-activated computers it is a short step to the development of robots we can interact with as though they were human beings. In fact, computer scientists at the Massachusetts Institute of Technology (MIT) feel they have already developed such a robot (Port, 1997). According to Isaacson (1998), we will provide so many thoughts and preferences to our computers of the future that they will ultimately be able to mimic our minds and act as our proxies. And yes, then they will probably build their own computers.

The preceding developments are relatively modest. Most of this increase in capacity has come about because the makers of silicon chips, on which all the software and memory of computers are stored, have devised ways to make them ever more efficient. This increased efficiency is accomplished by making the circuits that store information on the chips tinier and tinier. In about seven years, however, around 2008, the circuits will have to be the size of atoms, and silicon chips will no longer be a viable medium. At that point it is expected that computers based on the silicon chip will disappear, and some new model of computing will arise. Many feel that the real future of computing lies in nanotechnology (Rogers & Kaplan, 1998). A *nano* is one-billionth of a meter, and microscopic devices that have already been developed based on nanos may allow us to manipulate atoms and molecules. With this capacity we could literally create any substance we wanted. Computers of the future could thus, upon command, materialize a cheeseburger and fries, and the stove to cook them on, out of a primordial fog in our kitchens.

Along the same lines, a coalition of researchers from IBM, MIT, Oxford University, and the University of California at Berkeley recently reported that they created a computer in which the central processor consisted of atoms of hydrogen and chlorine, and used it to sort a list of unordered items (Markoff, 1998). The computer is based upon the principles of quantum physics and is assembled from units the size of molecules known as *cubits*. This development is considered especially exciting because unlike conventional computers, which are assembled from arrays of millions of digital switches that represent either a 1 or a 0, a cubit can represent 0, 1, or potentially many other states simultaneously. This potentiality could eventually enable machines that function millions of times faster than today's supercomputers.

At cutting edge computer labs all over the world, computer scientists are working on these and other future prototypes for computers. With the demise of the silicon chip, many scientists believe that computers of the future will be patterned much more closely on living creatures, and will no longer be based on the old desktop metaphor (Judge, 1997). For example, some computer scientists are studying how computers might be modeled upon ant colonies, which function perfectly with no central authority, or upon rushing rivers of data, or upon materializing three dimensional images in space (Gross, 1997) rather than the current binary (0/1) digital format.

No matter what form computers eventually assume, one thing is certain. In the past 20 years, the number of doctorate degrees in computer science has risen from 10 to 1,000 a year, with master's degree holders rising concomitantly. And it is advances in computer science that drive many of the other developments we discuss in this chapter.

Telecommunications and Netware

Today some 40% of the U.S. population regularly accesses the Internet via personal computers. By 2021, most telecommunications specialists predict that every man, woman, and child will be using information technology as an integral part of their daily lives (Port, 1997). If this state is to be achieved, however, the use of information technology must become as easy as driving a car. Most people can drive a car easily without knowing how the engine works. The use of the Internet needs to become equally simple.

Currently, the main obstacle to easy access and use of information technology is the difficulty of economically transporting broadband (video and audio) information with our current narrowband technology. Broadband technology is now in wide use for transmission of information, but most of the receiving sites (e.g., homes and offices) can accept only narrowband information. However, more and more organizations, such as the California State University system, are putting broadband technology in place for receiving information. In addition, Microsoft Corporation is in the process of launching a project they call *TELEDESC*, which will put into orbit a series of satellites to transmit two-way broadband information to anyone who wants to receive it, much like a giant cellular phone system. Finally, during the Clinton administration, Vice President Gore unveiled national plans to build a new Internet that can transmit at speeds that astound current users. The new Internet, dubbed *Internet 2*, will be able to transmit the entire *Encyclopedia Britannica* in one second and the content of the Library of Congress in less than a minute. In short, the future promises pervasive broadband technology combined with completely affordable computing power for all (Markoff, 2000).

What are the implications of readily available, portable Internet access? First of all, people will be walking around while online. Telecommunications specialists envision clothing that turns body heat into electricity in order to power the transmission and receipt of information (Gross, 1997). Your pacemaker will be able to send information directly to your doctor. Caps will have video visors that allow you to scan information constantly. Your watch will also access the Internet, giving you the entire planet's knowledge on your wrist (Kahu, 1998). Some pundits have coined the term *Homo cyberneticus* for these online people of the not-so-distant future (Flynn, 1997).

It is not just people, but their houses and appliances, that will be online. When you step on the scale, your weight will go to your physician (or your Weight Watchers group). Your refrigerator will receive your weight and decide what to feed you that day. It will also notice when you're low on milk or other groceries and order them directly from the market (Gershenfeld, 1999). The thermostat in your house will sense a shiver and turn up the heat, or sense perspiration and turn it down.

In academic settings, researchers from different continents can be part of visually rich virtual laboratories and participate jointly in discoveries. In medical settings, physicians will have the virtual reality techniques to conduct operations thousands of miles away. Such an operation has in fact already been conducted during the recent war in Kosovo (Margolis, 2000). In short, easy and inexpensive access to the Internet should have the same revolutionary effect on everyday life that the access to electricity did half a century ago (Davis & Wessel, 1998). It will simply permeate every aspect of human functioning.

Biotechnology and Artificial Life

As Isaacson (1998) notes, the digital revolution that we are in the midst of today is likely to "pale in comparison to the revolution in biotechnology that is just beginning" (p. 34). The most important aspect of this newest revolution is that humans now have the ability to replicate and modify their own DNA. The ability to modify our DNA has powerful implications for the treatment of disease. For example, several French infants with severe immune system disorders, which previously required them to live in sterile "bubbles," have now been cured via gene therapy (*New York Times*, 2000). We will also probably be able to select the characteristics of our offspring. The ability to replicate our DNA means that we will undoubtedly start to clone ourselves, despite all the current thrashing about with regard to the ethical implications of cloning. The researchers from Great Britain who cloned Dolly the sheep have already applied for and been awarded permission to look at certain aspects of human cloning.

Among the predictions floating around is that ultimately we will carry around our entire genetic makeup on a handy CD. A trip to the doctor's will entail an examination of the information on the CD, rather than a physical. If something is wrong with us, we will be given a shot designed to rearrange our DNA so as to make us immune to the illness.

Once we start cloning ourselves and selecting the genetic characteristics of our children, it is anyone's guess as to what is likely to happen to humans. One idea that immediately comes to mind is that there will be a huge preponderance of tall male offspring. Silver (1998) predicts that cloning technology will be too expensive for mass use, and thus will be used only by a small percentage of the population. He goes so far as to predict that this small percentage of the population will then proceed to clone itself into a different species.

Another exciting development appears to be a promising approach to the treatment of cancer (Kolata, 1998). Medical researchers have discovered two new drugs, angiostatin and endostatin, which operate by cutting off the blood supply that tumors require to grow. In trials with mice, the drugs have been shown to be effective for all types of known cancers, and the National Cancer Institute has made human trials its top priority.

The combination of a cure for cancer and genetic engineering certainly suggest that *Homo cyberneticus* could have a life span immensely longer than that of *Homo sapiens*. Again, as with revolutions in computer technology, our minds probably cannot grasp what changes advances in biotechnology are likely to produce.

One thing is certain. Unlike in previous decades, there is essentially no gap any more between what is in research and what is in production (O'Hamilton, 1997). For example, a glance at the reference list for this article shows that all but one of the references are dated between 1997 and 2000, the span in which this article was written. Further, although we reference mostly hard copy sources (books and magazines) for the convenience of the reader, all the information contained in those sources can be easily retrieved from the Internet.

Effects on Guidance Programs of the Future

The advances discussed thus far, in computer science, telecommunications, and biotechnology, have the potential to affect dramatically the guidance programs of the future. This impact could be felt on two fronts: the mechanisms through which the services of guidance programs will be offered, and how guidance programs will help prepare students to live and work productively in this new world.

How Services Will Be Offered

Traditionally, guidance programs have operated within a school site. But will schools as we know them exist in 20 years? Perhaps not. Most education can easily be conducted through virtual reality experiences via the Internet, especially once broadband transmission becomes universally available. Books and films need no longer be the media of choice. Further, with the technology of virtual reality, the boundary between training and doing may soon disappear. In short, with Internet access universal, inexpensive, portable, and easily available, there is absolutely no reason why a school as a geographical location needs to exist. Schools could probably function almost totally through their websites.

Once schools are operating primarily through telecommunication, it logically follows that guidance programs could do the same. Personal and career counseling are already being offered on some websites, and there is no reason to expect the trend to slow down, especially considering "Internet use has grown an astonishing 65 percent" just in the last year

(Jaco, 1998, p. 7).

We envision the guidance program of 2021 as potentially consisting of parents, teachers, students, and counselors communicating through the medium of networked computers. The counselors will be able immediately to transmit various kinds of information to interested subgroups via the twenty-first-century version of mailing list servers and bulletin boards. Group and individual counseling sessions could be conducted via interactive videoconferencing. Career development could be enhanced via virtual reality experiences with various occupations, culminating in virtual reality job interviews.

We qualify all the above statements with words such as *could* and *might* because schools (and their associated guidance programs) are notoriously slow to change. Most of us, in walking into a contemporary school, would find it little changed from the schools we attended 10, 20, or 30 years ago. It is true that we might find some computers there, but they would likely be old, out of date, and little used. And this situation is frequently exacerbated in poorer schools. Therefore, although we hope that guidance programs of the future will take advantage of the incredible developments in technology that are certain to occur, we fear that we may be overly optimistic.

The World for Which Students Must Be Prepared

Like Johnson and Johnson (1993), we believe (or at least we hope) that accountability in the form of results-based programs will dominate guidance models of the future. One of the major results for which guidance programs have always strived is to prepare students to become productive members of the workforce. If guidance programs of the future are to help prepare students to enter the workforce, the facilitators of these programs must have a clear picture of what the world of the future will look like, and an even clearer picture of what the world of work will look like. Once we can envision these worlds more clearly, we should be better able to prepare students to succeed in them.

In envisioning the world of 20 years hence, the scenarios tend to fluctuate between those from a pessimistic point of view and those from an optimistic point of view. The pessimists like to point out the problems and dangers inherent in the use of the new technologies. Sometimes these problems seem relatively trivial. For example, a refrigerator that is supposed to sense when you are out of milk and order it from the market would probably have to be designed with sensors to detect the weight of the milk carton. These sensors would only function properly if the milk were returned to the same place every time. But what if your child put the milk on the bottom shelf instead of the top shelf? (Guernsey, 2000) More frightening scenarios have been proposed by Joy (2000), who feels that "genetic engineering, nanotechnology, and robotics . . . carry a hidden risk of huge dimensions" (p. 9). With regard to genetic engineering and robotics, he points to the possibility of bio-engineered plagues and robots so much more intelligent than humans that they come to consider humans expendable. He also notes that the materials created with nanotechnology might be foreign to our environment and could destroy our existing biosphere. Of more immediate concern to counselors and educators, the data on whether computers actually aid learning in school are still not completely in. For example, there is evidence that reliance on computers for routine drills in math classes actually decreases math performance compared to instruction by a live teacher (Mathews, 2000). A pessimistic scenario for the future world of work is often articulated by Robert Reich, the former Secretary of Labor under the Clinton administration (McGuinn & Raymond, 1998). According to Reich, the "blue collar/white collar" labor classification that has dominated the work world since the industrial revolution is rapidly becoming a thing of the past. In our information society, good jobs will require more training than ever, and full-time positions will give way to freelance talent for hire. Most of these workers will telecommute to their offices.

With the demise of the blue collar job, Americans with only a high school education cannot ever expect to earn comfortable middle-class salaries as they have in the past. Robots are already capable of taking over all unskilled assembly work and can be expected to move rapidly up the ladder. At best, unskilled workers can probably expect to become low-paid personal service workers, although not many of those jobs will exist either, since most of them will be moved overseas or replaced by computers. Reich predicts that middle-class jobs will be those requiring training, especially upgrading of computer skills, beyond a high school diploma. He points to high-tech auto mechanics as an example, and suggests that most of these employees will be trained by community colleges and private technical schools. Finally, he believes that the upper class will consist of persons with advanced graduate degrees focusing on an intensive ability to manipulate knowledge and information.

Computer scientists, physicians, and investment bankers are a few of the professions he cites as comprising this twenty-first-century upper class. We view this scenario as more pessimistic because Reich tends to emphasize the kinds of jobs that are likely to be lost, the lack of financial security for individuals, and the difficulty of revamping the educational system when he talks of the future work world.

A more optimistic scenario of the future work world is often offered (Davis & Wessel, 1998), especially by those actually dominating the telecommunications industry, such as Bill Gates (Gates et al., 1998). Although Gates has recently been attacked by the Justice Department for monopolistic practices on the part of Microsoft Corporation, he clearly has been able to anticipate computing needs and future trends in the telecommunications world. He predicts that entire professions and industries will fade as new technologies develop, but he also predicts that new ones will flourish to replace them. He notes that the personal computer has altered and eliminated some companies (e.g., typewriter manufacturers) but that overall the microprocessor and personal computer have created a burgeoning new computer industry that has produced a substantial net increase in employment. Even most workers who were laid off by now-defunct companies have found employment within the computer industry. He draws the analogy to the time prior to the industrial revolution, when most people lived and worked on farms. "If someone had predicted back then that within a couple of centuries only a tiny percentage of the population would be needed to produce food, all those farmers would have worried about what everyone would do for a living. The great majority of the 501 job categories recognized in 1990 by the U.S. Census Bureau didn't even exist 50 years earlier" (Gates et al., 1998, p. 253).

Attali (1998) also believes that the majority of the jobs of the twenty-first century do not yet exist today. He predicts that occupations will continue to become more and more diverse. He notes, for example, that the 30 most common occupations of today employ only 50% of the population, whereas they employed 75% in 1900. Further, most of these 30 most common occupations now require some extent of computer literacy.

He predicts a fascinating compendium of occupations of the twenty-first century (Attali, 1998), some with titles already in use, some of which he has created. These titles include microsurgeon, corporate lawyer, computer repair person, software patent specialist, inspector of author rights for computer games, Internet advertising specialist, Internet conceptual technologies specialist, software graphics creator, director of high-tech companies, insurance agent for risky innovative software, genomician, esthetic engineer, nanotechnology specialist, genopharmacist, and cloning technician. He also outlines the occupations (many of them in the personal service field) that currently exist for which he believes there will always be considerable demand: gardeners, janitors, medical assistants, continuing education specialists, teachers, psychotherapists, counselors, resume specialists, human relation analysts, manicurists, actors, salespersons, cooks, and skilled artisans.

We would add to Attali's (1998) predictions that the explosive growth in Internet use will also mean that an ever greater percentage of the population will work from home. "By the year 2010, 40 percent of all Americans are expected to be self-employed" (Jaco, 1998, p. 7), and even large corporations are expected to be little more than networked computers.

The ideas presented in the previous paragraphs all suggest that in terms of "results," there is little doubt that guidance programs of 20 years hence must prepare the huge majority of their students to (a) enter technical fields, (b) adapt themselves to extensive telecommuting and the lifestyle that it entails, (c) prepare primarily for self-employment or freelance employment, and (c) live an extremely long time.

In this article we have tried to outline some of the features of the world of 2021 that we expect to be affected by current trends in computer science, telecommunications, and biotechnology. As is so often the case, however, the only things we can predict with any certainty are change and the ever-accelerating rapidity of change. For example, as we wrote this article, almost every day we came across a newspaper or magazine article, or information on the Internet, outlining a new technological development or new finding that we felt we should mention. If guidance programs of the future are to plan successfully for change, they must find a structure that allows virtually instantaneous adaptation and accommodation to new information and developments. We sincerely hope that if we walk into a school in 2021 and observe the guidance program in operation, we will see both a physical plant and a provision of services that would be unrecognizable in today's world. Otherwise, it would be unlikely that the school and guidance program had prepared successfully for change.

References

Attali, J. (1998). *Dictionnaire du XXI siècle*. Paris: Fayard.

Davis, B., & Wessel, D. (1998, May 5). Broadly shared prosperity: Why the middle class will do better in the decades ahead. *Wall Street Journal Interactive Edition*, HYPERLINK [Online]. Available: http://interactive.wsj.com/

Flynn, J. (1997, June 23). British Telecom: Notes from the ant colony. *Business Week* (European Ed.), 61.

Gates, B., Myhrvold, N., & Rinearson, P. (1998). *The road ahead*. London: Viking.

Gershenfeld, N. (1999). *When things start to think*. New York: Henry Holt & Co.

Gross, N. (1997, June 23). Into the wild frontier. *Business Week* (European Ed.), 44–52.

Guernsey, L. (2000, April 17). Is it smart to make refrigerators think? *International Herald Tribune*, p. 13.

Isaacson, W. (1998, April 13). Our century and the next one. *Time*, 30–35.

Jaco, J. L. (1998, March). Preparing for the future. *Counseling Today*, p. 7.

Johnson, S. K., & Johnson, C. D. (1993). *The new guidance: A systems approach to pupil personnel service programs*. Fullerton, CA: California Association for Counseling and Development.

Joy, B. (2000, April 19). The dangers of new technology. *International Herald Tribune*, p. 9.

Judge, P. C. (1997, June 23). MIT: Two big rivals on campus. *Business Week* (European Ed.), 56.

Kahu, M. (1998, March 16). As science finds answers, it uncovers questions. *Los Angeles Times*, p. B2.

Kolata, G. (1998, May 4). A cure for cancer? Elated doctors cautiously point to healthy mice. *International Herald Tribune*, pp. 1, 10.

Margolis, J. (2000, March 6). Cutting edge humanity. *Time*, p. 40.

Markoff, J. (1998, April 30). Quantum computing takes a quantum leap. *International Herald Tribune*, p. 12.

Markoff, J. (2000, April 24). Microsoft cofounder closes California research lab. *International Herald Tribune*, p. 11.

Mathews, J. (2000, May 2). Do computers aid learning in school? *International Herald Tribune*, p. 9.

McGuinn, D., & Raymond, J. (1998, February). Workers of the world, get online. *Newsweek*, 32–33.

New York Times. (2000, April 30). Success in gene therapy at last. *New York Times*, OpEd page.

O'Hamilton, J. (1997, June 23). Stanford: Eggheads and entrepreneurs. *Business Week* (European Ed.), 55.

Port, O. (1997, June 23). Dueling brainscapes. *Business Week* (European Ed.), 53–54.

Rogers, A., & Kaplan, D. A. (1998, February). Get ready for nanotechnology. *Newsweek*, 52–53.

Silver, L. (1998). *Remaking Eden*. New York: Avon.

About the Authors

Lynda Mitchell is most recently a professor in the Division of Administration and Counseling at California State University, Los Angeles. She holds a doctorate in counseling psychology from Stanford University and is the co-author of *Counseling Research and Program Evaluation* (Brooks/Cole, 1990), "Research in Human Decision Making: Implications for Career Decision Making and Counseling" (in the *Handbook of Counseling Psychology*, Wiley, 1984), and "The Social Learning Theory of

Career Decision Making" (in *Theory and Practice of Career Development*, Jossey-Bass, 1990). She is also the author of numerous articles in research and journal publications.

Philippe Hardy is a graduate of the Ecole Polytechnique in Paris and holds a master's degree in business administration from Stanford University. He has held positions at Bechtel, Hewlett-Packard, and McKinsey and Company (management consultants) and was a partner with the Telesis management consulting group before establishing his own consulting company, Strategicum. His consulting specializations include telecommunications and twenty-first-century technology.

Chapter Nineteen

Future Student Support Programs: Distinction or Extinction?

Sharon K. Johnson & C. D. Johnson

All contributing authors have identified and addressed changes for the future of student support programs from their perspectives. It becomes clear when speaking with student support professionals that without a blueprint of how the fields of school counseling, psychology, nursing, social work, attendance work, and other student support programs will change to address the future, extinction is guaranteed. Major changes are already occurring that affect the student support programs of the future.

Communities

In the present and in the future, a return to local communities will be common. "The global community of the future will be at its best a series of communities that are interdependent and diverse, embracing differences, releasing energy, and building cohesion" (Hesselbein, Goldsmith, Beckhard, & Schubert, 1998, p. xi). This return to a smaller, more knowable community reflects the basic need of humans to belong. The community includes families and homes, classrooms and schools, churches and recreation areas, and neighborhood businesses and industries. Currently, communities are being constructed around common missions and values, with the objectives of reducing gang involvement and increasing communication and collaboration among community members. The larger communities include towns, states, and nations—the political entities to which allegiance is pledged.

The student support professionals become a community within each educational community, addressing the needs of families, schools, neighborhoods, and other groups that constitute the whole. "Building the global community of the future is not the work of tomorrow. We are each called to build it today—to build it now" (Hesselbein et al., 1998, p. xiv). For student support professionals, the change in community focus is significant because it mandates that counselors give up a circumscribed role and learn to collaborate more effectively with others who make up the student support team. The student support team will become a more diverse community group, including more than just the traditional counselor, psychologist, nurse, and social worker. Ensuring that students are prepared to assume a productive role in the new community will necessarily involve an expanded focus on contributions, responsibilities, experiences, and opportunities outside the 8:00 a.m. to 3:00 p.m. school day, outside the school building, and with adults other than just professional educators. Given the current limited focus, student support staff members will need additional skills and, perhaps, mentoring experiences to expand their view of the possibilities within each community.

Computer Technology

Distance education is already an element of local educational institutions, including public schools and universities. The computer allows for more home schooling for students who learn better at home, for disruptive youth, and for academically accelerated youth. School-home communication by e-mail is already being used for auditing students' progress in academics, assisting with educational and career preparation, and sending report cards. Universities and many high schools have students and their parents enroll in classes through the use of telephone-computer technology. Teaching–learning style matching is now simplified by using available technology that we hope leads to better academic achievement. The information explosion has already accelerated cognitive growth and has caused a rise in national academic standards.

Acquiring the necessary competencies in interpersonal and intrapersonal relationships appears to be the area most neglected in this technological age. The coming years will bring a proliferation of interactive, voice-activated technology that can be designed to enhance social interaction skills among participants. Cameras attached to computer screens are available to allow users to see whom they are addressing. This technology will become common and may reduce the impersonal nature of computers. Kurzweil (1999) indicates that by 2009 computers will be embedded in our clothes, and the average household will have more than one hundred computers, and by 2019 they will be placed in our bodies. Use of computers to streamline paperwork formerly assigned to student support personnel has already begun, but attention will need to be refocused on how students can utilize computers for academic learning without losing the essential skills of getting along with others, being part of a learning community, contributing to others, and fulfilling their interpersonal needs for connection and belonging. If schools are allowed to focus only on academic achievement, leaving relationship-building to the family and community, many students will face a bleak, impersonal, and unfulfilling future. Counselors must assume leadership in helping educators find new ways to reach beyond computer technology to focus on the human being at the core of the learning process.

Families

There appears to be a return to the traditional family structure of original parents—that is, a reduction in divorces. However, most families will continue to have both parents employed in order to live their desired lifestyle. The fast-food craze may become a way of life, with more healthful prepared meals delivered to the home. Current developments in the health field indicate that individuals will visit health sites on a regular basis and, through submission of a blood sample, receive an individualized health plan with suggested meals, supplements, vitamins, and exercise regimens. Improved health awareness, as well as active involvement in school achievement, may become a family, school, and employer concern. Schools will extend their hours to incorporate family education options as well as wellness, recreational, and avocational activities. As families gain awareness of their importance within a school community, the family as a group will increase cohesiveness and participation in cooperative ventures.

The increased interactions among multiple cultures will affect how families view themselves, their collective roles, and their contributions within the larger community. These collaborations may result in healthier, more connected families with common goals and interests. New rituals of communication and interaction are needed to replace the traditional separation of families and schools. Shopping malls have become social centers. If schools take leadership in providing a focal point within the community, however, the role of counselors will become paramount in helping to structure positive and productive conversations within and between families, with families and schools working together to establish the family vision and the unique missions of each individual and family. Research clearly indicates that the more the family is involved in a student's education, the greater the student's success (Henderson & Berda, 1994). Traditionally there has been clear separation between home and school. It will become the counselor's responsibility to break down the separating walls and find new ways to integrate and support collaborative relationships between school and home, acknowledging the importance of each.

Education

Some believe that the current school organizations will never change regardless of what research has to contribute: The 50-minute class period and the 6 or 7 period-a-day schedule in high schools, the single-teacher classroom in elementary schools, the bus schedules, and the support schedules will be maintained because they serve a community function. It seems that students have fewer electives, causing more youth to leave high school without a regular or traditional diploma. There are fewer skill-related classes to prepare students to enter the workforce. Rituals in schooling that were established in the early 1990s have been difficult, if not impossible, to change. It has been said that there have been no substantive changes in the delivery of education in the last 100 years. Yet, the National Education Commission on Time and Learning (1994) found that the fixed clock and calendar is a hindrance to education reform and must be changed. They further believe that the schedule must be modified to respond to the changes that have reshaped and are reshaping American life outside school. "In the United States, we've concentrated on getting students ready for the next grade or pushing them into the university. And that's not the same as preparing them for a technological, information-based society" (Daggett, 1994).

The imminent changes in technology, families, and community may be the catalyst for significant changes that have been touted in many reform movements during the last 20 years.

More personalized educational plans and offerings, more efficient organizational structures, and more room for parent and community participation are key elements that promise meaningful change in student outcomes. Within the educational reform movement of the 1990s, mention of student support programs was conspicuously absent. Unless counselors assume leadership in defining their contributions to education as it changes, student support professionals from a variety of backgrounds will step in to fill the needs. This trend has already begun with nonschool professionals being utilized for specialized projects such as family counseling, safe school initiatives, drug and alcohol projects, teen suicide response teams, and a variety of other specially funded efforts. Counselors must demonstrate the importance of coordination and collaboration of efforts to ensure that all students receive the assistance they needed to become successful as students and in the future roles they will assume.

The Economy

The world economy is consistently growing in scope and quantity. The results are a massive growth in mergers and closures, fewer middle managers, a transient workforce, and an ever-increasing gap between those with money and those without, making the middle-class workforce smaller and smaller. The need for universal work skills is visible. The growth of world economies portends a more international scope in work, travel, lifestyles, and education. Student support personnel will need to identify clear, attainable student competencies related to comprehensive educational expectations in order to guide students toward relevant goals and plans.

Employees are expected to be mobile, to change not only types of employment but also locations. Companies now hire full-time temporary employees, thus cutting costs. There are few middle managers, leading to an increase in lower paid workers. Many firms hire consultants for specific jobs, which allows for cost savings but also requires worker mobility. There is a dramatic increase in the number of individuals who work out of their home, as both entrepreneurs and employees. These trends imply the expectation of lifelong learning competencies. As the economy changes, technology advances, and communities evolve, new worker skills are necessary. Therefore, family involvement in education is not limited to children and adolescents but can and does involve all family members. Counselors become essential in helping students and families adapt to the diversity around them, to embrace differences, and to see themselves as competent in meeting the many economic and work roles they will be expected to fulfill.

Results Orientation

Industries, businesses, education units, and many social and government agencies are demanding the achievement of specified results. The leaders demand quality, and they are almost always on a quota system themselves for product development. The current economy, with its many investors, has a forceful impact on top management's decision making, leading to closing businesses, moving manufacturing to other countries, or simply closing plants to reduce costs, thereby causing unemployment, worker mobility, or worker retraining. These actions affect employees and their families.

Leadership

The face of leadership has changed from the traditional military and sports models to a participative, inclusive management model of organizations (Senge, 1990). The increasing number of women in upper management positions has had an impact on the type of management skills required to maintain learning organizations. More time is being spent in planning, using the total quality management (TQM) processes, and in addressing continuous changes. As work-related leadership skills change, so do the parenting skills utilized at home. Providing opportunities for input from all workers provides a model for managing family groups. The use of family meetings, the practice of listening to all views, and development of a vision and goals for each family member and for the family as a whole have been suggested as winning strategies for the families of the future. Student support personnel need to become leaders in the school culture in order to effectively advocate for students and their families. As school leadership evolves into more collaborative team efforts, student support professionals need to become active in leading the way: teaching others how to listen, reflect, and clarify; sharing group process skills, such as those required for effective meetings; and developing and teaching other competencies that are a part of counselor training programs. Leaders find a way to adapt their skills to meet the needs of the group and each individual. Who better than counselors to fulfill this role?

How do these changes reflect the development of a coherent ecology? The concept of ecology speaks to the pattern of relations between living things and their environments, or to the interdependence of all organisms as manifest by community development and structure. Coherent means to be "logically consistent and ordered to become fittingly connected or unified by certain principles, relationships or themes in the pursuit of one purpose or idea" (Merriam-Webster, Inc., 1981).

Thus, educational changes must be integrated into the life of each community, large or small, if that community is to move ahead in a chosen direction. The development of coherent ecology mandates creation and acceptance of a shared mission, vision, and values; the opportunity to seek new methods, reflect on the results, and make additional adaptations; willingness to work in collaborative teams, learning from one another and creating momentum to fuel continued improvement; willingness to act, to experiment, and sometimes to fail in order to change and improve; as well as the encouragement of continuous improvement and striving for positive results. Coherent ecology bespeaks communities that are growing, vital, alive, and welcoming. We must learn that "whatever is flexible and flowing will tend to grow and whatever is rigid and blocked will atrophy and die" (Heider, 1985, p. 151).

Using available information on what is happening and what is projected, the opportunity has been created to suggest different metaphors or models for use in moving student support personnel professionals forward, heuristically changing their icalf pathsî to better meet new community values and conditions. Metaphors offer professionals the means to examine what they are doing compared to what they might be or will be doing in future years if they are to avoid extinction.

Each of the contributors to this book offers the reader different ways of examining what the contributions might be for each member of the student support team—counselor, nurse, psychologist, social worker, teacher, administrator, and other active members, including community members.

The professional learning community consists of numerous individuals who provide support services for youth from birth to age 18 (DuFour & Eaker, 1998). They may be assigned to different organizations and in different locations within the community. The student support professionals within the learning community might include social workers, nurses and other health specialists, school psychologists and counselors, other mental health workers, and counseling and clinical psychologists. In addition there may be family center personnel and recreational specialists. Using this information, there are numerous potential paradigms that might be considered "outside the box." These are offered as ideas to stimulate creativity.

1. Collaborative teams will be the resource to break down territorial boundaries among professionals, leading to a career lattice with a single mission: the educational achievement and mental health of all youth.

2. The teams may be assigned case management for families that have one or more children, working with those children from birth to 18 years of age or older. The team will be accountable for the children learning to learn, to work, to relate, to contribute to the community, and to maintain a balance of activities that provides a sense of wellness.

3. The teams might be organized to require collaboration with other community entities. The team leader will be selected on competence of leadership and not title or degree, such as school psychologist, school counselor, social worker, or administrator.

4. The student support team will be charged with implementing a comprehensive results-based student support program that centers on academic achievement for all students pre-K though grade 12 (or graduation from high school) or through grades 13 and 14, if not through four years of college.

5. School leadership will have to realign professional assignments in order to provide assistance for home schoolers, for those involved in distance learning, for those in college-high school programs, and for those students attending school in industries and businesses where their parents are working.

6. More districts may be contracting with out-of-school consultants for specific results and purposes, such as college planning, career planning, personal counseling, and mental health needs. Therefore, the school counselors, psychologists, social workers, and administrators will need competencies in managing others in the student support program areas.

7. Career ladders will cause current college and university preparation for student support personnel to change as well as expand. There are models of career ladders available; however, the future student support program career ladder will require a unique approach with clearly defined steps based on competence rather than specific educational degrees.
8. Parental involvement in students' education may take a different path, one in which parents are mandated to participate in certain functions planned to assist them in helping their children to achieve specific competencies related to preparing their children to become contributing citizens.
9. Schools may once again assume the role of being the center of the community life, because schools are the most permanent social institution. However, this change will necessitate changes in scope and flexibility.
10. Private practitioners will be a prime source of expertise for students and families in need. It may become common for schools to contract with clinical and counseling psychologists for ongoing assistance.

Conclusion

There are many possibilities for realigning available resources to provide better and more results without additional funding. The realignments must be evaluated on an ongoing basis to ensure the paradigms being used are delivering planned-for results in terms of academic achievement and wellness program implementation. These new paradigms must move us from established educational patterns into new, dynamic paradigms for the future. Student support programs will by necessity be different from what we know today, if they are to survive in the new millennium. Human beings are genetically encoded to grow and change—the challenge ahead is to make the educational and support communities flexible enough to accommodate the many environmental and human changes that lie ahead.

References

National Education Commission on Time and Learning. (1994). *Prisoners of time*. Washington, DC: Government Printing Office.

Daggett, W. (1994, June). Today's students, yesterday's schooling. *The Executive Educator, 16*, 18-21.

DuFour, R., & Eaker, R. (1998). *Professional learning communities at work*. Bloomington, IN: National Educational Service.

Garth, M. (1997). *Images of organizations*. Thousand Oaks: Sage.

Heider, J. (1985). *The tao of leadership*. New York: Bantam Books.

Henderson, A. T., & Berda, N. (1994). *A new generation of evidence*. Washington, DC: National Council of Citizens in Education.

Hesselbein, F., Goldsmith, M., Beckhard, R., & Schubert, R. (Eds.). (1998). *The community of the future*. San Francisco: Jossey-Bass.

Johnson, C., & Johnson, S. (1983). Competency-based training of career development specialists, or let's get off the calf path. *Vocational Guidance Quarterly, 30*(4).

Kurzweil, R. (1999, November 19). Will my PC be smarter than I am? Time, 155, 16-21.

Merriam-Webster, Inc. (1981). *Webster's third new international dictionary*. Springfield, MA: Author.

Senge, P. (1990). *The fifth discipline: The art and practice of the learning organization*. New York: Currency Doubleday.

Wheatley, M. (1994). *Leadership and the new science: Learning about organization from an orderly universe*. San Francisco: Berrett-Koehler.

About the Authors

C. D. "Curly" Johnson, Ph.D., has been a consultant for more than 30 years in the areas of education, counseling, mental health, and business. Currently president of Professional Update, an educational and business consulting firm, Dr. Johnson has consulted in 30 states and 16 countries on a variety of programs, including results-based school counseling, marriage and family counseling, student development, group counseling, and school-home partnerships. He has authored and co-authored books and articles in the areas of at-risk students and potential dropouts, family practices, parent-school partnerships, group leadership, therapeutic techniques, career development, program evaluation, and management for results. He resides and runs an active consultant practice from his residence in San Juan Capistrano, California. Dr. Johnson is the recipient of several achievement awards from national and state professional associations including PTA, NCDA, CACD, and CASC.

Sharon K. Johnson, Ed.D., is retired from her position as professor and coordinator of the Counseling and Educational Leadership Program within the Division of Administration and Counseling at California State University, Los Angeles. She has consulted nationally and internationally with educational and business organizations, as well as co-authoring articles and books in the areas of parent-school partnerships; group counseling; program development and evaluation; management training; marriage, family, and child counseling; career development; and multicultural issues. Dr. Johnson is a former teacher and school counselor, and was director of pupil services for the Howard County Public Schools in Maryland for 10 years. She has been active in many national and state professional associations, including PDK, AAUW, ASCD, AERA, and multiple divisions of ACA, representing group work specialists, counselor educators and supervisors, career development professionals, and school counselors. She is past president of the California Association of Counselor Educators and Supervisors, the Los Angeles chapter of Phi Delta Kappa, and the California Association for Counseling and Development.

AMERICAN SCHOOL COUNSELOR ASSOCIATION

One Vision   One Voice

The American School Counselor Association (ASCA) is a worldwide nonprofit organization based in Alexandria, Virginia.

Founded in 1952, ASCA supports school counselors' efforts to help students focus on academic, personal/social and career development so they not only achieve success in school but are prepared to lead fulfilling lives as responsible members of society. The association provides professional development, publications and other resources, research and advocacy to more than 12,000 professional school counselors around the globe.

American School Counselor Association
801 N. Fairfax St., Suite 310
Alexandria, VA 22314-1757
(703) 683-ASCA (2722)
fax: (703) 683-1619
www.schoolcounselor.org